CIRCA 1900

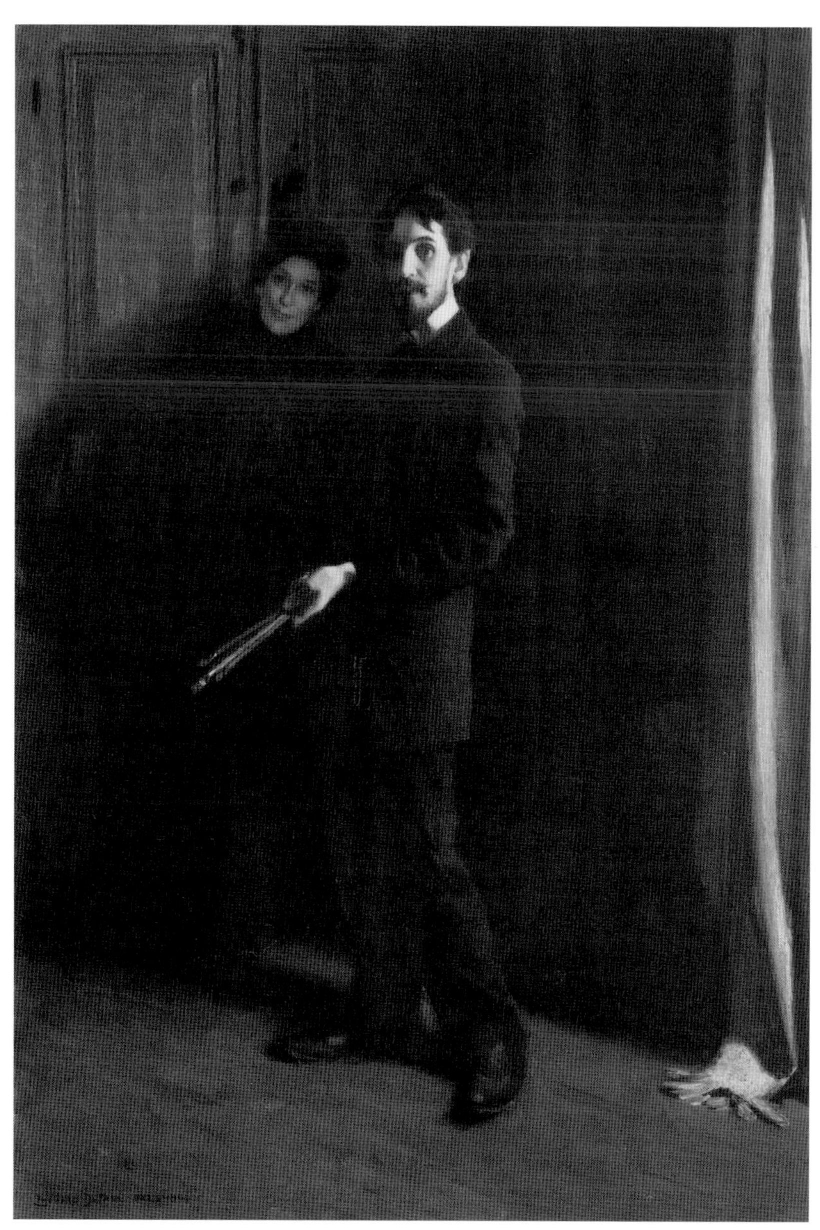

Organized by the Albright-Knox Art Gallery, Buffalo, New York

CIRCA 1900

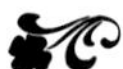

Essay and catalogue by Helen A. Raye

with a contribution by Claire Schneider

Albany Institute of History and Art

Albright-Knox Art Gallery, Buffalo

Everson Museum of Art, Syracuse

Herbert F. Johnson Museum of Art, Cornell University, Ithaca

Memorial Art Gallery of the University of Rochester

Munson-Williams-Proctor Arts Institute, Museum of Art, Utica

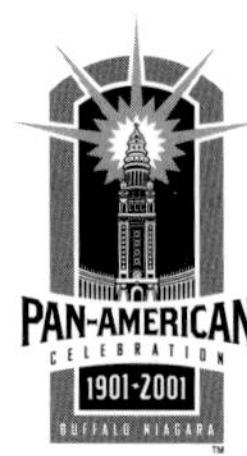

This catalogue is published on the occasion of the exhibition, *Circa 1900: From the Genteel Tradition to the Jazz Age,* organized by the Albright-Knox Art Gallery in conjunction with the centennial celebration of the Pan-American Exposition in Buffalo and on behalf of the Consortium of Upstate New York Museums.

Douglas Dreishpoon, Project Director, Albright-Knox Art Gallery
Helen A. Raye, Project Curator, Albright-Knox Art Gallery

Munson-Williams-Proctor Arts Institute, Museum of Art, Utica
March 3 – April 15, 2001

Albright-Knox Art Gallery, Buffalo
May 6 - August 19, 2001

Herbert F. Johnson Museum of Art, Cornell University, Ithaca
September 8 – November 25, 2001

Albany Institute of History and Art
December 14, 2001 – March 3, 2002

Everson Museum of Art, Syracuse
March 22 – May 26, 2002

Memorial Art Gallery of the University of Rochester
June 15 – September 15, 2002

Editor: Karen Lee Spaulding
Designers: Alex Castro and Kelly Parisi, Castro/Arts, Baltimore
Indexer: Marjorie Mahle

First published in the United States of America in 2001 by
The Buffalo Fine Arts Academy, 1285 Elmwood Avenue, Buffalo, New York 14222-1096.

Frontispiece, page 2: Edward Dufner, *In the Studio*, 1899, won a Bronze Medal at the Pan-American Exposition in Buffalo in 1901.

Library of Congress Cataloging-in-Publication Data
Circa 1900: from the genteel tradition to the jazz age / [essays by Helen Raye,
Claire Schneider].
p. cm.
Catalog of a traveling exhibition first shown at Munson-Williams-Proctor Institute,
Utica, N.Y., Mar. 3-Apr. 15, 2001.
Includes bibliographical references and index.
ISBN 0-914782-98-3 (alk. paper)
1. Art, American—Exhibitions. 2. Art, Modern—19th century—United States—Exhibitions.
3. Art, Modern—20th century—United States—Exhibitions. 4. Art, Europe—Influence—Exhibitions.
I. Raye, Helen, 1956- II. Schneider, Claire. III. Albright-Knox Art Gallery.
IV. Munson-Williams-Proctor Institute.

N6510.C57 2000
709'.04'107474762—dc21   00-062071

Contents

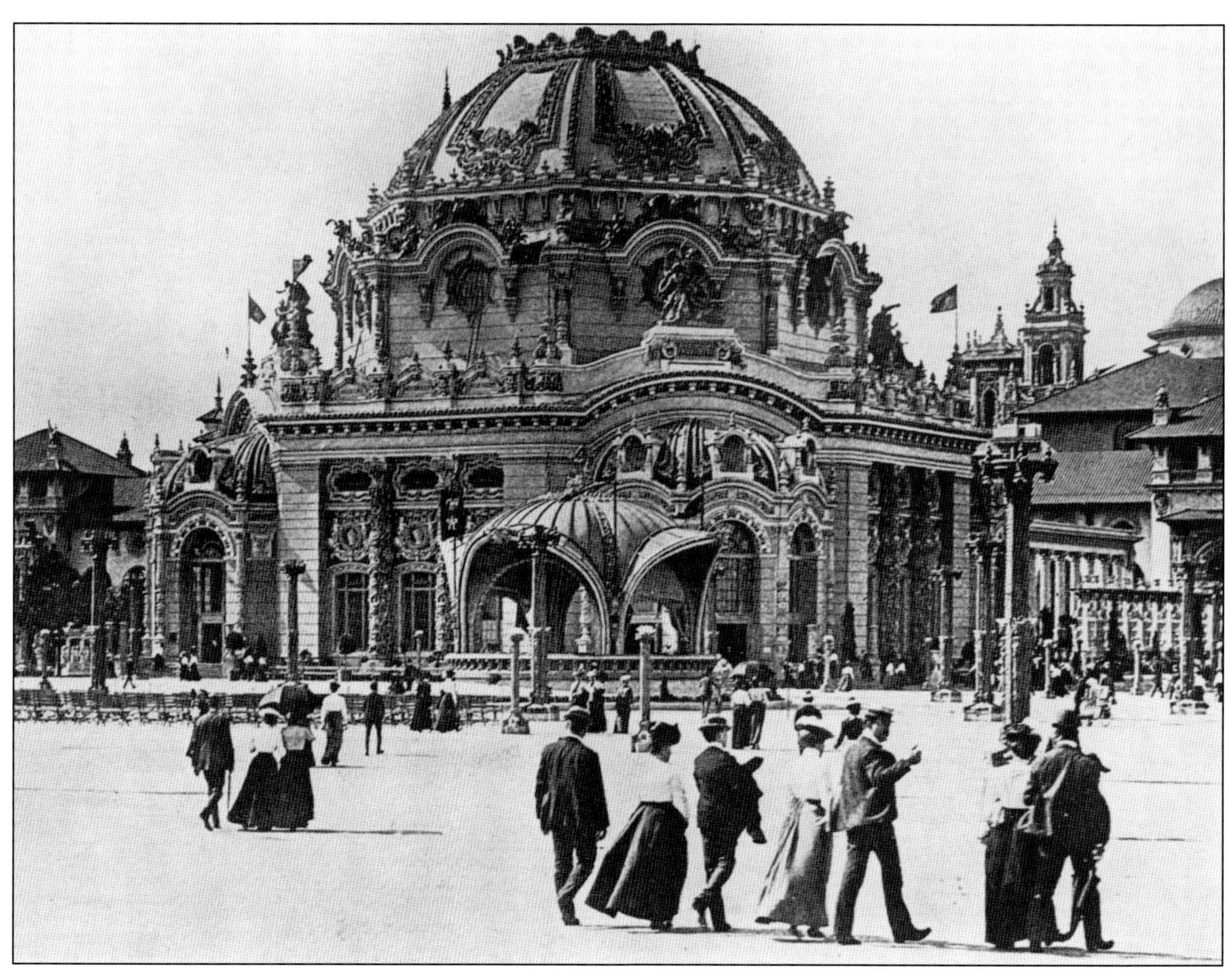

Temple of Music, Pan-American Exposition, Buffalo, 1901

FOREWORD

Since 1974, the Albright-Knox Art Gallery and its sister institutions in upstate New York have cooperated in organizing major exhibitions that highlight different aspects of their respective collections. American art, Far Eastern art, landscapes, master printmaking, and still–life painting have all been subjects of this rich and fruitful collaboration. This year, we celebrate the beginning of a new century by honoring the momentous changes in artistic expression taking place at the advent of the last century. The exhibition *Circa 1900: From the Genteel Tradition to the Jazz Age,* organized by the Albright-Knox Art Gallery, explores those changes by presenting outstanding works selected from its own collection and those of the Albany Institute of History and Art; the Everson Museum of Art, Syracuse; the Herbert F. Johnson Museum of Art, Cornell University, Ithaca; the Memorial Art Gallery, University of Rochester; and the Munson-Williams-Proctor Arts Institute, Museum of Art, Utica. At these institutions, all directors have been most hospitable and helpful: Grant Holcomb III in Rochester; Christine M. Miles in Albany; Franklin W. Robinson in Ithaca; Paul D. Schweizer in Utica; and Sandra Trop in Syracuse.

Circa 1900 opens in Utica at the Munson-Williams-Proctor Arts Institute, Museum of Art, in March of 2001. In May 2001, nearly one hundred years to the day that the Pan-American Exposition opened in Buffalo in 1901, the Albright-Knox Art Gallery has the pleasure of hosting the exhibition in conjunction with citywide centennial celebrations. This exhibition offers not only a view of the art admired at that time but also a broader perspective of the established academic tradition then being challenged and the radical changes in subject matter and style occurring thereafter. Although scholarship has explored the break from the Academy and the developments of modern art by the avant-garde, this is the first opportunity to visualize this change through artwork found in upstate New York collections.

Helen Raye, a specialist in nineteenth-century American art and Project Curator for this exhibition, has done a brilliant job of taking us from the Genteel Tradition, or the Gilded Age, occurring around 1880, to the beginning of the Jazz Age, around 1920. She has organized an exhibition of breadth and beauty and has written a masterwork of an essay that not only discusses works of art with clarity and insight, but also illuminates the social and historic changes that occurred at the turn of the century. Her contribution to this project is immense, and we are exceedingly grateful to her for all her hard work on behalf of the Gallery. Her colleagues at the Gallery, Curator Douglas Dreishpoon and Assistant Curator Claire Schneider, were important partners in this major endeavor.

It has been a pleasure for the Albright-Knox Art Gallery to take its turn as we look forward to the continued collaboration of the upstate New York museums well into this new century.

Douglas G. Schultz
Director
Albright-Knox Art Gallery

ACKNOWLEDGEMENTS

No exhibition is a solo endeavor, and in the case of a show like *Circa 1900: From the Genteel Tradition to the Jazz Age,* drawn from the riches of a consortium of upstate New York museums, the cooperative effort of the six participating institutions and their numerous staff members has been, indeed, monumental. Many thanks are due to the Albany Institute of History and Art; Everson Museum of Art, Syracuse; Herbert F. Johnson Museum of Art, Cornell University, Ithaca; Memorial Art Gallery of the University of Rochester; Munson-Williams-Proctor Arts Institute, Museum of Art, Utica, and, of course, the Albright-Knox Art Gallery, Buffalo, for generously parting with many prized items from their collections for the duration of the exhibition tour.

A number of individuals who truly extended themselves to help further this project deserve special thanks: At the Albany Institute of History and Art, Chief Curator Tammis Groft graciously hosted my visit to the Institute, guiding me through the collection and, along with her staff, ensuring the availability of their collection files for my perusal; also, Carolyn Wilson kindly followed through with additional requests for information and photographs. Thomas E. Piché, Jr., Senior Curator at the Everson Museum of Art, gave liberally of his time and assistance when Douglas Dreishpoon, Project Director for *Circa 1900,* and I came to view the museum's collection. Everson Registrar Michael Flanagan helped solve a number of knotty little conundrums that surfaced during the organizational process. Assistant Curator of Painting and Sculpture at the Herbert F. Johnson Museum, Sean M. Ulmer, provided ample help on all fronts. He introduced Douglas Dreishpoon and me to the Johnson Museum's collection of painting and sculpture on one occasion, brought forth the extensive collection of Tiffany glass for my review on another, supplied information on the collection, and adeptly filled the role of liaison in general. Nancy Green, Chief Curator at the Johnson Museum, also joined in furthering the formation of *Circa 1900* when she facilitated Albright-Knox Assistant Curator Claire Schneider's access to the museum's photography collection. Warren M. Bunn II, Registrar at the Johnson Museum, helped with organizational details, as did Curatorial Assistant Kasia Maroney, whose amiability when handling nitpicking questions was admirable. In Rochester, at the Memorial Art Gallery, Douglas Dreishpoon and I enjoyed a warm reception on the part of Director Grant Holcomb III; Marie Via, Curator of Exhibitions; Marjorie Searle, Curator of American Art; and Candace Adelson, then Curator of European Art. We benefited from the multitude of information and well-prepared presentation of their collection that they offered us. The continued assistance of the Memorial Art Gallery's curatorial staff, including the persevering and genial efforts of Curatorial Secretary Chrisa Katsampes and Monica Simpson, Permanent Collection Registrar, was a great boon. Director of the Munson-Williams-Proctor Arts Institute, Museum of Art Paul D. Schweizer was most cordial and hospitable. His willingness to share his time, expertise, and collection with Douglas Dreishpoon and me during our trip to Utica guaranteed that our visit there was as pleasurable as it was useful. Also at the Munson-Williams-Proctor Arts Institute, Museum of Art Registrar Maggie Mazzullo estimably picked up the reigns upon stepping into her position when *Circa 1900* was already in mid-stride and followed through on the matters in progress. Debora W. Ryan, formerly Registrar at the Munson-Williams-Proctor Arts Institute, Museum of Art and now Assistant Curator at the Everson Museum, has been of considerable help (in all her professional incarnations), as was her assistant at the Munson-Williams-Proctor Arts Institute, Museum of Art Adrienne Nardi.

My most heartfelt thanks go to those at the Albright-Knox Art Gallery with whom I have worked so closely over the course of many months. Director Douglas G. Schultz supported this project from its inception, when former Senior Curator Cheryl Brutvan (now Beal Curator of

Contemporary Art at the Museum of Fine Arts, Boston) first set the wheels in motion for a consortium exhibition to coincide with the festivities marking the centennial of the Pan-American Exposition. Douglas Dreishpoon, Project Director for *Circa 1900,* provided good company and knowledgeable insight on our tours of the consortium museums' collections, as well as valuable guidance and assistance throughout the evolution of the exhibition. Thanks to Assistant Curator Claire Schneider's interest in photography, the show has been enriched by the inclusion of that medium, just as the catalogue has been enhanced by her essay on photography. Holly Hughes, Curatorial Assistant, exercised her remarkable energy and efficiency in preparing much of the paperwork involved in the exhibition's organization. Head Librarian Janice Lurie, and the superb library staff have once again gone above and beyond the call of duty in compiling bibliographical information, searching out and gathering pertinent published material, and patiently handling many inter-library loans. Yvonne Widenor, Image Resources Librarian, has also helped greatly by conjuring up slides on short notice. Similarly, Daisy Stroud, Associate Registrar, has made sure that all photographs of objects from the Albright-Knox Art Gallery's collection needed for the catalogue were provided in a timely fashion. Without the dedication and skill of Senior Registrar Laura Fleischmann and her staff, along with the installation and handling crew, *Circa 1900* could not have physically come together, never mind toured. Robert Dickerson, Controller, and his team in the accounting office supplied much-needed budget figures and looked after all financial matters. The conscientious work of Development Officer Anne Hayes has helped secure the financial support that made this exhibition possible. The participation of Jennifer Bayles, Curator of Education; Mariann Smith, Associate Curator of Education; and all the others in the Education department has, in turn, made the show more accessible to the public. To Richard Cherry, Chief Technology Officer, and Bryan Gawronski, LAN Administrator, I owe humble thanks for bailing me out on the computer more times than I care to count. Carol Chur, a graduate student at the State University of New York at Buffalo and intern working on *Circa 1900,* brought to this project organizational skills and a rigorous attention to detail. Carol was invaluable in the compilation of the exhibition checklist, research materials, and assembling of catalogue illustrations; she also brought a persistence and positive attitude that I sincerely appreciated. Another SUNY at Buffalo intern, Meredeth Ferington, has won the gratitude of the Publications department for her exquisite competence in handling an extensive array of projects, a trait she shares with Betsy McCall, former Editor of Publications, who illuminated the department with her sunny personality on even the darkest days. Summer intern Karen Jenson helped as well in the final preparation of the manuscript. Working closely with Editor for Special Projects Karen Lee Spaulding was Alex Castro, who brought all of his experience and skill to his seventh significant collaboration with the Gallery, producing a book of great clarity and beauty. He was assisted in this major endeavor by his talented colleague Kelly Parisi. My final thanks go to Karen Lee Spaulding, my dear friend, who is possessed of super-human organizational skills, indefatigable energy, patience that transcends "saintly," and a truly magnanimous spirit. This book would not exist without her.

Helen A. Raye
Project Curator
Albright-Knox Art Gallery

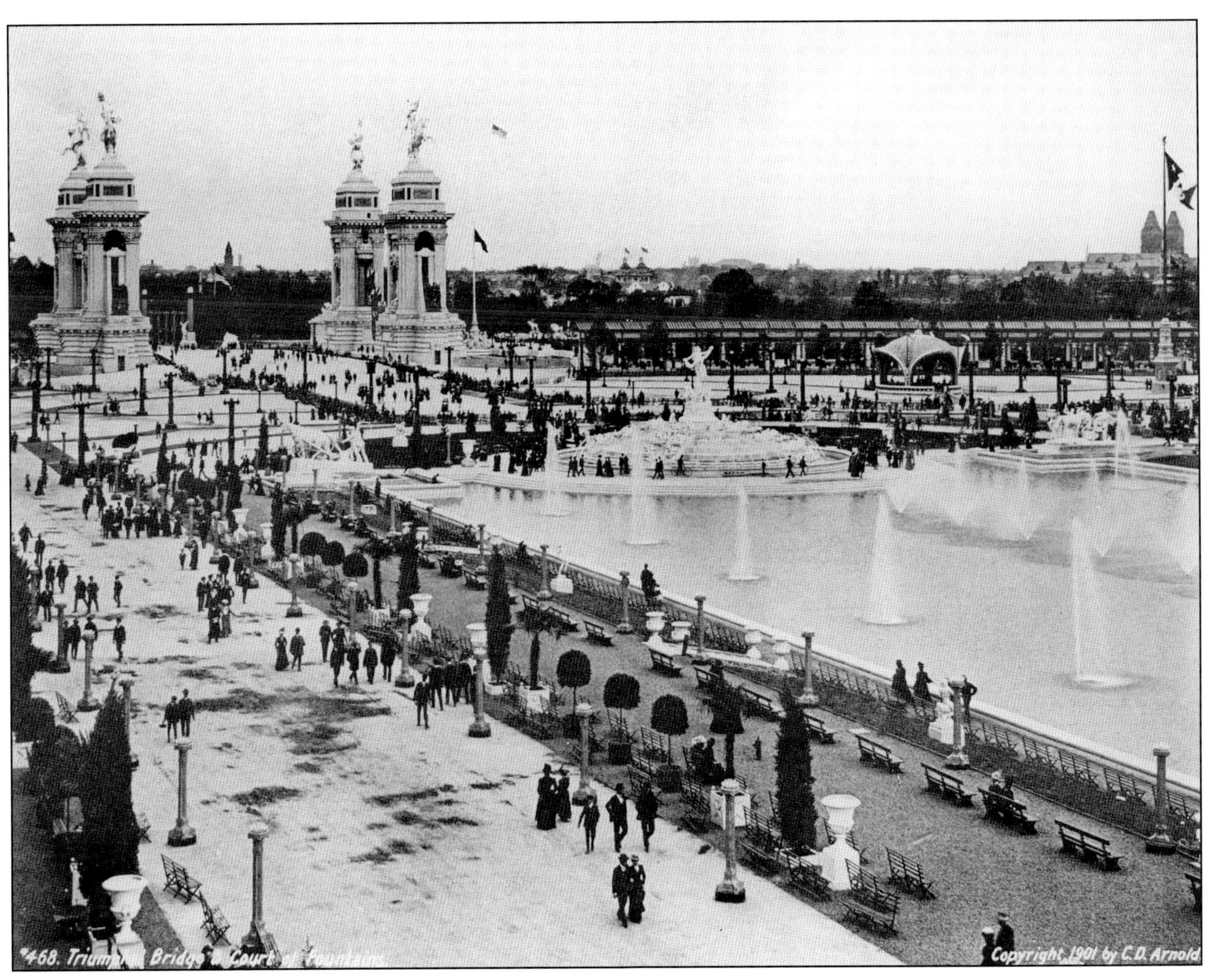

Triumphal Bridge and Court of Fountains, Pan-American Exposition, Buffalo, 1901

CIRCA 1900

FROM THE GENTEEL TRADITION TO THE JAZZ AGE

Helen A. Raye

AMERICA CIRCA 1900:
NEW FRONTIERS AND LOST HORIZONS

As we enter a new century, indeed, a new millennium, we find ourselves prompted by this chronological marker to review our past. Myriad publications, television programs, books and exhibitions, have been produced in response to our desire for cultural reassessment.[1] In such efforts, we reflect the same impetus that spurred our forebears to create grand expositions such as the spectacular Exposition Universelle in Paris in 1900. The United States also produced numerous expositions before and after the turn of the last century, beginning with the Centennial Exposition in Philadelphia in 1876 and continuing with the World's Columbian Exposition in Chicago in 1893, the Pan-American Exposition in Buffalo in 1901, the Saint Louis Exposition in 1904, and the Pan-Pacific Exposition in San Francisco in 1914. One may view these expositions as an indication of the nation's repeated attempts to summarize and assess the rapid changes that were occurring during this period as the United States transformed from a country comprised of small rural, agricultural communities to a major urban, industrial power. The Pan-American Exposition of 1901, in particular, took place at a crucial turning point in the development of foreign relations and the construction of a national identity.

Opening almost exactly one hundred years after the Pan-American Exposition, *Circa 1900: From the Genteel Tradition to the Jazz Age* also celebrates the advent of a new century by examining a crucial transformative period in the development of our art and culture. Different from the Exhibition of Fine Arts at the Pan-American Exposition, which included paintings, drawings, prints, and architectural renderings dating from 1876 to 1901 and almost exclusively by American artists,[2] our current exhibition encompasses not only American art but also some of the European art with which American artists interacted. Comprised of oil paintings, sculptures, photographs, ceramics, glass, and furniture, it offers a broad variety of media representative of the impact of evolving artistic theories, such as the concept of the unity of the arts, and developing technology, such as the growing interest in photography. In addition, the period covered by this exhibition begins at the onset of the Genteel Tradition or Gilded Age, about 1880, when new ideas about American art began to flower, and extends through the period of increasing interest in and acceptance of abstraction leading up to the dawn of the Jazz Age, around 1920. Selected from the exemplary collections of six major upstate New York museums, the works presented in this exhibition thus provide a means through which we can explore the evolution of American art and culture between 1880 and 1920 and form an understanding of how the United States viewed itself, its art, and its cultural and artistic relationship with Europe as it moved from the nineteenth into the twentieth century.

While the Pan-American Exposition is not the focus herein, taking place as it did in 1901, it does provide a fulcrum for the period under discussion, and an examination of the viewpoints inherent in the Exposition reveals the core issues underlying the cultural and artistic changes of that period. As art historian Elizabeth Broun has noted, the character of large expositions tends toward conservatism, even nostalgia, as opposed to prophecy of the future, despite all claims to the contrary by Exposition planners.[3] The Pan-American Exposition was not an exception in the respect that it embodied the prevailing social thought and reflected the impact of recent historical events.

One such event was the publication of Charles Darwin's *Origin of Species* in 1859 in which the British naturalist presented his theory of natural selection. As a result of studying the myriad species of flora and fauna that he observed during his extensive travels throughout the world, he concluded that life had developed over countless millennia through the process of survival of the fittest, with those species that were strongest and most adaptable to environmental changes enduring and evolving while others faded from existence. Darwin's theory shook the very foundation of long-established historical and religious beliefs: Nature no longer represented God's creative mandate and grace, and humanity no longer stood, apart from the rest of creation, at the center of the universe. Instead, the world suddenly appeared a place of uncertainty and threat, and the history of existence became one of brutal struggle and mindless chance, with humanity enmeshed in the chaos. Yet within this grim picture of evolution, chinks in Darwin's theory remained, which allowed those whom social historian George Cotkin has termed "reluctant modernists," such as English social philosopher Herbert Spencer, to insert older ideas: an anthropomorphic, selecting force (God or nature) could be added to the concept of natural selection; a "Creator" could be imagined working through natural laws; and a beneficial direction could be ascribed to the course of natural development.[4] Spencer's form of "Social Darwinism," offered an alternative vision of evolution in which mankind inevitably progressed from primitive, competitive, and violent origins toward an industrially and intellectually developed, cooperative, and peaceful apex. Despite its flawed reasoning based on initial prejudices and assumptions, Social Darwinism gained a fast following in the United States.[5] For the increasingly challenged White Anglo-Saxon Protestant elite, it reestablished the supremacy of man over nature, bolstered their threatened religious beliefs and social position, and supported their optimistic faith in the ascendancy of society to higher, more spiritual ends.[6]

Another major event that had recently jolted the American mind was the announcement in 1890 that population censuses had revealed that the frontier no longer existed.[7] If the United States were to continue to follow what was considered its destiny – to expand – it would have to look beyond its own borders. This line of thought was reinforced when in 1893 a great depression began, one that was to last throughout the better part of the decade. Businesses, plagued with dwindling markets and growing surpluses, began to look abroad for a solution to their problems. At the same time, fear of job shortages stimulated nativist tendencies and a call for immigration restriction. Further alarm created by increasing violent unrest on the part of poor, largely immigrant, labor (as demonstrated in Chicago in the Haymarket Square riot of 1886 and the Pullman strike of 1894) contributed to the growth of racism that, in turn, affected American relations with less developed countries and peoples.[8] By focusing on the superiority of European, especially Anglo-Saxon bloodlines, Americans found one way of defining themselves and justifying the nation's new imperial policies.[9]

The leadership role of the United States was implicit in the theme of the Exposition from the outset. According to the congressional papers relating to the Exposition, the purpose was "to fittingly illustrate the marvelous development of the western hemisphere during the nineteenth century by a display of the arts, industries, manufactures, and products of the soil, mines, and sea," and to do so by a "demonstration of the reciprocal relations existing between the American Republics and Colonies."[10] While businessmen with commercial aspirations and politicians with a taste for power were elated with this first step into the imperial arena and felt little need to modify a crassly economic, imperial interpretation of Spencer's Social Darwinist theory concerning survival of the fittest, the American middle class preferred a smoothness and absence of violence and disorder in the conduct of world affairs.[11] They sought to candy-coat expansionism with an emphasis on peaceful intent and democratic procedure. While the belief in white superiority remained intact, the prevailing thought centered on the upward progress of mankind as a whole, led by the civilizing example of the white race in general and the United States in particular. As civilized nations grew more enlightened, the theory maintained, "barbarian" nations would rise toward standards set from above; "backward" nations needed patient tutoring before becoming full-fledged world citizens. Mankind, it was believed, was moving inexorably toward eventual unity in peace and brotherhood.[12] Such was the outlook that manifested itself in the Pan-American Exposition and permeated turn-of-the century American culture.

Fortified by the reassuring theories of Herbert Spencer and his many followers,[13] Americans thus embraced a feeling of optimism and pride as their nation matured into an economic and political world power. Yet, at the same time, the concomitant undermining of traditional social, economic, and value structures that accompanied this growth generated an atmosphere of anxiety, regret, and confusion. The industrialization that helped to propel the country into its enhanced postition concurrently sapped individual autonomy, created demoralizing working conditions, and plundered the natural environment (while often producing poorly designed and shoddily manufactured goods). Public reaction thus was marked by a sense of disillusionment and a rejection of the emphasis placed on materialism as an end in itself.[14] A feeling that spirituality and beauty were being pushed out of contemporary life prevailed, and many, especially artists and their patrons, sought to escape such a harsh reality by reasserting the importance of both in the sphere of everyday life.

LIVING IN THE MATERIAL WORLD:
ART FOR ART'S SAKE / ART FOR LIFE'S SAKE

Beauty became a compelling issue in post-Civil War America with the blossoming of the Aesthetic Movement in the 1870s and 1880s. Originating in England and rapidly accepted in the United States where publications by such popular proponents of Aesthetic tenets as British art critic John Ruskin and Arts and Crafts advocate William Morris spread its message, the Aesthetic Movement offered a science of the beautiful or philosophy of taste.[15] United by an interest in promoting taste and beauty, Aestheticism's adherents were otherwise quite diverse; ironically, perhaps, the most distinctive trait of the movement was the variety of interpretations of beauty and the myriad, often contradictory, theories encompassed within its bounds. Its identity consisted more of a shared concern with atmosphere and mood than with a particular visual quality.[16] Two primary aspects of the movement that were in many respects opposed but that had equally significant impact in the United States were the ideology of art-for-art's-sake (a conviction that the appreciation of beauty, without concern for meaning or content, is a desirable end in itself) and the belief in the unity of the arts (a theory that underscored the merits of the arts conceived as a whole, unhampered by the traditional, hierarchical divisions of fine and decorative arts). By the 1890s, the two issues became polarized as the moral implications inherent in the concept of the unity of the arts (specifically, the amalgamation of art and life embodied in the Arts and Crafts Movement) diverged from the amoral art-for-art's-sake aesthetic.

Lionized art critic John Ruskin and renowned designer and social philosopher William Morris laid the philosophical groundwork for the Arts and Crafts movement. Ruskin's approach to design emphasized its moral implications. In his 1859 book *The Two Paths, Being Lectures on Art and Its Application to Decoration and Manufacture,* he turned his full attention to the issue of decoration, stressing its importance and placing it on the same level as the fine arts. Designs based on natural forms received his greatest praise since, Ruskin perceived, they evinced God's work as reflected in nature. For Ruskin, natural scale, form, and materials embodied truth, which he found essential to the creation of moral ornament.

Morris was perhaps the most outspoken and well-known proponent of handicraft, which lay at the heart of the Arts and Crafts Movement. He believed that in order to produce aesthetically pleasing objects, the worker must find satisfaction in the process of making the object, a circumstance that can only occur if he or she is involved in all aspects of its manufacture. In this respect, he joined Ruskin and others who contended that work itself could be ennobling or debasing and who looked to the Gothic era for its model of workmanship based on the lack of specialization and divided labor.[17] Morris also furthered the creed that beauty must be joined to usefulness.

The migration of Ruskin and Morris's ideas to the United States prompted a multitude of philanthropic and reform endeavors. These efforts ranged from the establishment of settlement houses like Ellen Gates Starr and Jane Addams's Hull House in Chicago (modeled on Toynbee Hall in London), in which handicraft training was aimed at endowing the poor with saleable skills and creative satisfaction, to attempts to reform factories and fashion a "new industrialism," in which workshop production would combine production with industrial education and thus merge school, studio, and factory into an organic whole.[18]

Primary credit for the dissemination of these ideas in this country may be given to two Americans with enterprises based in upstate New York, Gustav Stickley and Elbert Hubbard. Both men appeared to undergo a conversionary experience following trips to England in the 1890s, Hubbard after meeting Morris himself (according to Hubbard's own, somewhat questionable, account) and touring his Kelmscott Press in 1894, and Stickley after a visit in 1898 during which he saw furniture designed by prominent English Arts and Crafts designers C.F.A. Voysey and C.R. Ashbee.[19] Hubbard returned home catalyzed to found the Roycroft Press and

Community in East Aurora, New York.[20] Stickley soon turned his Syracuse, New York, furniture enterprise toward producing Craftsman furniture and began publishing the magazine *Craftsman*.[21]

Stickley's *Craftsman* and Hubbard's periodical *The Philistine* featured articles emphasizing the moral and health benefits of simple living, the importance of gaining satisfaction from one's labor, and the virtues of design based on simple forms, straightforward construction, and appropriate choice and treatment of materials. Desirable traits such as honesty, sincerity, individuality, and dignity were ascribed to objects as they would be to people, and thus the use and appreciation of objects so endowed could, it was thought, uplift the people who possessed them.[22] One can discern this design philosophy in Stickley's United Crafts *Magazine Rack* of ca. 1900 (cat. no. 50), with its clean lines, sturdy construction, and beautiful oak material and in the austere but well-proportioned, solidly built chair made at the Roycroft Shops around the same time (cat. no. 49). Stickley stressed the desirability of furniture that was as easy to care for (that is, durable and unencumbered by dust-catching ornamentation), as it was beautiful, and both his and the Roycroft piece would certainly meet his criteria. The use of leather and brass studs also typifies the Arts and Crafts penchant for natural materials.[23]

Concern for fulfilling creative work, appropriate use of materials, and simple beauty that would uplift taste and thought characterized, as well, the aims of the many art potteries that flourished at the time of the Arts and Crafts Movement. Upstate New York was a particularly active center for the development of art pottery. New York drew craftspeople for many differing reasons: The broad network of rail and canal lines that afforded easy transportation of raw materials and finished goods, the presence of the marketing mecca of New York City, the often skilled handicraft laborers among the masses of immigrants arriving at Ellis Island, and the beauty of New York's countryside all made the state a desirable location for various artists, arts and crafts associations and communities, and art potteries such as Buffalo Pottery (1901-56) and Tiffany Pottery in Corona, New York (1898-1920).[24] Furthermore, Englishman Charles Binns's establishment of the New York School of Clayworking and Ceramics at Alfred University in 1900 helped to attract students, like Adelaide Alsop Robineau, who went on to become major figures in the development of art pottery.[25] In 1899, Robineau and her husband Samuel created the Keramic Studio Publishing Company and produced the first issue of *Keramic Studio*, a magazine that, along with conveying technical information about ceramics, quickly became as influential as Stickley's and Hubbard's periodicals in spreading the aesthetics and aims of the Arts and Crafts Movement. After moving from New York City to Syracuse, New York, in 1901, Robineau, a painter turned china decorator, tired of painting on blanks and began making her own pottery forms (mostly in porcelain, although she created some stoneware).[26] Consequently, she started experimenting with glazes, developing a unique oxblood-flammé and crystalline glazes in blue, ivory, green, lilac, and gold.[27] One can admire such crystalline glazes in brown and green on her *Jar with Cover* of 1919 (cat. no. 44), a piece that also possesses an unusual lid incised to suggest the stem of a gourd and glazed in a deceivingly metallic brown. Her love of natural forms took shape, as well, in her *Crab Vase* of 1908 (cat. no. 43). With its low-relief decorations of crabs around the shoulder of the vase, its pierced and incised crab-embellished base, and its combination of flowing brown and tan matte glazes and aqua, blue, and orange crystalline glazes, this vase demonstrates the range and virtuosity of Robineau's technical and creative skills.

Flowing, natural forms of decoration such as those on Robineau's *Crab Vase* point to the growth of Art Nouveau toward the end of the nineteenth century. An offshoot of Aestheticism,

Art Nouveau profited from its progenitor's stress on freedom from exact imitation of historical styles and focused on the development of pleasing, original design for its own sake. Usually inspired by various flora and fauna, Art Nouveau decoration featured harmonious curvilinear motifs (especially the exaggerated "whiplash" curve) that suggested, rather than precisely depicted, biological phenomena.

Louis Comfort Tiffany's *Vase with Pansies* of ca. 1910 (cat. no. 47), a cylindrical stoneware form composed entirely of merging flowers, leaves, and stems, and glazed with a mottled green, displays an affinity with the Art Nouveau aesthetic. Most of Tiffany's pottery was mold-made and, like *Vase with Pansies,* produced by studio potters, though bearing Tiffany's monogram.[28] Tiffany Pottery, in operation from 1898 to 1920, was only one of Tiffany's enterprises and, in comparison with some of his other ventures, a relatively short-lived component of his business; by 1914, his interest in pottery had already waned.[29] His involvement with glass making, however, proved far more enduring, beginning with his experiments at commercial glasshouses in New York in 1873 and continuing throughout his life.[30] Yet even in many of his glass pieces, the Art Nouveau element prevailed, as is evident in the gentle organic swell and flare of his *Gold Iridescent Tulip Vase* (cat. no. 64).

Tiffany's versatile interests and multifaceted career exemplify the diverse and sometimes paradoxical character of American art and culture around 1900. Heir to his father's prestigious store, Tiffany & Co., in New York, Tiffany initially chose to pursue art rather than business and enrolled at the National Academy of Design in 1866 to study painting. Two years later, his studies took him to Europe where he became a pupil of French academic painter Léon Bailly for a brief period.[31] His desire to study in France and his subsequent travels throughout Europe, the Middle East, and North Africa mirrored the aspirations and activities of many young American artists of his generation who wished to establish their place in the world of art by claiming access to the same artistic, historical, and cultural training as their European peers. While seeking cultural status by association, these young artists also reflected the aggressive nationalism of the period by practicing a sort of cultural imperialism, selecting and combining elements from a cornucopia of cultures and historical periods to create what they felt would be a genuinely American art. Unified by the aims of the Genteel Tradition — to raise simultaneously the level of aesthetic standards and the moral value of art — the eclectic productions of this generation of artists demonstrated both the underlying cultural insecurity and the aspirations of a country purportedly at the apex of societal evolution.[32]

The cosmopolitan delight in the beautiful and exotic offerings of foreign cultures, the elevated ideals of the Genteel Tradition, and the ebullient nationalism driving a desire to create and excel on a grand scale all manifested in the subsequent career of Louis Comfort Tiffany. In 1879, he founded an interior decorating firm, L.C. Tiffany & Associated Artists, in New York along with two other painters, Samuel Colman and Lockwood de Forest, and Candace Thurber Wheeler, a textile designer and founder of the Society of Decorative Art in New York. Each partner exercised a particular expertise, but they pooled their knowledge, often bringing in other respected artists, to design complete environments.[33] Their highly ornamented interiors integrated elements juxtaposed in terms of historical period, place of origin, and style through harmonious arrangements of color, tone, and texture. Collections of art pottery, oriental porcelains, and paintings, for example, would become part of an overall scheme including mosaics, glass fireplace tiles, opalescent glass screens, embroidered hangings, and a profusion of patterns on walls and ceilings.[34] Tiffany, who would sketch the overall scheme but turn the details over to his associates,[35] liked to think of his business as a Renaissance atelier, like that of Della Robbia, in which a master initiated and oversaw the work carried out by gifted artisans and apprentices.[36] With his involvement in so many media, Tiffany revealed a desire to rival the original multi-talented "Renaissance man," as did many of his confreres who similarly turned their skills as painters, architects, and sculptors towards collaborative projects that united the various arts.[37] In tandem with this trend, businessmen like the Vanderbilts who had recently amassed great fortunes possessed the means as well as the desire to play the role of modern Medicis, acquiring vast collections of rare and valuable objects and engaging artists and decorators to design suitably elaborate interiors in which to house them. Indeed, such analogies drawn between the ideals and practices of the Italian Renaissance and those of late nineteenth-century America, in addition to the popularity of Renaissance-related styles (most comprehensively embodied in the "White City" of the World's Columbian Exposition in Chicago), have earned the period the appellation of "the American Renaissance." [38]

"BUT IS IT ART?": PHOTOGRAPHY COMES INTO FOCUS

At once forward and backward looking, Tiffany and others of his generation relied heavily on the past for inspiration and validation of their artistic and moral standing, while simultaneously pursuing new business strategies and modern technologies to attain their goals. Tiffany, for instance, began using photography as early as the late 1860s, taking pictures that he then employed to help him frame scenes and organize the compositions of his landscape paintings.[39] Again, he was not alone in such endeavors.

Photography in and of itself was not an entirely new technology at the end of the nineteenth century. Indeed, the concept of the camera dated to the Renaissance, but its potential to produce images by recording the action of light on chemically treated materials (paper, metal, or glass) only began to be explored at the very end of the eighteenth century. Yet not until nearly the last quarter of the nineteenth century were methods of fixing and printing negatives perfected to the point that the medium became quick and easily portable. Simultaneous with these advances in chemical procedures were improvements in camera lenses, shutters, and camera design, and in 1888, George Eastman, a photographic supply manufacturer residing in Rochester, New York, created a handheld camera that contained a roll of sensitized paper (plastic film replacing the paper by 1891), for which his company would supply photofinishing.[40] His inventions revolutionized photography by making it easy and available to not just the professional or dedicated amateur but to the public at large.

Popular as it became by the end of the nineteenth century, photography was, as it had been from its inception, plagued by debates about its very nature: could it be a new form of art, or was it a simply a mechanical means of visual documentation? No doubt there were many who concurred with artist Joseph Pennell when he scoffed,

> In a word, the photographer is the bold independent who has broken loose from tradition and asserted his individuality, not by the cultivation of his hand and his brain and his eye... no, by sticking his head into a black box, and at the crucial moment letting a machine do everything for him.[41]

Conversely, photography's validity as an art form had numerous vocal advocates such as the British physician-turned-photographer Peter Henry Emerson whose book *Naturalistic Photography for Students of the Art,* published in 1889, advanced the case for pictorial photography. Emerson's preference for quiet, atmospheric images stemmed from an appreciation of scientist Hermann von Helmholtz's studies on human optics. According to von Helmholtz, the human eye can focus clearly only on a central field; objects in the distance thus appear hazy. In photography, Emerson contended, truth to nature required the photographer to imitate the limitations of the eye by adjusting the lens to focus sharply only on the center of the composition, allowing the rest of the picture to become increasingly unfocused toward the distance.[42] *Twixt Land and Water* (cat. no. 69), a direct, non-sentimental view typical of the photographs he took during the late 1880s in the marshlands of East Anglia, demonstrates his theory put into practice.

Pictorial photography gained attention and respect in the United States largely due to the efforts of photographer, editor, and gallery director Alfred Stieglitz. From 1897 until 1902, his magazine *Camera Notes* informed readers about innovative photographic processes, provided critical reviews of exhibitions, and presented fine reproductions of contemporary photographs. Discouraged by the difficulty he encountered in stimulating American camera clubs to organize exhibitions with sufficiently high aesthetic standards, Stieglitz, together with friends Gertrude Käsebier, Clarence H. White, Edward J. Steichen, and others, formed the Photo-Secession in 1903.[43] Despite his early encouragement of photographers to experiment with various procedures in the darkroom that could increase the options for individual artistic expression in the final print, Stieglitz generally preferred not to manipulate the negative. He relied instead on choosing a subject and then patiently waiting to shoot until the perfect moment when the lighting and placement of figures serendipitously allied with his aims. For example, he reported once standing for several hours in a snowstorm in order to get his picture, a tale that comes to mind when one views *The Street, Fifth Avenue* (cat. no. 34).[44]

Stieglitz's efforts to promote pictorial photography eventually succeeded, providing encouragement for regional camera clubs like the Photo-Pictorialists of Buffalo and leading to recognition by prominent art museums like the Albright Art Gallery in Buffalo, where the Photo-Pictorialists of Buffalo exhibited in 1907 and Stieglitz organized the landmark *International Exhibition of Pictorial Photography* in 1910.[45] Nevertheless, success did not preclude unrest among the supporters of photography as an art form. Although photography ultimately became established as legitimate, artistic medium, during the course of its evolution, even some of its original proselytizers shifted allegiance. Emerson, convinced by scientists that the control of tones that he sought in the process of development was unachievable, issued a pamphlet in 1891 titled "The Death of Naturalistic Photography" in which he recanted his earlier position that photography was an art.[46] Stieglitz, while continuing to believe in the artistic value of photography, nonetheless eventually turned his attention solely to straight photography.

For those who regarded photography essentially as a tool for documentation, however, there was greater consensus: it served well. Always in demand for portraiture, photography also answered such diverse purposes as recording the wild grandeur of the west during the 1870s and exposing the dreadful living conditions of the working poor, largely immigrant, urban populations in the 1880s and 1890s. Further technological developments, such as the use of the halftone print process that allowed photographs to be transferred to metal plates (called the photogravure process) so that the pictures could be reproduced in magazines, newspapers, and the like, proved as much of a boon to art as to news reporting or advertising. Photographs of all types of art from different historical periods and geographical origins, made widely available through popular graphic media, helped to provide a rich visual source for artists, promote an interest in art among the public, and promulgate contemporary art theories and criticism. Moreover, art and technology could work in concert in pursuing the scientific exploration of movement, anatomy, and perspective, a circumstance evinced by the collaboration between British-born photographer Eadweard Muybridge and American painter Thomas Eakins.

Muybridge began his study of movement in the 1870s when he was commissioned by former California governor Leland Stanford to settle a bet he had wagered on his claim that a horse in full gallop had all four feet off the ground at one time. Setting up a row of cameras at intervals along a racetrack, each camera attached to a thread crossing the course, Muybridge contrived to photograph the precise motion of the horse as it ran through the threads, triggering the cameras and thus producing a chronological series of pictures breaking down the movements of the animal into individual, still shots. This study generated widespread interest, including that of Eakins, who had been investigating animal locomotion through artistic means and had also not only used photography as a tool to assist in his painting but had made some technological contributions to the process as well.[47] Eakins began corresponding with Muybridge in 1879, and when the provost of the University of Pennsylvania later contracted Muybridge to continue his experiments in Philadelphia under the auspices of the University, Eakins became supervisor of the project. The two worked together from 1884 through 1885, and during that time, Muybridge produced approximately 30,000 negatives that he published in 1887 under the title *Animal Locomotion*. *Animal Locomotion (woman at wash stand)* (cat. no. 72), an example of those published photographs, reveals how mundane activities, broken down into images exposed in increments of 1/2000 of a second, can transform into a narrative of fantastic detail.

ACADEMICIANS, EXPATRIATES, AND ARTISTIC AGITATORS: A VARIED PICTURE OF PAINTING

Perhaps Eakins acquired his interest in photography when he studied in Paris during the 1860s with the French academic master Jean-Léon Gérôme, who pioneered the use of photographs as a form of preparatory documentation for painting.[48] Gérôme traveled extensively in the Near East, North Africa, Spain, and Portugal between 1854 and 1872 in search of exotic subjects like that of the belly dancer or "almeh" depicted in *Almeh Performing the Sword Dance* (cat. no. 53). His dedication to exactitude in painting, in this instance, led to his engaging a dancer he saw in a café to pose in his studio where he could sketch and photograph her so that he might paint her picture with the aid of these and other props (he bought her costume for this purpose!) at a later time.[49] One of the most popular teachers among the young Americans pouring into Paris from the late 1860s onward, Gérôme stressed the importance of drawing and accurate representation of the figure, requiring his students to draw from casts of classical sculptures and then from live models before finally allowing them to paint. Hence, his style promoted the use of intellect over imagination, line over color, and a precise, disciplined handling of form and values (or tones, that is, the range of light to dark) over an expressive, more softly naturalistic treatment of color, atmosphere, and light. This emphasis on drawing was shared by many of the French academicians of the time, such as the enormously popular Adolphe William Bouguereau whose *Young Priestess* of 1902 (cat. no. 74) professes the endurance of classical motifs and painstaking attention to drawing and detail into the early twentieth century.[50] Some American painters adopted the academic style wholeheartedly, as can be discerned from Daniel Ridgway Knight's exactingly painted peasant girl in *Springtime* (cat. no. 14). Others, while profiting from academic lessons in mental discipline and knowledge of the human form, adopted a looser, more expressive handling of brushwork and a more atmospheric treatment of color and light. Eakins's *Music* (cat. no. 10), for example, displays an objective command of perspectival relationships and rendering of figures while moving beyond documentation into subjective expression by means of softening brushwork and subdued, gently modulated light and color that contribute to the painting's reflective, even nostalgic mood. Eakins, it should be noted, also studied with Léon Bonnat, one of a number of academic French painters who encouraged a more painterly approach than Gérôme or Bouguereau. Thomas Couture, for instance, taught his students to compose in masses and imparted a sensitivity to the handling of tones, and Charles Emile Auguste Carolus-Duran, unlike both Couture and Gérôme, made brushwork rather than charcoal drawing the foundation of his method, had his students paint light figures upon a dark ground, and allowed them to paint from the outset. His methods, in fact, paralleled those taught at the Bavarian Royal Academy in Munich, Germany, which, though superceded in popularity by the Parisian academies, nonetheless attracted such American painters as Frank Duveneck and William Merritt Chase who became important teachers, and thus disseminators of this type of painting, upon their return to the United States from Europe. Although later in his career Chase, under the influence of French Impressionism, lightened his palette, elements of the Munich style – dramatic contrasts of light and dark and bravura brushwork reflecting the current admiration for Baroque masters Frans Hals and Diego Velázquez – are still evident in *Memories* (cat. no. 84).[51]

In addition to the technical mastery – in composition, drawing, shading, and above all, in depicting the human figure – acquired from study with academic painters and examination of works by Old Masters, young Americans absorbed other artistic lessons during their sojourns in Europe. An alternative influence originated in the small French village of Barbizon near the forest of Fontainebleau where earlier in the century a group of painters (most notably, Jean-François Millet, Camille Corot, and Théodore Rousseau) had developed a style of painting that opposed what they perceived as the artificiality of academic painting. Their works, painted out-of-doors rather than in the studio, featured unedited views of nature, composed in flat, broad masses of tone with little modeling or detail and a brushy application of paint entirely unlike the enamel-like surfaces of much French academic painting. By these means, they captured the transitory immediacy of nature while maintaining an underlying sense of continuity and stability. George Inness, an older American painter previously associated with the detailed landscape mode of the Hudson River School, embraced the Barbizon style after his first exposure to it in the 1850s and helped establish its precedence among younger American artists. A convert to the teachings of Swedish mystic Emanuel Swedenborg, Inness had come to believe that God resided in the unseen and that the Ideal lay in the artist's spiritual vision of nature rather than in the objective imitation of nature itself. Through his landscapes, he sought to reveal the "correspondences" between the spiritual world and the material world. The Barbizon method better enabled him to achieve his expressive aims, as exemplified in *Early Moonrise in Florida* (cat. no. 77), in which a mystical harmony between man and nature is suggested by the lone figure, reaching toward the moon and united with the surrounding landscape by an all-encompassing, atmospheric haze. One may also detect an element of Japanese influence in Inness's late work, as seen in the flattening of the illusion of three-dimensional space and in the silhouetted, stylized patterning of the trees against the sky in *Early Moonrise in Florida.*

Japan arose as the most fashionable exotic cultural source in contemporary European and American art at the end of the nineteenth century. Virtually cut off from the West until it was opened by the American Commodore Perry in 1853, Japan exercised the lure of mystery upon the western imagination, and its products were not often seen in the occidental world before the 1860s. In London, the Japanese exhibit at the International Exposition there in 1862 set off an explosion of Japanese mania that permeated everything from the English Aesthetic movement to the burgeoning art of French Impressionism. The construction of an entire Japanese village, presented at the Centennial Exposition in Philadelphia in 1876, had a similar impact upon all the arts in the United States. Flattened spatial perspective, patterning, massing of form and color, asymmetrically balanced composition, and graceful stylization of natural forms characterized the Japanese aesthetic.

American expatriate painter James Abbott McNeill Whistler, a flamboyant innovator whose works excited both great admiration and great controversy at the London and Paris Salon exhibitions, incorporated Japanese artistic concepts into his art-for-art's-sake approach to painting. His contribution to the spread of such ideas in the form of his *Ten O'Clock Lecture* of 1885 and his *Gentle Art of Making Enemies* of 1890 had a marked impact on the minds of his compatriots. At the core of his aesthetics lay the conviction that

> Art should be independent of all clap-trap – should stand alone, and appeal to the artistic sense of the eye or ear, without confounding this with emotions entirely foreign to it, as devotion, pity, love, patriotism, and the like. All these have no kind of concern with it and that is why I insist on calling my works "arrangements" and "harmonies."[52]

Even in a small example of his work such as *The Sea, Pourville, No. 2* (cat. no. 94), Whistler's theories are visibly present in the flattened pictorial space, the subtle play of gray tonalities uniting browns, blues, and greens, the simple three-tiered horizontal composition alluding to land, sea, and sky, and the casual smear of creamy paint that somehow conveys a sense of crashing waves, thereby injecting a contretemps of life and movement into an otherwise static and subdued painting. Here, the artist's response to and expression of nature outstrips in importance the role played by nature itself. In fact, the "subject" of nature essentially becomes a vehicle for displaying the art of painting.

While American artists responded enthusiastically to Whistler's concepts of "harmonious" arrangements of forms, colors, and tones, they rarely, if ever, succeeded in freeing their paintings from "all clap-trap." Indeed, within the very search for gratification of the senses through formal means lay a paradox that a generation of painters strove to reconcile, for to the American painter, beauty in itself carried meaning: Beauty represented moral goodness. For the young, generally European-trained American artists of the period, the desire to convey uplifting ideas through poetic, emotionally evocative paintings created the problem, as art historian Susan Hobbs has phrased it, of "how to invest an objectively depicted subject with abstract or spiritual significance."[53] The wide appeal of Whistler's model of abstraction derived directly from its potential to fulfill this need. Thus, despite some skepticism on the part of American artists toward the more stringent aspects of Whistler's art-for-art's-sake creed, his idea of evoking musical effects through the use of color, tone, and form reverberated throughout late-nineteenth century American painting. While his American contemporaries might have rejected his assertion that "subject matter has nothing to do with harmony of sound or of color," they nevertheless embraced his belief that "nature contains the elements, in color and form, of all pictures, as the keyboard contains the notes of all music…. As music is the poetry of sound, so is painting the poetry of sight…."[54] In fact, the association of abstract elements of composition with poetry and music helped endow painting with inherent meaning in the eyes of American artists.[55] Poetry and music, after all, served to uplift the intellect and spirit just as did visual beauty. Moreover, this emphasis on synesthesia (imaginatively experiencing something through a sense other than that receiving the stimulus, as when one "hears" color) enhanced the significance of the new, broad style of painting that young artists were bringing back from Munich, Paris, and Barbizon by imbuing technique with content.

Characterized by soft, unifying tonalities, crepuscular lighting, and mist-enshrouded moodiness, the style of painting developed by Whistler, Inness, and like-minded artists has, in recent years, come to be called Tonalism. At a time of economic, social, and cultural upheaval, this new art provided the contemplative viewer with an experience of harmony, unity, and repose generally absent from the hectic milieu of everyday life.[56] *Landscape,* an early painting by John Twachtman (cat. no. 93), and *Portrait in a Brown Dress,* by Thomas Wilmer Dewing (cat. no. 76) both communicate an experience of solitude and reverie. Twachtman's *Landscape,* devoid of human presence and subdued by an overcast light that seems to dissolve the solidity of land and trees into a moist green atmosphere, offers the viewer an intimate glimpse, through the artist's eyes, of the enduring flux of life or spirit that animates the ephemeral countenance of nature.[57] Dewing's portrait of a sylphlike young woman, apparently alone in a sparse interior setting, suggests a similar instance of individual withdrawal into contemplation. Seated in a chair and absorbed by the book she holds in her hand, she has left the physical world and the company of the artist/viewer for an inner world of meditative thought where intellect and spirit reside. Whether depicting the natural landscape or a figure within an interior, American artists like Twachtman and Dewing claimed their responsibility in furthering the progress of civilization by creating works of quiet beauty that spoke to the higher self. Through ethereal images that shed the vestige of physicality, they created secularized icons meant to draw the art lover into the mystery of art and thus into the realm of refined thinking and spiritual feeling.[58]

Many American critics received the art produced by Tonalist painters such as Twachtman and Dewing – along with that by other Americans whose work reflected various European influences – with enthusiasm when it began to appear on the walls of America's established art institutions. When the National Academy of Design in New York opened its spring exhibition in 1874, a writer for *Harper's* magazine noted

> The effect was startling. Their canvases were like windows unexpectedly opened upon
> a fair and hopeful prospect. They showed us figures well drawn and solidly painted;
> powerful portraits; bold effects of atmosphere; a rich tone and rugged handling in land-
> scape, all but unknown in American work until then.[59]

Returning from abroad, the young artists whose work caused this sensation soon broke from the National Academy of Design. In 1877, a number of them joined in forming a rival organization, the Society of American Artists, devoted to exhibiting the products of this varied group of rebels whom critics (rather indiscriminately) grouped together under the vague moniker "The New Movement." Yet, at a time of rapid transformation, that which was once considered new soon became the established norm, and by 1900 the work of European-trained Americans dominated the country's showing at home and abroad. Although European critics reviewing the

United States' contribution to the Exposition Universelle in Paris in 1900 often noted the diversity of styles among American artists, much of the commentary was complementary, and American painting and applied arts garnered numerous prizes. American critics, however, spoke of a distinctly American school and favored what is now termed Tonalist painting (then viewed as an American alternative to French Impressionism) as the most home-grown American style.[60]

Certainly the young American artists in Europe at the end of the nineteenth century would have been exposed to European Impressionist painting from its inception. The Impressionists had exhibited as a group for the first time in Paris in 1874, when their style acquired its name, courtesy of critics who panned Claude Monet's painting, *Impression: Sunrise* (a scene painted out-of-doors at daybreak, depicting red rays of sunshine flickering over misty, gray water) for its lack of clearly defined form or three-dimensional perspective. Heir to the Realist strain of painting developed by French artists such as Gustave Courbet and the Barbizon painters, the Impressionists sought to capture the transient quality of everyday life by imitating in paint the optical response to light and color as it plays over solid forms, dissolving them in atmospheric luminescence. Their interest in current scientific theories concerning color and optical perception led them to attempt to break light down into its component colors, applied in short brushstrokes of unmixed pigment, that they believed the eye would blend when the viewer stood at a distance from the canvas. Hence, their works characteristically featured a light palette of bright, usually unblended colors, choppy brushstrokes, and compositions that appeared spontaneous, created entirely of color with little or no modeling of form and a limited sense of spatial perspective. *Woman Sewing* (cat. no. 17) by Berthe Morisot, a member of the French Impressionist circle, demonstrates many of these traits, including the quotidian choice of subject, casual composition, splintery brushwork, and unifying play of light woven in dabs of color. At first employed in a more intuitive rather than scientific manner, the rules concerning color and optics eventually became more rigorously applied by some, evolving into Neo-Impressionism or Divisionism, a style that stressed the ways in which the reflected color of closely situated objects and the interaction of juxtaposed colors affect the quality of light. As one may observe in a Neo-Impressionist painting such as *Peasants in the Fields, Eragny* (cat. no. 20) by Camille Pissarro, light has been broken down into a complex matrix of numerous, distinct, contrasting colors applied more methodically in uniform dashes throughout the entire composition.

Yet, neither Impressionism nor its immediate successors initially held great appeal for American artists, perhaps because European artists sought a primarily objective, visual impression whereas American artists pursued an essentially subjective, emotional, or spiritual impression. George Inness put his finger on the difference between his idea of impressionism and French Impressionism when he wrote:

> Long before I heard of Impressionism, I settled to my mind the underlying law of what may properly be called impressionism of nature.... Whatever is painted truly according to any idea of unity will, as it is perfectly done, possess both the subjective sentiment – the poetry of nature – and the objective fact to give the commonest mind a feeling of satisfaction and through that satisfaction elevate to a higher idea.... In the art of communicating impressions lies the power of generalizing without losing that logical connection of parts to the whole which satisfies the mind. The elements of this are solidity of objects, the transparency of shadows in a breathable atmosphere through which we are conscious of spaces and distances.[61]

While Inness never warmed to French Impressionism, others began to gravitate toward its heightened palette and broken stroke. By the mid 1880s, French Impressionism made its way to the United States through the means of major exhibitions in Boston, New York, and Chicago, the 1886 New York exhibition of approximately three hundred paintings, organized by the influential art dealer Paul Durand-Ruel, proving most pivotal in exposing to the general public that which many American artists had already begun to embrace. A significant number of those previously associated with Tonalism ultimately converted to a style closer to the French mode, including Chase, Twachtman, and Twachtman's close friend, Julian Alden Weir. Weir's portrait of his daughter (cat. no. 38) displays a feathered touch and delicate play of color quite different from the earlier, dark-hued paintings by this former student of Gérôme and admirer of Whistler. Nevertheless, the figure in the portrait retains a greater sense of solidity than her French counterparts, a distinction typical of American painting. Even in its most French incarnation, American Impressionism rarely broke completely with Inness's preference for a clear relationship between distinct forms and a deference to natural coloration. Childe Hassam, today widely considered the most completely Impressionist of American painters, and Theodore Robinson, viewed by his peers as the truest American follower of French Impressionism, both met the more rigorous tenets of the European style with a casual independence.[62] They often eschewed its bright spectrum of unmixed colors for a more naturalistic, modified palette including some darker, earthier hues as can be seen in Hassam's *Rocks and Sea, Isles of Shoals* (cat. no 55) and Robinson's *The Berme Road* (cat. no. 56). Also, both artists, thoroughly trained in academic drawing and composition, revealed in their works a disinclination to abandon solid form altogether. *Rocks and Sea, Isles of Shoals,* for example, captures the transience of light glancing off water and rocks in broken brushstrokes of varied colors, but the craggy boulders, their masses defined with dark shadows, remain an immovable bulwark against which the heaving sea shatters into foam. Nevertheless, in comparison to the Tonalist and academic paintings with which the American public had become familiar by the twilight of the century, this Impressionism still appeared radical in the 1880s and 1890s. Thus, in 1897, when Chase, Twachtman, Weir, Hassam, Robinson and a number of other painters resigned from the Society of American Artists in order to mount their own exhibitions, their group (called simply "The Ten") replaced its predecessor as the new American avant-garde.[63]

By early in the first decade of the twentieth century, however, American Impressionism had become a widely accepted style of painting in the United States, and soon a new group sprung up to challenge conservative ideas and institutions. Following in the footsteps of The Ten, a circle of painters led by Robert Henri, critically christened "The Eight," caused an uproar in 1908 with their first exhibition at the Macbeth Gallery in New York.[64] Less a rejection of Impressionism, per se, than a rebellion against the genteel cult of beauty ensconced among the artists of the National Academy of Design (with which the Society of American Artists had reunited in 1906), the exhibition of The Eight stressed the participating members' artistic individuality and independence from accepted artistic ideals.[65] Indeed, the sensibilities of the eight artists diverged considerably: Arthur B. Davies, for instance, created paintings of nymph-like women inhabiting dreamy landscapes that were abstruse in meaning, idiosyncratic in style, and closer in spirit to works like the mystical *Temple of the Mind* (cat. no. 22) by eccentric veteran American painter Albert Ryder than to anything by his fellow exhibitors. Maurice Prendergast presented a distinctly personal style – exactly conforming neither to Impressionism nor to any of its offshoots – featuring images constructed with large dabs of color, reminiscent of mosaics or stained glass. Ernest Lawson, on the other hand, maintained a more decipherable connection to Impressionism, although his rugged brushwork and preference for urban industrial subjects introduced a new grittiness to the genre. Henri himself painted in a manner recalling the Munich school with its dramatic contrasts of light and dark and its bravura brushwork inspired by Hals, traits that are evident in his painting *Dutch Soldier* (cat. no. 88), which was included in the Macbeth exhibition. His style, albeit embodied in vivid, unidealized portraits of contemporary people, was not as radical as were his ideas regarding art and teaching.

In the early 1890s, Henri had taught at the Women's School of Design in Philadelphia and held gatherings at his studio that attracted a number of young men who were both students at the Pennsylvania Academy of Art and newspaper illustrators, including John Sloan, George Luks, Everett Shinn, and William Glackens (later all members of The Eight). There he began his career, continued in New York from the late 1890s onward, as one of the most influential art teachers of the era. Abhorring sentimentality or artificiality of any kind, Henri pitted himself against tradition and the philosophy of art-for-art's-sake, espousing instead complete immersion in all life experiences and instructing his students to paint honestly and vividly what they saw and felt as real. He encouraged his pupils to develop their own means of expression rather than imitate his or any other single style, thereby reflecting in his teaching method his generally liberal and democratic views.

Sloan, Luks, Shinn, and Glackens all responded to Henri's optimism, vitality, and "art-for-life's sake" views, which reinforced the interest in direct observation of life, solid depiction of form, and straightforward painting that they derived from their studies with Thomas Anshutz at the Pennsylvania Academy. Anshutz had studied with Eakins and thus provided a direct conduit for Eakins's teaching to a younger generation. Enflamed by Henri's rhetoric, Sloan, Luks, Shinn, and Glackens thereby proceeded to build a vigorous, unvarnished realism upon the foundation laid by older American artists like Eakins and Winslow Homer. By the early 1900s, they had all moved to New York where they threw themselves into portraying the urban industrial environment and the vibrant life teeming in the city's streets, bars, theaters, and tenements with a reportorial ardor enhanced by their experience as newspaper illustrators. Whereas their desire to paint scenes of contemporary life that were unmistakably American differed little, on a superficial level, from the aim of earlier American Impressionists to give their style a nationalist interpretation, these young artists' choice of city over country, slums over parks, and laborers and tenement-dwellers over middle-class maidens and businessmen posed a marked departure from conventionally cherished ideas of what constituted American identity. Accused of coarseness and vulgarity, their works had been rejected by the National Academy of Design (an occurrence that helped to spur the organization of the Macbeth exhibition), and their brash style and unrefined subject matter ultimately gave rise to their becoming dubbed the "Ashcan School."

Despite their renunciation of artistic formalities, either in technique or subject, the Ashcan painters, in fact, were less revolutionary than they at first appeared. In many ways, their intention to create a fundamentally American art, their liberal and reformist social views, and their desire to reveal the dignity, vitality, and positive potential of their subjects linked them firmly to the prevailing cultural belief in America's place at the forefront of social evolution: They rejected tradition only as an obstacle to progress. The exposure of social ills, they optimistically thought, would lead to necessary reform, and scientific, technological, and industrial developments would fuel the country's race toward the goal of a socially enlightened, utopian state. Although eschewing the strictly middle-class affiliation of those working in more traditional modes, the Ashcan painters did not engage in the social alienation and cynicism of many of their European contemporaries, as that suggested by the painting of a prostitute, *Woman Lifting Her Chemise* (cat. no. 25), by Henri de Toulouse-Lautrec. Toulouse-Lautrec chose to immerse the viewer in the seamy underbelly of modern city life, showing a woman lifting her slip, probably in preparation for a required, routine health examination by a government physician. By contrast, John Sloan emphasized the camaraderie, industriousness, and dignity of working-class women in his painting *Scrubwomen, Astor Library* (cat. no. 92).

BRONZE AND SHAPELY:
CHANGES IN SCULPTURE AT THE TURN OF THE TWENTIETH CENTURY

Not all European artists, of course, shared Toulouse-Lautrec's perception of life among the poorer denizens of society. Belgian sculptor Constantin Meunier, for example, honored the integrity and stoic perseverance of industrial workers in his quietly moving portrayals of laborers, like that of *The Hammerman* (cat. no. 29). Even so, his individual figures carry vestiges of hardship and resignation in their reflective demeanor, unlike the lively and cheerful competence with which Sloan imbued his scrubwomen. Meunier's realism, apparent in the relaxed pose and naturalistic modeling of his figures, has been often compared to that of his contemporary, Auguste Rodin, and although Rodin's fame as a bold innovator has since eclipsed Meunier's renown, the latter's work was internationally acclaimed around the turn of the century.[66] Rodin ultimately pushed impressionistic modeling to an extreme in his effort to express the interior psychology underlying the exterior appearance of his portrait subjects, as in his *Head of Balzac "C"* (cat. no. 58), one of the many studies he made in preparation for his monumental standing sculpture of the poet.

Sculpture, in general, began to enjoy a resurgence in innovation and popularity during the second half of the nineteenth century. Previously stalled in a neoclassicism that had become dry and static, sculpture in the late nineteenth century was revitalized, in part, due to the demand for sculptural decoration created by the flourishing activity of Beaux-Arts architects. Paris's Beaux-Arts academies, such as the Académie Julian, Académie Colarossi, and the school in the Jardin des Plantes, became a magnet for American sculptors as well as painters. French masters, like François Jouffroy, infused the formulaic naturalism of neoclassicism with a new vigor and animation, incorporating decorative qualities into both subject matter and form, and passed this style along to their American students.[67] Beaux-Arts naturalism dovetailed well with the needs of Americans whose culture – at once blatantly materialistic and devoutly idealistic – called for sculptures that combined a naturalism compatible with materialism and an idealized imagery reflective of the country's sense of pride and destiny.[68] Augustus Saint-Gaudens, a pupil of Jouffroy, successfully adapted his Beaux-Arts training to an American idiom in works such as *The Puritan* (cat. no. 59), originally cast in a full-size version for the city of Springfield, Massachusetts.[69] Its daunting presence and masterly execution epitomize the vitalized naturalism, heroic characterization of patriotic figures, and elevated standard of professional workmanship that Saint-Gaudens brought to American sculpture.[70] However, Saint-Gaudens's powerful portrayal of a historic American figure also exposed an ambivalent strain often repeated in art of the period. While the choice of subject bolstered a sense of national heritage, thus underscoring a line of evolutionary ascent supportive of the prevailing nationalism, it simultaneously hinted at a nostalgia for the past that belied the country's apparently sanguine embrace of rapid change. That the American middle-class still clung to its traditional mores in the midst of massive social, economic, and political transformation could not be more aptly illustrated than in its reception of Frederick MacMonnies's *Bacchante with Infant Faun* (cat. no. 81). MacMonnies, who had begun his career as an assistant to Saint-Gaudens and subsequently studied with Jouffroy's star pupil, Jean Alexandre Joseph Falguière, had already achieved considerable success in Paris before he began a series of impressionistic, animated sculptures of pagan creatures in the early 1890s.[71] His infatuation at that time with a vivacious Parisian model, Eugénie Pasque, led to his portrayal of her in the guise of a bacchant. Notwithstanding its classical reference (provided only by the inclusion of the mythical faun-child), the sculpture was essentially an exuberant, unidealized full-length portrait of a real woman. When MacMonnies's friend, prominent architect Charles F. McKim, presented the statue to the city of Boston in 1894 to adorn the courtyard of the public library that he had designed, public outrage over its perceived promotion of licentiousness and inebriation ensued. Pressure from sources as diverse as Harvard Art History professor Charles Eliot Norton and the Women's Christian Temperance Union succeeded in effecting the withdrawal of McKim's gift.[72] Ironically, the victory of these conservatives only enhanced MacMonnies's fame: the Metropolitan Museum of Art in New York readily accepted the rejected sculpture (despite protests by the American Purity League and the Social Reform League), and the French government, perhaps in mockery of American priggishness, commissioned a replica for the Luxembourg Museum in Paris.[73] MacMonnies continued to produce lively, allegorical sculptures well into the twentieth century, but by the beginning of the first World War, his method of embodying abstract ideas in naturalistic forms had been challenged by the rise of abstraction and soon became obsolete.

Avant-garde developments in Europe at the outset of the twentieth century presented a far more radical departure from earlier modes of sculpture and painting than that with which most Americans were familiar. Indeed, MacMonnies's charming allegorical figures appear to belong to another time and another world than the one in which Henri Matisse produced his *Reclining Nude I* of 1907 (cat. no. 28) or Pablo Picasso his *Woman's Head* of 1909 (cat. no. 30). Rodin's precedence, evident in the rugged modeling of the sculptural surfaces and the resulting dramatic and active play of light and shadow, remained as the primary link between these works and earlier sculpture. In other respects, Matisse's and Picasso's treatment of the human form introduced formal and expressive liberties entirely new to western art. Both Matisse and Picasso had become acquainted with African sculpture probably sometime in 1906, and its profound effect can be seen in paintings and sculptures that they subsequently produced.[74] Proportion in African sculpted figures is determined by the significance invested in various body parts rather than by a desire to reproduce the natural (albeit often somewhat idealized) proportions of the human figure as in traditional western art. Furthermore, those body parts are themselves stylized into streamlined, geometrical forms rather than naturalistically rendered images of muscle and bone. Matisse employed this same exaggeration of body parts in his *Reclining Nude,* with its prominent breasts and hips dramatically juxtaposed by the twisted pose of the figure, thus creating a dynamic rhythm of curving forms, complemented by the lively handling of the surface.[75] Pleased with the results himself, Matisse included the image of this sculpture in many of his later paintings.

Picasso's attraction to African art, along with his admiration for the paintings of the French Post-Impressionist master Paul Cézanne, and his interest in contemporary theories concerning the nature of time and space, contributed to the development of Cubism. Working in concert with his colleague, Georges Braque, from about 1907, Picasso not only began to explore the iconic and abstract properties present in African and other forms of what was considered primitive art but also to build upon the new approaches toward color, form, and spatial structure established by Cézanne. Like many French artists at the end of the nineteenth century, Cézanne came to find Impressionist painting deficient in terms of solid form and structure. He sought stability in his views of nature and perceived basic geometry — the cone, cube, and sphere — underlying all of nature's forms. Yet, in his effort to grasp the essence of every object, his paintings became anything but static, as he created a complex pictorial order through the distortion of spatial perspectives that combined different viewpoints of each object into single, highly descriptive images of those objects. Moreover, he united drawing and color by using blocks of pigment to build forms, relying on the optical capacity of color to control the sense of depth and weight (reds and yellows appearing to come forward, blues and greens seeming to recede in space, and deeper colors producing an illusion of fullness of form). In his painting *The Sea at L'Éstaque* (cat. no. 75), for example, one can observe this process and the way in which related and interlocking shapes unite the different planes of space.

Picasso found that Cézanne's ambiguous treatment of space and depiction of objects from multiple viewpoints lent themselves well to providing a visual expression of current philosophical and scientific theories regarding time and space. Prior to the popularization of Albert Einstein's theory of relativity in the 1920s, when the fourth dimension became defined as time, the concept of the fourth dimension in physical and metaphysical terms stirred great interest on the part of scientists, philosophers, artists, and the general public.[76] Several mystical themes became central to the discussion of the fourth dimension: the concept of infinity suggested the illusionary nature of time and space and the absence of spatial orientation or limitation; philosophical monism proposed the unity of all things spiritual and material, an absolute oneness of which the self was simply a part; and the idea of the evolution of consciousness offered the possibility of an enlightenment in which the distinction between the ego and the external world, between subject and object, would dissolve.[77] In the same vein, the influential writings and lectures of the contemporary French metaphysicist Henri-Louis Bergson emphasized the role of intuition as a means of perceiving reality by imaginatively or empathetically entering into the objective world. Only by so doing, he believed, could one truly comprehend the continual flux of memory, momentary perception, and anticipation that comprise experience.[78]

Picasso and Braque sought to give visual expression to these concepts by breaking down objects into myriad viewpoints, thereby evoking the flux of perception and memory associated with intuitive experience and the fourth dimension. In *Woman's Head,* Picasso presented a series of interlocking shapes that create an active structural interplay extrapolated from the basic form of his mistress's head and neck. Naturally, in Cubist paintings, the spatial ambiguity of interpenetrating and shifting planes became even more pronounced, sometimes eroding depicted objects almost beyond all recognition.

The Cubist style generated by Picasso and Braque soon began to metamorphose in various ways in the hands of other artists. Fernand Léger, for example, produced a distinctive form of

Cubism based on his idea of dynamic contrasts, juxtaposing solid and ephemeral substances, angular and curvilinear forms as evident in his painting *Smoke* (cat. no. 15) in which rounded shapes representing billowing smoke contrast with architectural structures. Robert Delaunay contributed another aspect to Cubism with his Orphic paintings, so named by art critic Guillaume Apollinaire because he associated the abstract, expressive quality of Delaunay's work with that of music (the latter art linked to the mythical hero Orpheus). Since the Impressionists, color had been increasingly liberated from its naturalistic, descriptive role. Whereas the Impressionists and Neo-Impressionists had broken light down into its component parts, hence supplying a potpourri of brilliant, contrasting colors instead of more subdued, natural hues, Post-Impressionist and Symbolist artists like Vincent van Gogh and Paul Gauguin had eschewed solely representational coloration and used color rather to express and elicit particular emotions. Cézanne, in turn, blazoned the trail for placing color at the service of structure. Finally, by the early twentieth century, Matisse and a handful of colleagues broke altogether with tradition and applied color in an apparently arbitrary way, concerned only with its emotive capacity and formal structural and rhythmic purposes within their paintings; thus they earned themselves the title "Fauves," or "Wild Beasts." Delaunay, building upon these developments, executed paintings such as *Sun, Tower, Airplane* (cat. no. 7) in which he combined the shifting, interpenetrating planes of Cubism with the optical properties of bright, contrasting colors that appear to advance and recede in space. Here, residual images of the Eiffel Tower, a biplane, and a ferris wheel (representative of the new technologies of modern life) on the right defy gravity as they merge into the wheeling cosmos of color (the disc symbolizing, for Delaunay, the universe) at the left.

During the first decade of the twentieth century, the rapid and radical transformation of art in the hands of the European avant-garde received little attention in the United States and thus remained virtually unknown to most Americans. A few American artists who traveled to Paris, however, found this new art compelling and by pursuing it themselves began to sow the seeds of modernism back home. Max Weber, one such artist, spent the years 1905 to 1908 in Paris where he became interested in the work of Cézanne and studied briefly with Matisse. Acquainted with Picasso and Delaunay, as well, he participated in the Cubist and Fauvist experiments. Elements of all these influences are evident in his *Figure Study* of 1911 (cat. no. 27). The heightened torque of the figure's pose, together with its bold, rhythmic outline, recalls a similar painting, *Blue Nude,* by Matisse and also Matisse's sculpture *Reclining Nude,* while the angular distortions of the body relate to Picasso's early Cubist paintings and point to Picasso and Weber's shared fascination with African sculpture. For Weber and his peers, primitive art embodied the spontaneity, energy, and sincerity that they believed western cultures had lost and that native peoples still possessed. Their interest in achieving direct expression of the emotions, sensations, and urges of the unconscious mind stemmed largely from the burgeoning popularity of psychology spurred by the studies of Sigmund Freud. Freud's publications, such as *The Interpretation of Dreams* printed in 1900, catalyzed a shift in values and attitudes that placed the importance of instinct above that of rational thought as a key to unlocking the source of human behavior. This emphasis on the subconscious, in turn, enhanced the role of an artist's intuition in the creative process and dovetailed neatly with the mystical aspect of subjective experience associated with theories of the fourth dimension. Weber himself contributed significantly to the dialogue about the fourth dimension in his article "The Fourth Dimension from a Plastic Point of View" that appeared in Stieglitz's *Camera Work* magazine in 1910.[79]

Camera Work, Stieglitz's successor to *Camera Notes* and published from 1903 to 1917, provided an essential journalistic venue for the promotion of modernism in the United States and, as such, complemented the activities and aims of Stieglitz's Little Galleries of the Photo-Secession, located at 291 Fifth Avenue in New York City and better known as simply "291".[80] Founded by Stieglitz in 1905, it became a haven for modernists who practiced a wide variety of styles but united in their stance against the antimodernist attitudes then prevalent in American society. Stieglitz himself scorned the public-at-large as ignorant and devoted to a culture of crass commercialism; mass production and mass education, in Stieglitz's view, were equally responsible for lowering standards of aesthetic and individual perfection. For him, the artist assumed a noble, heroic stature, nurturing beauty amidst vast opposition, and the creative process itself he associated with mystic phenomena and the most profound expression of the individual spirit.[81] Given these views, it seems natural that his support of artists would reach beyond exhibiting their work and promoting them through publications to actually subsidizing them on occasion, as he did when he put Weber up in a room behind the gallery and when he advanced money to the painter Marsden Hartley to fund his return from a trip to Europe.[82]

In 1912, Hartley traveled to Paris where he became immersed in avant-garde circles, but he discovered a greater rapport with the German Expressionist painters that he met during his stay in Berlin from 1913 to 1917 and was particularly influenced by the art and theories of the Russian artist Wassily Kandinsky. Kandinsky's book, *Concerning the Spiritual in Art* of 1910, applied ideas related to current discussions of synesthesia, intuition, monism, and evolution of consciousness to painting, promoting an art of pure color and shape.[83] Hartley's *Painting No. 46* (cat. no. 13), one of a series of works inspired by his friendship with a German soldier and featuring German military insignia, melds a cubist, collage-like layering of forms with the boldly expressive use of color and shape espoused by Kandinsky. Although not entirely abstract, *Painting No. 46* epitomizes Hartley's quest (begun originally in landscapes bearing the mystical stamp of his early idol, Ryder), to convey the significance and personal meaning his subjects held for him through means of color, line, and form. Throughout his European sojourn, Hartley kept Stieglitz apprised of his thoughts and experiences, and Stieglitz supported his artistic explorations by exhibiting Hartley's German paintings upon his return to the United States.

Stieglitz maintained a reciprocally stimulating relationship with the artists and modern art enthusiasts with whom he worked. As early as 1908 he had begun exhibiting drawings by Rodin and Matisse that received rough treatment at the hands of bewildered, conservative critics but started to educate and inspire those with open minds. He also launched Weber and the painter Alfred Maurer with an exhibition in 1909 and caused a stir the following year with *Younger American Painters*, a show including works by Edward Steichen (a painter as well as photographer), Arthur B. Carles, Arthur Dove, John Marin, Maurer, Hartley, and Weber. In turn, Stieglitz learned a great deal about contemporary European art from Weber and other American artists like Maurer, Marin, Dove, Carles, and Steichen who had spent time in Europe during the early years of the twentieth century.[84] As a result, he began to show the works of Toulouse-Lautrec, Cézanne, Picasso, and others, thus providing for many, like Hartley, an initial introduction to their art.

Although Stieglitz played perhaps the most central role in supporting early modernism in the United States, his nearly religious fervor in promoting it was shared by a number of other prominent Americans at home and abroad. In Paris shortly after the turn of the century, the Pennsylvania-born, avant-garde writer Gertrude Stein and her brother Leo Stein, an artist himself, began collecting the works of Cézanne, Matisse, Picasso, and other revolutionary artists. Through their collecting activities and artistic pursuits, they met and cultivated acquaintances not only with artists the caliber of Matisse and Picasso but also with equally unconventional authors, musicians, dancers, intellectuals, collectors, art dealers, and socialites. Until about the outbreak of The Great War, their Parisian apartment became the meeting place of those shaping the revolution in the arts, and many young American artists arriving in Europe gleaned their first introduction into avant-garde circles there through the Steins.

On the other side of the Atlantic, the Buffalo native and wealthy socialite Mabel Dodge established a similar salon as the Steins' at her Fifth Avenue apartment in New York City. Between 1912 and 1917, avant-garde artists (many of whom were also members of Stieglitz's circle) might rub shoulders with political radicals such as John Reed and Emma Goldman, columnists and muckrakers such as Walter Lippman and Lincoln Steffens, contemporary dancers such as Isadora Duncan, social reformers such as birth-control advocate Margaret Sanger, and any number of other liberal and creative individuals involved in the cultural ferment taking place during those years. Dodge, though not an artist or art dealer herself, actively supported the arts, as when she assisted Isadora Duncan in establishing a dance school and when she supplied money and publicity for the Armory Show of 1913, a large, watershed exhibition of modern art.[85]

Mary Louise and Walter Conrad Arensberg hosted a comparable salon in New York City, as well, from 1914 to 1921. Like Dodge, they attracted many of the same people involved with the Stieglitz group, and indeed, mutual respect rather than competition characterized the relationship between the overlapping circles. Unlike Dodge, however, the Arensbergs were directly involved in the arts, "Lou" as a musician and Walter as a journalist, poet, founder and patron of the avant-garde literary periodical *Others,* and translator of modern French poets from Charles Baudelaire to Stephan Mallarmé. Naturally, literary figures comprised a significant component of their gatherings and included Wallace Stevens, Amy Lowell, and William Carlos Williams, among others. Another aspect of the Arensbergs' salon that set it apart was its marked association with the early manifestations of Dadaism in America. Dada (the name itself a nonsense word) originated with a group of artists and writers in Zurich, Switzerland, during World War I and expressed a critical reaction to the hysteria and madness of the world at war through art, music, poetry, theatricals, and lectures that featured the effect of intuition (unmediated by reason), chance, cacophony, and general chaos. Their madcap, often biting, humor threw into question the validity not only of the traditions of art but also of the morals, ideals, beliefs, and structures of the cultures from which the war had sprung.[86]

With the arrival of French artists Francis Picabia and Marcel Duchamp in New York in the mid-1910s, the seeds of what would become Dada were sown in the United States. Both artists benefited from their initial association with Stieglitz, but they found themselves most comfortable within the Arensbergs' circle; Duchamp, with his satirical humor and complex intellectual wit, in fact became the center of the group and received substantial support from Walter Arensberg. Although early works by Picabia and Duchamp displayed the faceting and multiple viewpoints of Cubism, they turned those tools to a task more expressive than formal. Picabia's *Figure Triste* of 1912 (cat. no. 19), for example, with its ambiguous title translatable as "sad face," "sad figure," or "metaphor for sadness," offers a fractured view of a mother comforting a child, all painted in harsh tones of black, gray, white, and cold blues.[87] Duchamp's contemporary painting *Nude Descending a Staircase,* picturing a splintered figure in several simultaneous positions along a stairway, already suggested a tongue-in-cheek approach to the sophisticated, abstract formality of Cubism, an attitude that soon blossomed into the blatant iconoclasm of his subsequent art. His challenging, conceptual, and ironically humorous art struck a responding chord in a number of American artists, such as Man Ray, who ultimately converted from his early Cubist style to a fully Dadaist mode. Dada's primary impact on American modernism remained short-lived, however, for Picabia and Duchamp returned to Europe, Ray departed for Europe, as well, in 1921, and the Arensbergs left New York for California in 1922. Yet, the Arensbergs' legacy to the establishment of modern art in the United States remained, with their extensive collection of art eventually bequeathed to the Philadelphia Museum of Art.

The turning point in America's introduction to modern art, however, took place not in Stieglitz's gallery, nor in the Steins' Paris apartment, nor at a salon hosted by a wealthy socialite or collector, but at the Sixty-ninth Regiment Armory in New York City where the *International Exhibition of Modern Art*, organized by a group of American artists, opened on February 17, 1913. Many American artists at the turn of the century had come to feel that, despite the efforts of Stieglitz and a handful of other art dealers and supporters, the taste of American collectors for traditional, primarily European, art had become ossified and that the brittle grip of the National Academy of Design, a collaborator in the preservation of that taste, needed to be broken. Views akin to those of Robert Henri, a champion of artist-organized exhibitions, with no juries and no prizes, were shared by contemporary artists of both realist and less representational persuasions. A few successful attempts at such efforts (most notably, the Independent Artists exhibition held in a New York City loft in 1910), catalyzed the formation of a group called the "Association of American Painters and Sculptors" dedicated to promoting contemporary American art. At first dominated by Henri's circle, with J. Alden Weir as president, disagreement among differing factions within the group soon led to Weir's stepping down to be replaced by Arthur B. Davies. It was Davies, a more liberal-minded artist with a wider knowledge of current artistic developments, who spearheaded the organization of the groundbreaking Armory Show. Inspired by the catalogue of a large exhibition of modern art in Germany, the *Sonderbund* show in Cologne in 1912, Davies sent his assistant, painter Walt Kuhn, overseas to view the show, ultimately joining him there. With the assistance of the art critic Walter Pach and other Americans then involved in the European art community, Davies and Kuhn arranged loans for the most extensive exhibition of avant-garde European art ever shown up until that time, either in the United States or Europe. To the European works they added a wide variety of contemporary American art (albeit with an emphasis on the more radical end of the spectrum), assembled under the direction of William Glackens. Essentially two exhibitions in one, the Armory Show sought to present a history of the development of modern art, beginning with the early nineteenth-century paintings of Jean-Auguste-Dominique Ingres and Eugène Delacroix and extending through the most recent works of current artists. Several factors resulted in a distinctly French bias: Few German Expressionist painters were included because the organizers deemed their work imitative of the French; the Italian Futurists were absent because they had refused to participate if not shown as a group; and other than Kandinsky's paintings, little Russian art appeared, due to unavailability at the time of the exhibition. Some American artists also protested the weight given to foreign and radical art. Nonetheless, the exhibition represented a massive undertaking and won great success. Largely unprepared for the telescoped history of unfamiliar and challenging European art, the American general public responded with alarm, ridicule, and rapt fascination, and the vituperative and uncomprehending reviews of many critics only fanned the flames of this *succès de scandale*. As the show traveled to Chicago and Boston, newspapers filled with charges associating the new art with everything from anarchy and bolshevism to degeneracy, immorality, and insanity. Duchamp's *Nude Descending a Staircase* became the butt of numerous jokes, parodies, and satirical cartoons, and in Chicago, Pach, Matisse, and the sculptor Constantin Brancusi were burned in effigy. Yet the exhibition, containing roughly sixteen hundred works, attracted more than a quarter of a million visitors by the end of its tour, and more than three-hundred works (including nearly all thirty Cubist pieces) were sold. A number of major private collections of modern art, the Arensbergs' among them, began with the Armory Show, and the Metropolitan Museum of Art in New York City led major museums in the acquisition of modern art by purchasing a Cézanne for its collection. The Armory Show injected a new vigor into the flagging American art market, forcing artists and public alike to take up the gauntlet thrown down by the exhibition. Not a passing fad, as some conservatives hopefully claimed, modernism had arrived and found a permanent home in the United States. By the end of 1913, new galleries that featured avant-garde art began springing up, and exhibitions of contemporary art began to proliferate.[88]

One important exhibition following in the wake of the Armory Show, for example, took place at the Carroll Galleries in New York City and represented the American debut of Morgan Russell and Stanton MacDonald-Wright's Synchromist painting. Though both American, the two artists did not meet until 1911 in Paris where they had fallen under the spell of Cézanne's work, absorbed the Impressionists' and Post-Impressionists' lessons in light and color, and sought a new way to systematically apply the color theories of Michel-Eugène Chevreul and Herman von Helmholtz that had so affected their predecessors. Like Delaunay (to whose Orphism they owed a debt that they vigorously denied), they were interested in the relationship of painting and music and in developing color rhythms in painting. By pursuing that course, they believed they could surpass traditional painting, in which a static image exists solely in space, and create paintings that appeared to unfold in time, like music. They felt that their work reached beyond Delaunay's in expressing these ideas through pure form, liberated from all material representation, an opinion that they flaunted in their European-style Synchromist manifestos accompanying a joint exhibition in Paris in 1913. Indeed, Russell's *Cosmic Synchromy* of 1913-14 (cat. no. 91) eschews the sort of residual imagery still present in Delaunay's *Sun, Tower, Airplane.*

Russell chose to show *Cosmic Synchromy* at another subsequent, important exhibition at the Anderson Galleries in New York City in 1916: *The Forum Exhibition of Modern American Painters* came about at the instigation of a group of art dealers, critics, and artists who felt the need to establish standards of value, not entirely met at the Armory Show, in the selection and presentation of American modernism. Stieglitz, Henri, and MacDonald-Wright's brother, the critic Willard Huntington Wright, were among those who assembled the two hundred works by sixteen artists for this exclusively American showing of modern art. In an effort to better educate the public and thus encourage a greater understanding and sympathetic embrace of contemporary art, the sponsors provided an exhibition catalogue containing explanatory statements by each of the participating artists. Russell wrote of *Cosmic Synchromy,* "...I was concerned with the elimination of the natural object and with the retention of color rhythms.... The principle [sic] idea in this canvas is a spiralic plunge into space, excited and quickened by appropriate color contrasts."[89] His emphasis on the absence of objective subject matter and his desire for pure art echoed, for the most part, the aspirations of the majority of his fellow artists, since even those who retained some recognizable objects in their work voiced the importance of abstract means and ideas.

The culmination of the anti-Academy revolution in American art occurred in 1917 with the Independents' exhibition organized by the Society of Independent Artists in which approximately twenty-five hundred works by thirteen hundred artists from thirty-eight states represented the apotheosis of Henri's ideal of the artist-organized, non-juried, non-judged exhibition. Encompassing every conceivable style and level of skill, it definitively broke the National Academy's conservative and restrictive hold on determining artistic taste in America. Extensive as it was, however, the Independents' exhibition could not compete with the success of the Armory Show in terms of structure, vision, or foresight, and its impact was further overshadowed by a more profound event: the country's entry into the first World War.

World War I, then euphemistically termed "the war to end all wars," brought to an end the ingenuous optimism and faith in western civilization's proximity to perfection that had managed to prop up the aging Genteel Tradition into the early twentieth century. The mutual atrocities committed among civilized nations and the unprecedented horrors unleashed by modern technology's contribution to warfare, such as the submarine and the airplane, bore greater witness to Darwin's cruel biological determinism than to the gentler, quasi-religious social evolution proposed by those like Spencer and Fiske. Neither could the cultivation of beauty uplift the mind and spirit of humanity above the call of war, nor could a nostalgia for handicraft withstand the progress of machine technology, industrial standardization, mass-production, and corporate consolidation. Efficiency became the catchword of an era epitomized by the embrace and application of "scientific management" (a method of achieving maximum productivity at minimum cost), first proposed by the engineer Frederick W. Taylor in the 1890s and developed in the following years to blossom fully when the United States rapidly mobilized for war.

However, on the eve of the 1920s, American optimism, though tempered, remained largely intact: The country had emerged from the world conflict richer and more powerful; the growth of bureaucratic organization in government and industry had rendered both more focused, efficient, and effective; and the advances of science and technology had begun to transform peoples' thinking and their lives. Electricity, its promise so grandly stated by the Electric Tower and sparkling lights of the Pan-American Exposition in 1901, was spreading throughout homes, as well as businesses, paving the way for the introduction of numerous household appliances. Automobiles were rolling off production lines in increasing numbers, contributing to the burgeoning of an ever more mobile society and affecting the economy and the culture.

Such changes colored the optimism they helped to support by creating disruptive challenges to long-established values and beliefs. Women's roles began to shift, within the home with the arrival of the new appliances, and outside the home with more educational opportunities, greater access to professional employment, and the achievement of voting rights. Strict sexual mores began to erode as young men in new automobiles whisked off young ladies (without benefit of chaperone) to social functions, and strident new forms of popular music accompanied the daring youth in dances considered exceedingly risqué by traditional standards. Conservatives tenaciously resisted this flow of events, and the current of change carried within it some remnants of the past. Yet, the overall course of society had shifted irrevocably. Poised on the brink of a decade alive with the possibilities of prosperity and expansion, America blindly forged ahead toward radios, telephones, and "talkie" movies, Prohibition, Al Capone, and the Great Depression.[90]

Along with the culture as a whole, American art had matured as well. Emerging from the national artistic isolationism that had predominated just prior to the Civil War, American artists during the last quarter of the nineteenth century had claimed their place in the procession of western culture by traveling to Europe and studying alongside their European peers at the prestigious academies. Also exposed in Europe to revolutionary artistic trends, such as Barbizon and Impressionist painting, these artists had returned to the United States to invigorate the American Renaissance with masterfully executed academic works and to develop the distinctly American, quiescent mode of Tonalist painting. The Arts and Crafts movement had flourished in the United States, raising design standards for mass-produced goods as well as for handcrafted items, and American photographers had contributed significantly to the development of photography, both as a technology and as an art form. American Impressionism, though slow to take hold and retaining a more naturalistic bent, had eventually come into its own, for a time dominating the American art scene. Furthermore, its practitioners, epitomized by The Ten, had successfully extended the assault begun by the artists of The New Movement on conservative, restrictive exhibiting policies in the United States. During the early twentieth century, although largely ignorant of and indifferent to radical developments among the European avant-garde, America had produced a distinctive, socially conscious Realism, in the works of the Ashcan School, that acknowledged the nation's rough edges while reflecting its optimism. Finally, primed by the efforts of adventurous artists, such as Max Weber, and ardent promoters of modernism, like Alfred Stieglitz, the public's ultimate (if hesitant) acceptance of the avant-garde art presented in the Armory Show had marked a crucial turning point in thinking and taste. Although a strong strain of Realism continued to persevere and evolve, the move toward abstraction had been firmly planted and grew to dominate American art.

American acceptance of modernism resulted from the tremendous cultural and technological transformations that they shared with the rest of the developed world. With the advances in rapid transport and travel and breakthroughs in communications technologies, the United States, for better or for worse, was no longer insulated from foreign ideas, concerns, or events. Americans were as fascinated and affected by the theories of Bergson, the ideas of Freud, and the new hypotheses in physics, for example, as were Europeans, and the formal visual means – introduced by Cézanne, Picasso, Matisse, and others – used to express these ideas answered the needs of a volatile modern world.

Naturally, the exchange between the United States and Europe involved ideas and technologies that originated on both sides of the Atlantic. In cultural terms, the balance of origination tipped toward Europe at first, but in time it began to shift. American artists adapted and invented ways of conveying their responses to contemporary life that reflected the character of their specifically American experience. Certain viewpoints that had originated toward the end of the last century continued to inform the new art, even as they were expressed in modern terms. The artist's role had become increasingly culturally marginalized as the twentieth century progressed, yet the alienation and disappointment that pervaded the avant-garde did not intrinsically disassociate it from the upper middle-class elite with which most American artists had identified since the late nineteenth century. Hence, though the belief in the power of art to uplift may have receded (its likelihood of success, in the views of its adherents, applying to an ever shrinking portion of the population), it did not cease. Stieglitz's scornful, elitist attitude toward the perceptive and intellectual capacity of the general public, for instance, essentially echoed that of the Tonalist painter Thomas Dewing, who had refused to exhibit his work at the Pan-American Exposition because he felt the public would be incapable of understanding or appreciating it.[91] American artists, then, continued to uphold their esoteric creations as a repudiation of the materialism, greed, and dehumanization of an increasingly industrialized, bureaucratic culture, while eschewing the tactics of some of their European counterparts, who launched frontal attacks on contemporary society through deliberately offensive or bitingly critical artwork.[92]

Instead, artists like Arthur Dove, Marsden Hartley, and Georgia O'Keeffe built upon the same nature mysticism that inspired earlier artists, such as John Twachtman; whereas Twachtman strove to suggest through expressive, representational landscapes the unifying, mystical force that many believed permeated the universe and manifested through nature, these artists sought to imply the mysterious life-force through abstract paintings in which form and color alone imitated the immaterial rhythm of nature's pulse. Thus, they filtered the ideas of Bergson and the theories associated with the fourth dimension that had so affected European modernists through the American tradition of Transcendentalism to concoct a new blend of philosophical conception and abstract visual expression. Moreover, their receptivity to Kandinsky's relation of music, art, nature, and spirit in his book, *Concerning the Spiritual in Art,* no doubt resulted, in part, from their familiarity with Whistler's previous exploration of synesthesia and his application of musical terms to color and composition. Georgia O'Keeffe, for example, created a series of paintings in 1919 in which she attempted to translate music into visual art. *Black Spot No. 3* (cat. no. 18) exemplifies her quest to create "equivalents" of natural forces and sensations through fully abstract means, much as Whistler suggested subjective moods and musical effects through the use of subtle tonalities, delicately balanced compositions, and graceful (if representational) forms.[93] Like Whistler, Twachtman, Dewing, and other Tonalist artists, O'Keeffe, Hartley, Dove, and their confreres found in both art and nature a balm for mind and spirit.

Similarly, a number of artists who extended the use of representational imagery into the second decade of the new century maintained another distinctly American perspective. Painters as diverse as Abraham Walkowitz, Preston Dickinson, and Charles Demuth adapted modern formal techniques to the portrayal of the American city. Although they focused on the physical, urban-industrial environment rather than upon the lives of its inhabitants, their choice of subject matter, like that of the Social Realists, acknowledged the modern metropolis as the exemplar of America's fundamental character. Both groups' depictions of urban vitality offered an updated vision of the dynamically active, brashly confident, and aggressively industrious nation so eloquently championed by the nineteenth-century poet Walt Whitman. Walkowitz, inspired by Kandinsky's theories, composed swaying triangular forms and animated patterns of dots and lines into a nearly abstract expression of the city's teeming activity and upward architectural thrust in his *Improvisation of New York City* (cat. no. 26). In *Fort George Hill* (cat. no. 87), Dickinson employed the shattered geometries of Cubism, the bright colors of Fauvism and Synchromism, and the flat patterning of naïve and folk art to construct an alternative image of city life, capturing with sharp-edged, streamlined forms and staccato color rhythms the pace and tenor of twentieth-century New York City. The flattened space, confined color areas, and precisely delineated forms in Dickinson's painting appeared again, more muted and refined, in Demuth's later Precisionist painting, *Nospmas. M. Egiap Nospmas. M.* (cat. no. 86), depicting grain elevators in Lancaster, Pennsylvania.[94] Despite its provocatively enigmatic title, *Nospmas* presents an objective, mechanized interpretation of industrial America quite different from the emotive expression of Walkowitz's painting and reaching beyond Dickinson's work in its formal reserve and static, architectonic austerity. Demuth's synthesis of Cubist formal structure and realist imagery – exacting, unsentimental, and aloof – reflected clearly the "scientific" efficiency that enthralled and informed American industry and culture as the third decade of the twentieth century began.[95]

Whether objective or subjective, representational or abstract, or some combination of the two, American art at the close of the 1910s bore little visual resemblance to that produced between the last two decades of the nineteenth century and the first of the twentieth. Yet the fundamental needs it was called upon to fulfill – to identify the unifying, national characteristics, both spiritual and material, of a culture engaged in transformation – were much the same. In fact, the continuity in artistic examination of distinct themes – most notably, the quest for mystical experience through nature and art and the Whitmanesque embrace of objectivism, pragmatism, and confidence – suggest some success at answering this call. From Eakins's visual dissection of the moving body to Demuth's acute observation of industrial architecture, from Inness's "correspondences" to O'Keeffe's "equivalents," from Whistler's lyrical "nocturnes" to Walkowitz's raucous "improvisations," American artists born in different generations and using varied means responded to similar motivations. In so doing, they wove the threads of enduring themes into a bridge spanning four decades, from the era of the Genteel Tradition to the onset of the Jazz Age.

1 For example, the recent exhibition *1900: Art at the Crossroads,* organized by the Royal Academy in London and the Solomon R. Guggenheim Museum in New York, examined "the artistic landscape of the 1900s" reflected in the range of art and artists selected for the Exposition Décennale (of international art) and the Exposition Centennale (of French art), both part of the Exposition Universelle in Paris in 1900. Although the curators of *1900: Art at the Crossroads* did not attempt to recreate exactly the earlier exhibitions, by sketching the artistic context of the period, they sought to examine the burgeoning, within that context, of those artists now considered modern masters.

2 The *Exhibition of Fine Arts* at the Pan-American Exposition included roughly 1,600 works by more than 650 artists, sculptors, and architects. Although the vast majority of the art shown was by Americans (including American expatriates such as James A. McNeil Whistler, John Singer Sargent, Daniel Ridgway Knight and Gari Melchers), one gallery was set aside for an exhibition of Canadian art. Art from South America and North American provinces, such as Newfoundland, were displayed in the International Section. See William A. Coffin, "The Exhibition of Fine Arts," *Official Handbook of Architecture and Sculpture and Art Catalogue to the Pan-American Exposition* (Buffalo, New York: David Gray, 1901), pp. 86 – 91.

3 Elizabeth Broun, "Research in Progress: American Art at the World's Fairs" paper presented at *Decorating Our Nation: Art and Architecture in the Public Eye,* Delaware Symposium on American Art, University of Delaware, Newark, April 21, 1989.

4 George Cotkin, *Reluctant Modernism: American Thought and Culture, 1880-1900* (New York: Twayne Publishers, 1992), pp. 2-3.

5 Ibid., p. 10.

6 For additional examinations of the impact of Darwinism on American religious, social, and artistic development see Jackson Lears, *No Place of Grace: Antimodernism and the Transformation of American Culture 1880 –1920* (New York: Pantheon Books, 1981) and Kathleen Pyne, *Art and the Higher Life: Painting and Evolutionary Thought in Late Nineteenth-Century America* (Austin: University of Texas Press, 1996).

7 J. Leonard Bates, *The United States 1898-1928: Progressivism and a Society in Transition* (New York: McGraw-Hill Book Company, 1976), p. 12.

8 Ibid.

9 These policies first took shape with the Spanish-American War of 1898. When Spain, in a struggle with its Cuban colony, refused to completely acquiesce to the United States' demands that it withdraw from the western hemisphere, the United States stepped in to oust the Spanish and in the process gained control of the Philippines and Puerto Rico. In the flush of success, Congress also voted by joint resolution to acquire Hawaii.

10 Quoted in John G. Milburn, "The Purposes of the Exposition," *Official Handbook of Architecture and Sculpture and Art Catalogue to the Pan-American Exposition,* p. 7. Many journalists noted the desire of the government to replace the European nations as the main trading partners of the Latin American nations; this aim was accepted as a logical economic extension of the beloved Monroe Doctrine. An exposition to further these aims was first proposed in 1895 by Secretary of State James G. Blaine, who organized the first Pan-American conference in 1890, and Captain John M. Brinker, a Buffalo citizen who wished to promote business for his city. Originally planned to take place in 1899, the fair was merely postponed, rather than derailed, by the Spanish-American War. See Joann Marie Thompson, "The Art and Architecture of the Pan-American Exposition, Buffalo, New York, 1901" (Ph.D. diss., Rutgers University, 1980), p. 6.

11 Robert H. Wiebe, *The Search for Order 1877-1920* (New York: Hill and Wang, 1967), p. 237.

12 Ibid. Wiebe notes that, while the middle class believed in the continual progress of mankind and the potential to uplift the "barbarians," no government official before 1913 accepted such views. On page 234, Wiebe explains that the power-minded circle of men that gathered around McKinley and Roosevelt felt no need to justify expansionism as simply a means of helping less advanced societies to progress. Wiebe quotes McKinley's Secretary of State John Hay who said imperialism was "a fine expression of the American spirit," and noted that Lyman Abbott, editor of *The Outlook* magazine and a supporter of the government's policies, expressed the opinion that "barbarism has no rights which civilization is bound to respect."

13 John Fiske, for example, was one of Spencer's most prominent American disciples. His 1884 book *The Destiny of Man Viewed in the Light of His Origins* offered a description of the growth of human civilization from the "savage" to the modern ideal in which he shifted Spencer's secularized language into overtly religious terms. The views of Matthew Arnold, an Englishman, were also widely circulated in the United States. Although he retained a more secular approach, he still promoted the idea of the linear evolution of civilization toward perfection, suggesting that that ideal was close to fulfilling its potential in America. He urged those involved in the arts, in particular, to meet the challenge of uplifting culture with objects whose beauty drew from art of the past but culled from it only its best offering, presenting it in a new and original way. For a discussion on the impact of Arnold on turn-of-the-century art, see David C. Huntington, "The Quest for Unity: American Art Between World's Fairs 1876-1893," *The Quest for Unity* (Detroit, MI: Detroit Institute of Arts, 1983).

14 For an extended study of the major socioeconomic issues that arose in the United States following the Civil War, the accompanying cultural changes, and the lasting effect of those transitions taking place during the last quarter of the last century, see Alan Trachtenberg, *The Incorporation of America: Culture & Society in the Gilded Age* (New York: Hill and Wang, 1982).

15 Elizabeth Aslin, *The Aesthetic Movement: Prelude to Art Nouveau* (New York and Washington, D.C.: Frederick A. Praeger, 1969), p. 14.

16 Ibid., p. 15.

17 Morris, however, did not entirely eschew the machine, for he realized the necessity of working within the mechanical and financial context of his time in order to change it. "As a condition of life," he observed, "production by machinery is altogether evil; as an instrument for forcing on us better conditions of life, it has been, and some time yet will be, indispensable." Quoted in Peter Stansky, *Redesigning the World: William Morris, the 1880s, and the Arts and Crafts* (Princeton, NJ: Princeton University Press, 1985), p. 64. In fact, Morris established a very successful design firm in 1861 (reorganized in 1875 as Morris & Co.) in which he engaged in some machine production.

18 See Robert Judson Clark and Wendy Kaplan, "Reform in Aesthetics: The Search for an American Identity," in Wendy Kaplan, *"The Art That is Life": The Arts & Crafts Movement* *in America, 1875-1920* (Boston: Little, Brown and Company with Museum of Fine Arts, Boston, 1987), p. 58 and Eileen Boris, "Reform in Craftsmanship," in Kaplan, *"The Art That is Life,"* pp. 208 and 212.

19   Clark and Kaplan, "Reform in Aesthetics," in Kaplan, *"The Art That is Life,"* p. 57.

20   While Hubbard's Roycroft Community was essentially a business, not a commune, with shops producing printed matter, furniture, metalwork, stained glass and leather goods, it still retained a strong element of reform idealism. The Roycroft "campus" included, in addition to buildings housing various workshops, a chapel, an inn, houses and also dormitories for workers, enhanced with facilities for leisure activities. At times, people working in diverse areas would be called upon to collaborate on a project that would benefit the community. Roycroft was only one, albeit the most prominent, of a number of Arts and Crafts communities in New York. Stickley also at one time planned to establish a cooperative community, Craftsman Farms, near Morris Plains, New Jersey, although this goal was never achieved. For more information on the Roycroft Community and other Arts and Crafts communities and associations, see Marie Via and Marjorie Searl, *Head, Heart and Hand: Elbert Hubbard and the Roycrofters* (Rochester, NY: University of Rochester Press, 1994), and Coy L. Ludwig, *The Arts and Crafts Movement in New York State 1890s – 1920s* (Hamilton, NY: Gallery Association of New York State, 1983).

21   Stickley also learned about the ideas of Ruskin and Morris through his acquaintance with Syracuse University professor Irene Sargent, who was also of great influence in promoting the Arts and Crafts Movement in Syracuse and, through her articles in *Craftsman,* nationally. See Boris, "Reform in Craftsmanship," in Kaplan, *"The Art That is Life,"* p. 216.

22   Just as reform of arts and crafts, labor, and society represented the recurrent themes in Stickley's and Hubbard's magazines, education, pleasant working conditions and meaningful work lay at the center of both men's business philosophies. Yet, being successful entrepreneurs, they reinterpreted the British socialist concept of new industrialism to accommodate American capitalism. Both were as interested in making useful, well designed and crafted items widely available at modest prices to the middle class as they were in creating positive work experiences for laborers. Neither eschewed the use of machinery in their handicraft studios, nor did either entirely eliminate division of tasks in the production of goods. Stickley found the idea of organized labor an anathema, and Hubbard (who had previously developed his considerable marketing skills – and his fortune – at the Larkin Company) endeared himself to the corporate world with his insistence that only if workers demonstrated sufficient initiative, loyalty, and thoroughness should they keep their jobs. See ibid., pp. 216-19.

23   Stickley preferred to use quarter-sawn oak, finished with fumed ammonia that served as a preservative while bringing out the grain and tone of the wood. See Ludwig, *The Arts and Crafts Movement in New York State,* p. 63.

24   Ibid., p. 9.

25   Binns, who is credited with having "all but founded American studio pottery," also contributed significantly to the entry of women into prominent roles in the profession. In addition to Adelaide Robineau, Binns counted Mary Chase Perry Stratton, founder of Pewabic Pottery in Detroit, among his students. See Ulysses G. Dietz, "Art Pottery 1880 – 1920" in Barbara Perry, ed. *American Ceramics: The Collection of Everson Museum of Art* (New York: Rizzoli and Syracuse, NY: Everson Museum of Art, 1989), pp. 63 and 65. See Joan Siegfried, "American Women in Art Pottery" *Nineteenth Century* (Philadelphia), Spring 1984, pp. 12-18.

26   Robineau's entry into the field by way of china painting was typical for a woman of the period. The education of women was a concern of many art potteries, and indeed, the arts and crafts movement, like the reform movement in general, provided for women a toehold in the professional world previously open only to men. Nevertheless, their roles were usually limited to those associated with the domestic sphere such as the beautification of the home through arts and crafts or the nurturing of the poor through social work. Only in rare cases, such as those of Robineau and Stratton, did women achieve status not only as decorators but as potters, too. Traditional gender roles, so clearly drawn (if not always obeyed) in the Victorian and Edwardian periods, affected the field of art pottery as they did everything else. Women were usually confined to the "feminine" area of china painting and decoration (males might design decoration, but women usually carried it out), whereas men participated in the "male" areas of glazing, throwing, and firing (considered manly because of the requirement of scientific knowledge and/or physical strength). See Dietz, "Art Pottery 1880 – 1920" in Perry, ed., *American Ceramics,* pp. 63 and 91.

27   Ibid., p. 91.

28   The molds themselves, however, were made from handcrafted pottery that was either thrown on a pottery wheel or sculpted by hand, with extra ornamentation or carving done by hand as well. While his employees at Tiffany Pottery produced the ceramics, Tiffany himself was experienced in ceramic work and had taken time to ensure that his company's pottery, presented publicly for the first time at the Saint Louis Exposition in 1904, was of mature high quality. See Alastair Duncan, *Louis Comfort Tiffany* (New York: Harry N. Abrams, Inc., in association with The National Museum of American Art, Smithsonian Institution, 1992), pp. 128-31.

29   Perry, ed., *American Ceramics,* pp. 112-13.

30   See chronology in Duncan, *Louis Comfort Tiffany,* pp. 146-49.

31   Tiffany was more inclined toward the atmospheric treatment of color and light found in the works of the American painter George Inness (with whom he had associated in New York) than he was taken with the strict academic emphasis on drawing over color embraced by Bailly. Ibid., p. 17.

32   For an extended discussion of these issues, see Richard Guy Wilson, "The Great Civilization," *The American Renaissance 1876-1917* (New York: The Brooklyn Museum, 1979), especially pp. 28-34.

33   Wheeler specialized in textile design and art embroidery, de Forest developed a fascination with carving and furniture, Colman was preoccupied with color and designed flat patterns for walls and ceilings, and Tiffany indulged his love of stained glass. See Marilynn Johnson, "The Artful Interior," in *In Pursuit of Beauty: Americans and the Aesthetic Movement* (New York: Rizzoli, in collaboration with The Metropolitan Museum of Art, 1986), p. 124.

34   Ibid.

35   Ibid.

36   Wilson, "The Great Civilization" in *The American Renaissance,* p. 117, and Robert Koch, *Louis C. Tiffany, Rebel in Glass* (New York: Crown Publishers, 1966), p. 64.

37   One of the large cooperative efforts in which Tiffany participated was the Pan-American Exposition, at which he was engaged to design the exhibition court for the Arts and Crafts display in the Manufacturers and Liberal Arts Building. For this, he enclosed the court with four clear glass domes and created a large fountain of colorful Favrile glass as the court's centerpiece. Other exhibitors, including the National Arts Club of New York, occupied spaces around the perimeter of the court. See Ludwig, *The Arts and Crafts Movement in New York State,* p. 55.

38   Wilson in "The Great Civilization," mentions the various names applied to the period and in his essay discusses at length the relatively recent coinage of the term "American Renaissance." Although the elaborate interior of the American Renaissance described above might fall within the purview of Aestheticism both in terms of the unity of the arts and of art-for-art's-sake appreciation of the beautiful and exotic in its own right, it would seem to preclude a strong moral element. Yet the Genteel Tradition's goal of uplifting moral character and spirit by elevating taste was not absent from Tiffany's agenda. Particularly after the rapid expansion of his industrial-art manufactory that he began as a glass furnace in 1893 in Corona, New York, he produced a plethora of household articles ranging from lamps and flower vases to toilet articles that disseminated his aesthetic vision throughout the American middle-class by means of affordable, mass-produced items. Despite the use of mass production rather than handcrafting, Tiffany did not diverge entirely from Morris's Arts and Crafts ethic, for he wished to make utilitarian things beautiful and furthermore make that beauty available to the general public. See *The American Renaissance,* p. 117.

39   Duncan, *Louis Comfort Tiffany,* p. 19.

40   Beaumont Newhall, *The History of Photography* (New York: The Museum of Modern Art, 1982), p. 129.

41   Joseph Pennell, "Is Photography Among the Fine Arts?," *Contemporary Review,* vol. 72, 1897, reprinted in Vickie Goldberg, ed., *Photography in Print* (Albuquerque, NM: University of New Mexico Press, 1988), p. 212.

42   Emerson's theories caused an uproar among those who thought photography should emphasize sharp, accurate detail throughout the entire image. Even his supporters often misconstrued his advocacy of allowing the lens to be slightly unfocused; the extreme liberties taken by some in creating unfocused and/or highly manipulated photographs led to charges that he promoted "fuzziness." He objected to this accusation, saying "Such persons are labouring under a great misconception; we have nothing whatever to do with any 'fuzzy school.' Fuzziness, to us, means *destruction of structure.* We do advocate broad suggestions of organic structure, which is a very different thing from destruction...." Peter Henry Emerson, "Naturalistic Photography," 1889, reprinted in Goldberg, ed., *Photography in Print,* p. 196.

43   He chose this name in reference to artist groups in Europe who used the appellation *Sezession* to stress their rebellion against the academies. Stieglitz explained, "Its aim is loosely to hold together those Americans devoted to pictorial photography in their endeavor to compel its recognition, not as the handmaiden of art, but as a distinctive medium of individual expression." See Alfred Stieglitz, "The Photo-Secession," *The Bausch & Lomb Lens Souvenir* (Rochester, NY: Bausch & Lomb Optical Company, 1903), reprinted in Beaumont Newhall, ed., *Photography: Essays & Images* (New York: The Museum of Modern Art, 1980), p. 167. Bausch & Lomb, a Rochester manufacturer of lenses, produced this brochure to commemorate the winners of a contest the company organized for the best photographs taken with their lenses.

44   For Stieglitz's account of this experience, see Alfred Stieglitz, "The Hand Camera – Its Present Importance," *American Annual of Photography,* 1897, reprinted in Goldberg, ed., *Photography in Print,* pp. 216-17.

45   The 1910 exhibition was extremely successful, leading the Albright Art Gallery to purchase twelve of the exhibited photographs and establishing the importance of the movement. Stieglitz expressed his feeling of triumph at the time in a letter to German critic Ernst Juhl that is translated and reprinted in Newhall, *Photography: Essays & Images,* p. 189. For a comprehensive discussion of the Photo-Pictorialists of Buffalo, see Anthony Bannon, *The Photo-Pictorialists of Buffalo* (Buffalo, NY: Media Study/Buffalo, 1981).

46   Peter Henry Emerson, "The Death of Naturalistic Photography," 1891, reprinted in Goldberg, ed., *Photography in Print,* pp. 197-98.

47   Prominent among those influenced by Muybridge's investigations was French physiologist Dr. Etienne-Jules Marey, who proceeded to build on Muybridge's discoveries by developing alternative, more accurate ways of recording motion, inventing the first crude motion-picture camera in 1888. Eakins, aware of Marey's work, himself devised a precursor to the motion-picture camera in the early 1880s, allowing him to make action studies even more precise than those of Muybridge and considered important enough for publishing. His interest in serial photography ended, however, once he felt he had learned what he needed in order to master the issues of perspective and anatomy involved in painting the human figure in motion. It was Thomas Edison who ultimately perfected and capitalized on the motion-picture camera in the 1890s. See William Innes Homer, *Thomas Eakins: His Life and Art* (New York: Abbeville Press, 1992), pp. 146-53, and Newhall, *Photography: Essays & Images,* pp.117-23.

48   Roger Benjamin, *Orientalism: Delacroix to Klee* (Sydney, Australia: The Art Gallery of New South Wales, 1997), p. 17.

49   Sarah D. Benson, Franklin W. Robinson, Anthony H. Sarimento, and Faith Short, eds., *A Handbook of the Collection: Herbert F. Johnson Museum of Art* (Ithaca, NY: Cornell University, 1998), p. 138.

50   Although Bouguereau, who had studied the work of Renaissance and Baroque masters in Italy, devoted his early career to painting largely classical and religious subjects condoned by the Academy, he eventually added themes of mothers and children, peasants, nudes, nymphs, and other mythological creatures to his repertoire. These latter works, though warmly received by the public, were the sort of paintings that Eakins found affected and profoundly disliked, as he preferred the documentary accuracy of Gérôme. See Homer, *Thomas Eakins,* p. 36.

51   Chase's choice of subject, a lovely young woman, was among the most popular in American art around the turn of the last century. The American woman held a place of iconic significance in the nation's culture and art at the end of the nineteenth and beginning of the twentieth-century. Portrayed as cultured, intelligent, capable, spiritual, and, ironically, as beautiful as she was chaste, the American woman symbolized the ideal of American culture: a domestic goddess devoted to her family and the guardian of moral rectitude. Often depicted in contemplation of nature or art, or withdrawn in profound introspection, this generally passive, domesticated image of woman was in many ways at odds with the actual modern woman, who was actively involved in social reforms, desirous of the vote, and eager to enter the professional world outside the home. However, in a society still dominated by the upper- and middle-class White Anglo-Saxon male, and in which distinct gender roles were emphasized, women seeking advancement in art and

other professions found many obstacles remained in their way. The issue of gender in nineteenth-century culture and art has been extensively discussed in current scholarship. See, for example, Martha Banta, *Imaging American Women: Ideas and Ideals in Cultural History* (New York: Columbia University Press, 1987); Ann Douglas, *The Feminization of American Culture* (New York: Knopf, 1977); Mary Kelley, ed., *Woman's Being, Woman's Place: Female Identity and Vocation in American History* (Boston: G.K. Hall & Co., 1979); and Lears, *No Place of Grace*, Burns, *Inventing the Modern Artist*, and Pyne, *Art and the Higher Life*, mentioned elsewhere in this essay.

52 James Abbott McNeill Whistler, *The Gentle Art of Making Enemies* (New York: 1890), reprinted in John W. McCoubrey, ed., *American Art 1700–1960: Sources and Documents* (Englewood Cliffs, NJ: Prentice-Hall, Inc., 1965), p. 186.

53 Susan Hobbs, "John LaFarge and the genteel tradition in American Arts 1875–1910" (Ph.D. diss., Cornell University, 1974), p. 7.

54 Whistler, *The Gentle Art of Making Enemies*, in McCoubrey, ed., *American Art 1700–1960*, p. 185.

55 In this sense, American painters shared a closer affinity with the European Symbolists, such as Edvard Munch or Paul Gauguin, who endeavored to convey meaning and emotion through line and color, than they did with art-for-art's sake theorists. However, Americans eschewed the moral decadence and extreme social alienation associated with European Symbolism. For more discussion on this fear of degeneration in art see, for example, Sarah Burns, "Fighting Infection: Aestheticism, Degeneration, and the Regulation of Artistic Masculinity," in *Inventing the Modern Artist: Art & Culture in Gilded Age America* (New Haven, CT: Yale University Press, 1996).

56 The need for mental and physical rest became a predominant theme in the United States during the 1880s and 1890s, "repose" and "relaxation" becoming catchwords (Pyne, *Art and the Higher Life*, pp. 27–29). Herbert Spencer's claim that humanity progressed from low beginnings marked by coarseness and crudity, toward manifestation of a higher spirit evident in fineness and delicacy gave rise to the notion that slight, fair persons of great sensitivity (in other words, upper-class persons of Anglo-Saxon descent) represented the most intelligent, most developed form of humanity. He warned Americans, whom he believed the most advanced and thus the most likely to suffer from overactivity, overwork, and nervousness, that they needed to protect their sensitive constitutions so that they could prevail in the evolutionary battle of survival of the fittest. In 1881, Dr. George M. Beard published *American Nervousness: Its Causes and Consequences*, in which he outlined a new, primarily American affliction that he termed "neurasthenia," a form of nervous exhaustion resulting from refined indoor living and the stress of greater brain activity. Its symptoms included everything from anxiety and depression to general physical weakness and, in women, interference with nurturing and reproductive functions. One of the most popular remedies to circumvent this problem was the mind cure, which included the closely associated practices of meditation and aesthetic experience, both thought to relax conscious control of the ego and allow the practitioner to become more spiritually at one with God or the life force or the universe, as one might choose to phrase it. See also Lears, "A Psychic Crisis: Neurasthenia and the Emergence of a Therapeutic World View," in *No Place of Grace*, and Burns, "Painting as Rest Cure," in *Inventing the Modern Artist*. For studies on the effect of these issues on the work of individual artists, see, for example, Sarah Burns, "Old Maverick to Old Master: Whistler in the Public Eye in Turn-of-the-Century America," *The American Art Journal* (New York) vol. XXII, no. 1, 1990, pp. 29-49; Kathleen Pyne, "Evolutionary Typology and the American Woman in the Work of Thomas Dewing," *American Art* (New York) Fall 1993, pp. 12-29; and Kathleen Spies, "Figuring the Neurasthenic: Thomas Eakins, Nervous Illness, and Gender in Victorian America," *Nineteenth Century Studies* (Charleston, SC), vol. 12, 1998, pp. 85-109.

57 Twachtman's landscape, indeed Tonalist painting as a whole, embodied the resurgence of interest in the Transcendentalist philosophy of Ralph Waldo Emerson that occurred during this period. Transcendentalism, a philosophy that valued the spiritual and intuitive above the material and empirical experience of the universe, encouraged the individual to seek the divine immanent in the self and in nature through immersing oneself in meditative reflection and appreciation of the natural environment. As such, Transcendentalism meshed well with the interest in oriental culture and philosophy that prevailed in America in the late nineteenth century. It also adapted well to Spencerian views, as Emerson's unified, harmonious, and ever-changing universe provided a model similar to Spencer's society of harmonious complexity toward which humanity supposedly was evolving. In relation to art, in particular, Pyne has explained: "For Emerson, art could be a mode of communion in which man's mind met with divine law as symbolized in the natural order." That is, the beauty of art helped unite the individual and universal, aesthetic and spiritual. See Kathleen Pyne, *Immanence, Transcendence, and Impressionism in Late Nineteenth-century American Painting, vols. I-III* (Ph.D. diss., University of Michigan, 1989), p. 50.

58 The use of art, during the late nineteenth century, to spiritually uplift is thoroughly examined in Kathleen Pyne, "Portrait of a Collector as an Agnostic: Charles Lang Freer and Connoisseurship," *The Art Bulletin* (New York), March 1996, pp. 75-97.

59 George Parsons Lathrop, "The Progress of Art in New York," *Harper's* (New York), April 1893, pp. 740-52.

60 See Diane P. Fisher, ed., *Paris 1900: The "American School" at the Universal Exposition* (New Brunswick, NJ: Rutgers University Press, 1999), especially Linda J. Docherty, "Why Not a National Art? Affirmative Responses in the 1890s," and Gabriel P. Weisberg, "The French Reception of American Art at the Universal Exposition of 1900."

61 George Inness, quoted in James Thomas Flexner, *History of American Painting (vol. 3): That Wilder Image* (New York: Dover Publications, Inc., 1970), p. 266.

62 See William Gerdts, *American Impressionism* (New York: Artabras, 1984), especially pp. 91-103.

63 The Ten American Painters included Frank Weston Benson, Joseph Rodefer De Camp, Thomas Wilmer Dewing, Frederick Childe Hassam, Willard Leroy Metcalf, Robert Lewis Reid, Edward Emerson Simmons, Edmund Charles Tarbell, John Henry Twachtman, Julian Alden Weir, and (after Twachtman's death) William Merritt Chase. The group continued to exhibit together until 1918, by which time they had come to represent the conservative element in the American art world. For a concise discussion of the founding of The Ten and its role in establishing Impressionism as an accepted style in the United States, see Ulrich W. Hiesinger, "Impressionism and politics: the founding of the Ten," *Antiques* (New York), November 1991, pp. 780-93.

64 The Eight included Robert Henri, Arthur B. Davies, William J. Glackens, Ernest Lawson, George B. Luks, Maurice B. Prendergast, Everett Shinn, and John Sloan. Although not originally planned to tour, the MacBeth exhibition ultimately traveled to Philadelphia, Chicago, Toledo, Detroit, Indianapolis, Cincinnati, Pittsburgh, Bridgeport (CT), and Newark (NJ). The venues that took the show were, in seven cases, art museums and, in two cases, public libraries that also served as art galleries, thus indicating an institutional acceptance of art considered insurgent by the National Academy of Design in New York. Varied but generally balanced and favorable critical response in the various cities where the exhibition was shown also suggests the nation was less culturally provincial than has been thought, as art historian Judith Zilczer has pointed out. In addition, she has noted that the MacBeth show set a precedent for independently organized modern art exhibitions that traveled to major American cities, most significantly the Armory Show of 1913 in which a member of The Eight, Arthur B. Davies, was a primary organizer. See Judith Zilczer, "The Eight On Tour, 1908 - 1909," *The American Art Journal* (New York) Summer 1984, pp. 21-48.

65   For a comprehensive treatment of Henri and The Eight, see William Innes Homer, *Robert Henri and His Circle* (New York: Hacker Art Books, 1988). Also see Milton W. Brown, *American Painting from the Armory Show to the Depression* (Princeton, NJ: Princeton University Press, 1955), pp. 9-38.

66   Respected art critic Christian Brinton, in a catalogue essay accompanying an exhibition of Meunier's work at the Albright Art Gallery in Buffalo in 1913, drew parallels between Rodin and Meunier, noted that both had worked in Brussels at the same time (although unknown to each other), and maintained that both adapted sculpture to contemporary life while continuing the plastic principles and objectivity of the ancient Greeks (pp. 50-54). He also prefaced his essay with a quote from Belgian Symbolist, Maurice Maeterlinck, who named Rodin and Meunier as the only contemporary sculptors to successfully uphold the exclusivity of sculpture among the arts. See Christian Brinton, *Constantin Meunier* (New York: Redfield Brothers, Incorporated, 1913).

67   Wayne Craven discusses the attraction that the French academies held for American students of sculpture in the late nineteenth century and the subsequent impact that the French style exercised upon American sculpture of the period. See Wayne Craven, *Sculpture in America* (Newark, DE: University of Delaware Press, and New York and London: Cornwall Books, 1968; revised 1984), pp. 418-19.

68   Ibid., p. 373.

69   Saint-Gaudens, originally planning to represent an actual historical figure, Deacon Samuel Chapin, ultimately created this embodiment of the Puritan character. It was so admired that the New England Society of Pennsylvania commissioned a replica for Philadelphia, and around 1900, the artist cast a number of smaller replicas in bronze, perhaps in response to sales demands after the full-size statue had won the Grand Prix at the Exposition Universelle in Paris in 1900. Ibid, pp. 384-85.

70   Ibid., p. 392.

71   Ibid., pp. 420-21.

72   In addition to summarizing the controversy that this sculpture engendered, Craven also notes that the publicity later contributed to the sculptor's work being featured at the Pan-American Exposition. His *Horse Tamers,* originally made for the Exposition, later found a home at Brooklyn, New York's Prospect Park, where they flank the entrance. Their embodiment of the concept of the mind exercising power over brute force typifies the Beaux-Arts method of conveying an abstract idea through natural forms. Ibid., pp. 423–24.

73   Later, around 1901, two more castings were made from the original: the one for the Luxembourg Gallery and another for New York collector, Charles Tyson Yerkes. After Yerkes's death in 1905, the sculpture was sold at auction to the Boston art philanthropist, George Robert White, and eventually handed on through his family to the Museum of Fine Arts in Boston in 1930. The pedestal intended for the *Bacchante* in the Library fountain remained empty, however, for 97 years, until as part of the historic renovation of the Library in the late twentieth century, the sculpture was recast from molds made from the Museum of Fine Arts' version. In 1993, the *Bacchante* finally returned to the Boston Public Library in triumph, long outliving her detractors. See Jonathan Leo Fairbanks, "MacMonnies' Bacchante: Its Trial, Condemnation and Restoration," *Sculpture Review* (New York) vol. 42, no. 2, 1993.

74   For various discussions of the effect of African and other tribal art on the development of modern Western art, see William Rubin, ed., *Primitivism in 20th Century Art* (New York: The Museum of Modern Art, 1984). An alternative view from that presented in the exhibition catalogue, critiquing that publication for not acknowledging the inherent colonialist dynamics involved in modernism's absorption of African and Oceanic art, is available in Marianna Torgovnick, *Gone Primitive: Savage Intellects, Modern Lives* (Chicago, IL: University of Chicago Press, 1993). See especially chapter 6: "William Rubin and the Dynamics of Primitivism."

75   Art historian Jack D. Flam discusses the traditional African treatment of the human form and its impact on Matisse, referring to *Reclining Nude*, in particular, as an "African Venus." See Jack D. Flam, "Matisse and the Fauves," in *Primitivism in 20th Century Art,* pp. 211-39.

76   For an examination of the effect of early theories of the fourth dimension on art, see Linda Dalrymple Henderson, "Mysticism, Romanticism, and the Fourth Dimension," in Maurice Tuchman, ed., *The Spiritual in Art: Abstract Painting 1890–1985* (New York: Abbeville Press, 1986), pp. 219-37. (A broader study is available in Linda Dalrymple Henderson, *The Fourth Dimension and Non-Euclidean Geometry in Modern Art* [Princeton, NJ: Princeton University Press, 1983]).

77   Ibid., pp. 221-23.

78   Many art historians have discussed the impact of Bergson's ideas on the development of modern art. For example, in an essay on the beginnings of American modernism, Charles Eldridge not only mentions how Americans were exposed to these ideas, noting that an extract of Bergson's *Creative Evolution* appeared in the October 1911 issue of Stieglitz's magazine *Camera Work,* but he goes on to give a succinct and insightful summarization of the main thrust of Bergson's theories and how American artists assimilated them. See Charles C. Eldridge, "Nature Symbolized: American Painting from Ryder to Hartley," in Tuchman, ed., *The Spiritual in Art,* pp. 113–29.

79   Henderson devotes a substantial sub-section of her essay "Mysticism, Romanticism, and the Fourth Dimension", pp. 224-27, to Weber and his interpretation of the fourth dimension and its application to art.

80   For a comprehensive source on Stieglitz and his involvement with the growth of modernism in the United States, see William Innes Homer, *Alfred Stieglitz and the American Avant-Garde* (Boston: New York Graphic Society, 1977).

81   Brown also discusses Stieglitz and his views at some length in *American Painting,* pp. 39-41.

82   Abraham A. Davidson, *Early American Modernist Painting 1910-1935* (New York: Harper & Row, Publishers, 1981), p. 20.

83   While Henderson includes Kandinsky in her general discussion of the fourth dimension in "Mysticism, Romanticism, and the Fourth Dimension," Eldridge examines Kandinsky's effect on Hartley, in particular. See Eldridge, "Nature Symbolized," in Tuchman, ed., *The Spiritual in Art*, pp. 118-21.

84   In *American Painting*, p. 42, Brown mentions that as late as 1907, Stieglitz and Steichen had laughed at Cézanne's work when they saw it on exhibition in Paris, and that Stieglitz later admitted that it was Weber who really taught him about modern art.

85   When James Gregg, in charge of publicity for the Armory Show, asked Dodge to write an article for a special edition of the magazine *Arts & Decoration* to be distributed at the exhibition, she contributed a piece titled "Speculations" that featured her praise-filled critique of Gertrude Stein's written "Portrait of Mabel Dodge at the Villa Curonia," Dodge thereby launched both herself and Stein into the public eye. She also assisted with the Armory Show by locating appropriate pictures in private collections and persuading the collectors to lend their possessions to the show. When she wrote A. B. Davies a note mentioning her support of the show, Davies had it printed on cards that were handed out to visitors at the exhibition. In 1914, Dodge attempted to promote contemporary art in her home town of Buffalo when she arranged an exhibition of Hartley's paintings there, but she was disappointed with the confused and unenthusiastic response it received. See Mabel Dodge Luhan, *Intimate Memories (vol. 3 of 4): Movers and Shakers* (New York: Harcourt, Brace and Company, 1935), pp. 254-55. For biographies of Dodge less biased than her own memoirs, see Emily Hahn, *Mabel: A Biography of Mabel Dodge Luhan* (Boston: Houghton Mifflin Company, 1977); Winifred L. Frazer, *Mabel Dodge Luhan* (Boston: Twayne Publishers, 1984), and Lois Palken Rudnick, *Mabel Dodge Luhan: New Woman, New Worlds* (Albuquerque, NM: University of New Mexico Press, 1984).

86   The information in the preceding paragraph is drawn, in part, from Davidson's chapter on the Arensberg Circle in *Early American Modernist Painting*, pp. 74-116. Davidson also aptly notes the difference in spirit between American Dada, which tended to be ironic and sometimes playful, and European Dada, which could be disturbingly nihilistic. He attributes the difference to the relative youthfulness, innocence, and optimism of the United States in comparison to the aggression, tension, and urgency that held Europe in its grip. See pp. 5-6.

87   Steven A. Nash with Katy Kline, Charlotta Kotik, and Emese Wood, *Albright-Knox Art Gallery: Painting and Sculpture from Antiquity to 1942* (New York: Rizzoli International Publications, Inc., 1979), p. 427.

88   The paragraph above concerning the Armory Show is based on the information provided by Brown in *American Painting*, pp. 47-59. The following paragraphs covering the Synchromists' exhibition at the Carroll Gallery, the Forum Exhibition, and the Independents' Exhibition also draw primarily from Brown, *American Painting*, pp. 64-66. For more extensive information on the Armory Show, including a checklist of the exhibition, see Milton W. Brown, *The Story of the Armory Show* (New York: Abbeville Press, 1988).

89   *The Forum Exhibition of Modern American Painters,* exhibition catalogue (New York: Anderson Galleries, March 13 - 25, 1916) unpaged, quoted in Gail Levin, "Morgan Russell (1886-1953) *Cosmic Synchromy,*" in Paul D. Schweizer, ed., *Masterworks of American Art from the Munson-Williams-*

Proctor Institute (New York: Harry N. Abrams, Inc., Publishers, 1989), p. 115.

90   A useful summary of the cultural changes taking place in the United States just before and during the 1920s can be found in Bates, *The United States 1898-1928*, especially chapter 15: "The 'Golden Twenties'."

91   Pyne, *Art and the Higher Life*, p. 202.

92   Recently, many respected art historians have discussed the issue of relative conservatism among late-nineteenth and early-twentieth century American artists in comparison to the avant-garde experimentalism of many of their European peers. Lois Finck suggests that this conservatism was associated with the desire for a link with artistic tradition and a cultural lineage. She points to the prevalence of Social Darwinist ideas in post-Civil War America as the source of this desire: If civilization evolved in a linear manner, then in order to place at the most civilized end of the line it was necessary to connect with the preceding line of cultural evolution. See Lois Marie Fink, *American Art at the Nineteenth-Century Paris Salons* (Washington, DC: National Museum of American Art Smithsonian Institution, and Cambridge, England: Cambridge University Press, 1990), pp. 278-89. Both Kathleen Pyne and Michael Leja have, in recent articles, made note of the identification of late-nineteenth and early-twentieth century American artists with the middle class, their concomitant sense of superiority and need to uplift the lower classes, and their reluctance to "*épaté la bourgeoise.*" Leja also remarks on the similarity of aims between the more conservative academic artists, the less conservative Tonalist artists, and indeed even the early modernist artists, all of whom sought to access and shape the soul and to inculcate the lower classes with upper middle-class values. See Kathleen Pyne, "Resisting Modernism: American Painting in the Culture of Conflict," in Thomas W. Gaehtgens and Heinz Ickstadt, eds., *American Icons: Transatlantic Perspectives on Eighteenth- and Nineteenth-Century American Art* (Santa Monica, CA: The Getty Center for the History of Art and Humanities, 1992), pp. 288-318, and Michael Leja, "Modernism's Subjects in the United States," *Art Journal* (New York), Summer 1996, pp. 65-72.

93   O'Keeffe was encouraged in this endeavor by her teacher Arthur Bement. See Eldridge, "Nature Symbolized," in Tuchman, ed., *The Spiritual in Art*, p. 125. Also see Nash, *Albright-Knox Art Gallery*, p. 527.

94   The title *Nospmas. M. Egiap Nospmas M.* has never been conclusively deciphered. Read backward, it seems to spell the name "M. Sampson Paige M. Sampson," but the significance of that name, if any, remains a mystery. See Betsy Fahlman, "Charles Demuth (1883-1935) *Nospmas. M. Egiap Nospmas. M.,*" in Schweizer, ed. *Masterworks of American Art*, p. 127.

95   For a discussion of the relation of Whitman's positive views on science and technology and the aims of the Precisionist artists, see Miles Orvell, "Inspired By Science and the Modern: Precisionism and American Culture," in *Precisionism in America 1915 - 1941: Reordering Reality* (New York: Harry N. Abrams, Inc., in association with The Montclair Art Museum, 1995), pp. 52-59.

A View of the Exhibition

Reproductions are arranged chronologically within each medium.

Painting

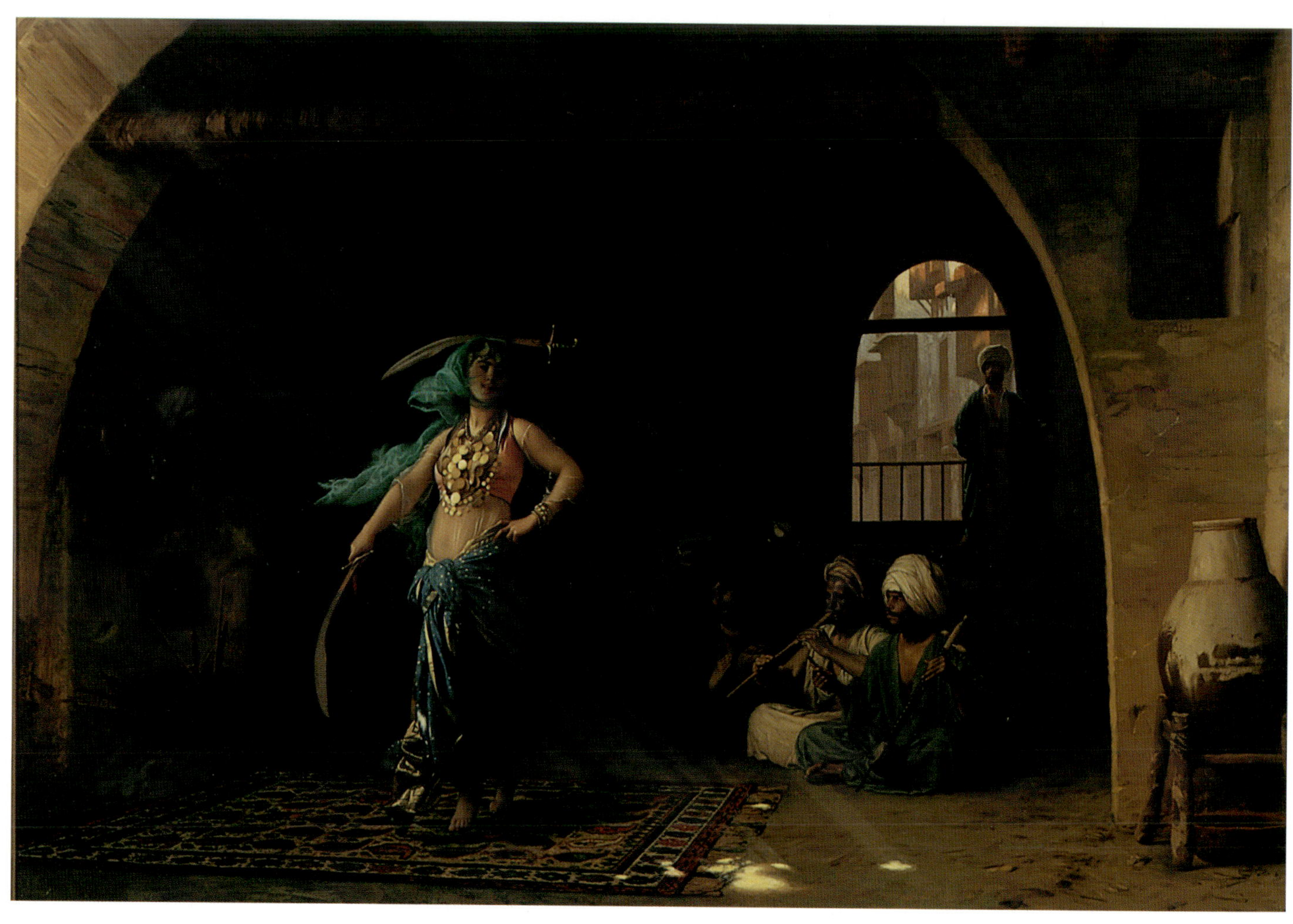

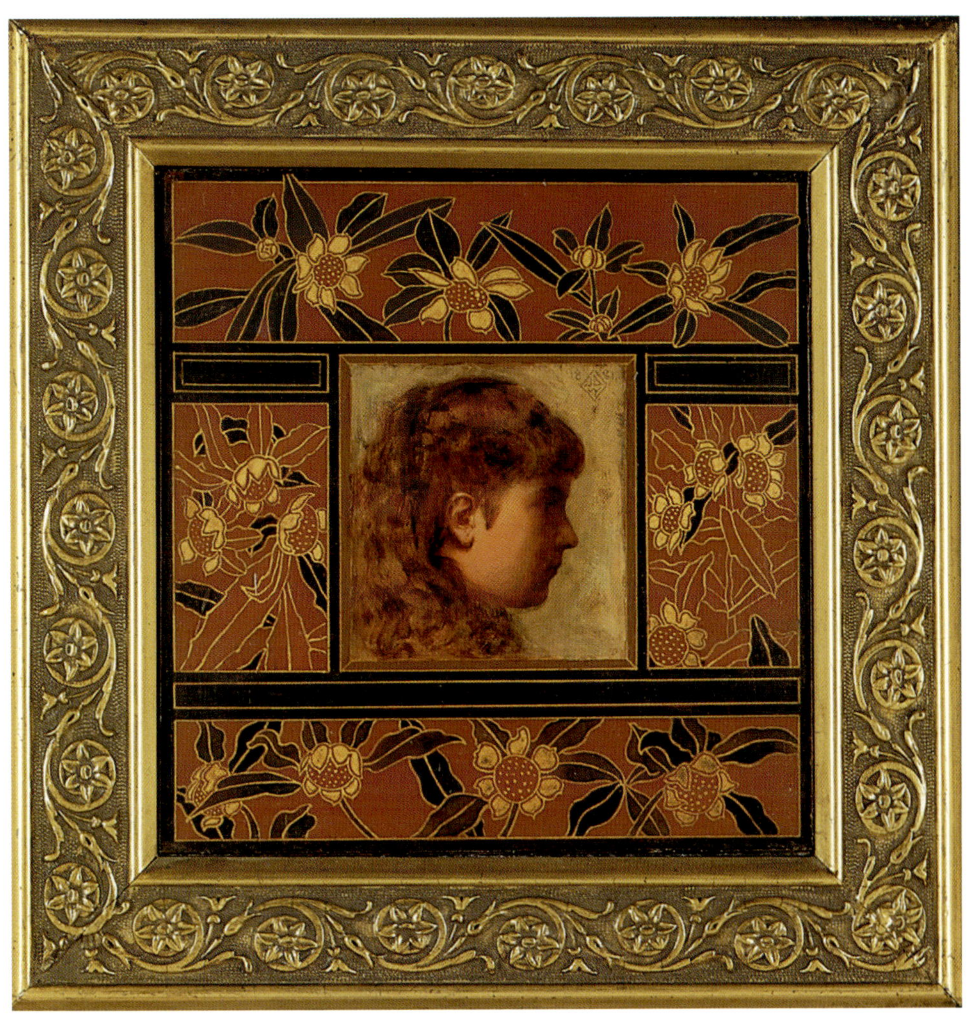

WALTER LAUNT PALMER (AMERICAN, 1854 – 1932)
DWARF SUNFLOWER, 1875-81

oil on wood panel, 9 x 9" (22.9 x 22.9 cm.)
painted border by Will H. Low, 1875, 13 1/8 x 13" (33.3 x 33 cm.)
Collection Albany Institute of History and Art, New York
Gift of Miss Louise A. Benson and William W. Benson, 1942
CAT. NO. 3

Walter Launt Palmer, son of the prominent sculptor Erastus Dow Palmer, benefitted from exposure to the
many talented artists who frequented his family's Albany home, as well as from studying portraiture with
Charles Loring Elliot and painting with the famous Hudson River School artist Frederic E. Church. No
doubt his father's influential connections also facilitated Walter's journey to Paris to study with Charles
Emile Auguste Carolus-Duran, as they did for Walter's friend and fellow Albany artist Will H. Low.
W. L. Palmer's delightful little portrait of an unidentified girl, set like a gem within a frame of sunflowers
and leaves painted by Low, epitomizes the spirit of the American Renaissance, when artists valued both
the fine and the decorative arts and willingly assumed versatile and collaborative roles.

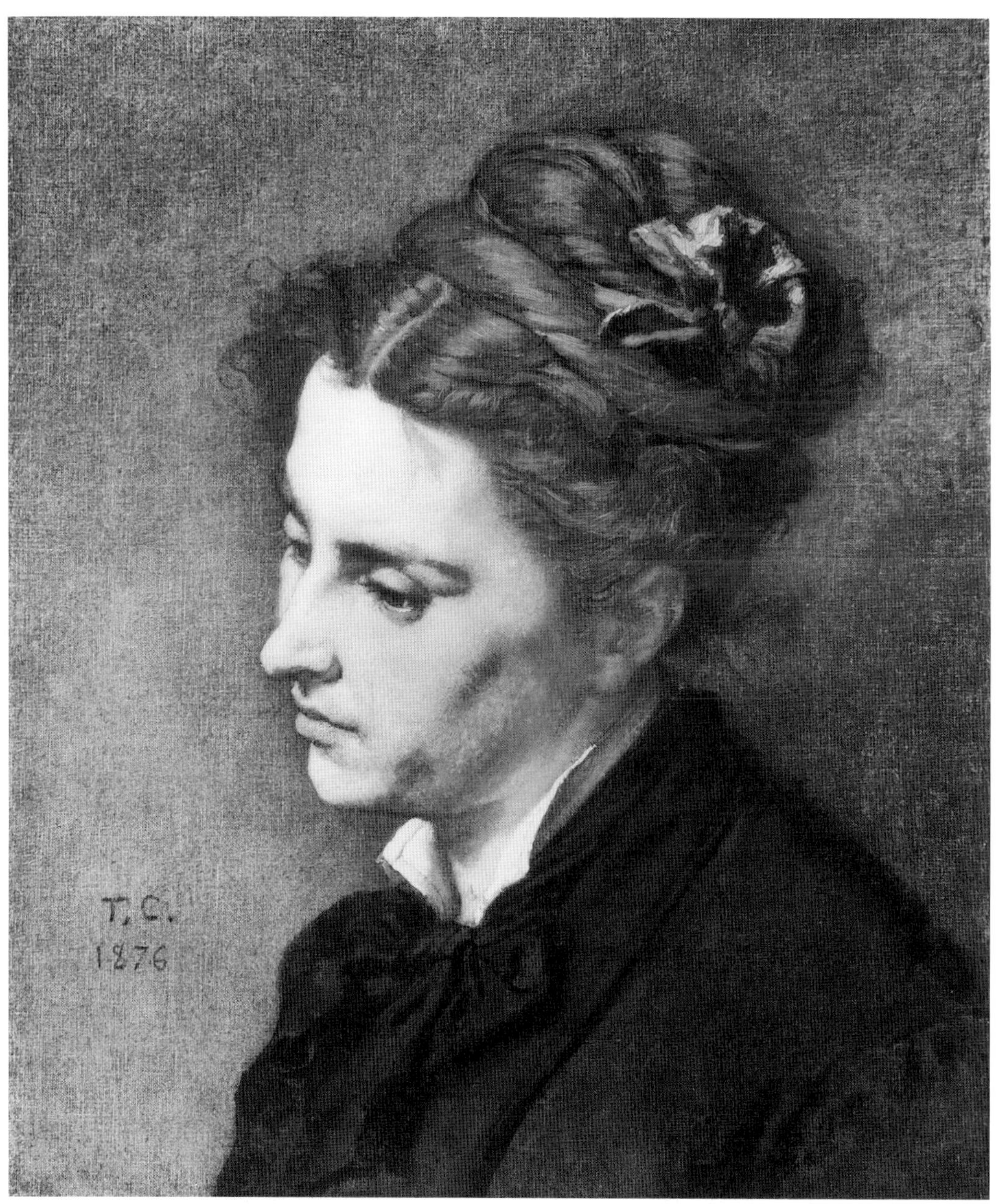

THOMAS COUTURE (FRENCH, 1815 – 1879)
HEAD OF A WOMAN, 1876

oil on canvas, 18 x 15" (45.7 x 38.1 cm.)
Collection Albright-Knox Art Gallery, Buffalo, New York
Elisabeth H. Gates Fund, 1930
CAT. NO. 6

One of the French academic masters most popular among the young American painters studying in
Paris at the end of the nineteenth century, Couture taught a looser, more painterly technique than some
of his colleagues, such as Jean-Léon Gérôme or Adolphe William Bouguereau. In this portrait (possibly
of Eleanor Norcross, an American artist studying in France), one can observe his use of rich, warm
tones and application of impasto in the face, collar, and ribbon.

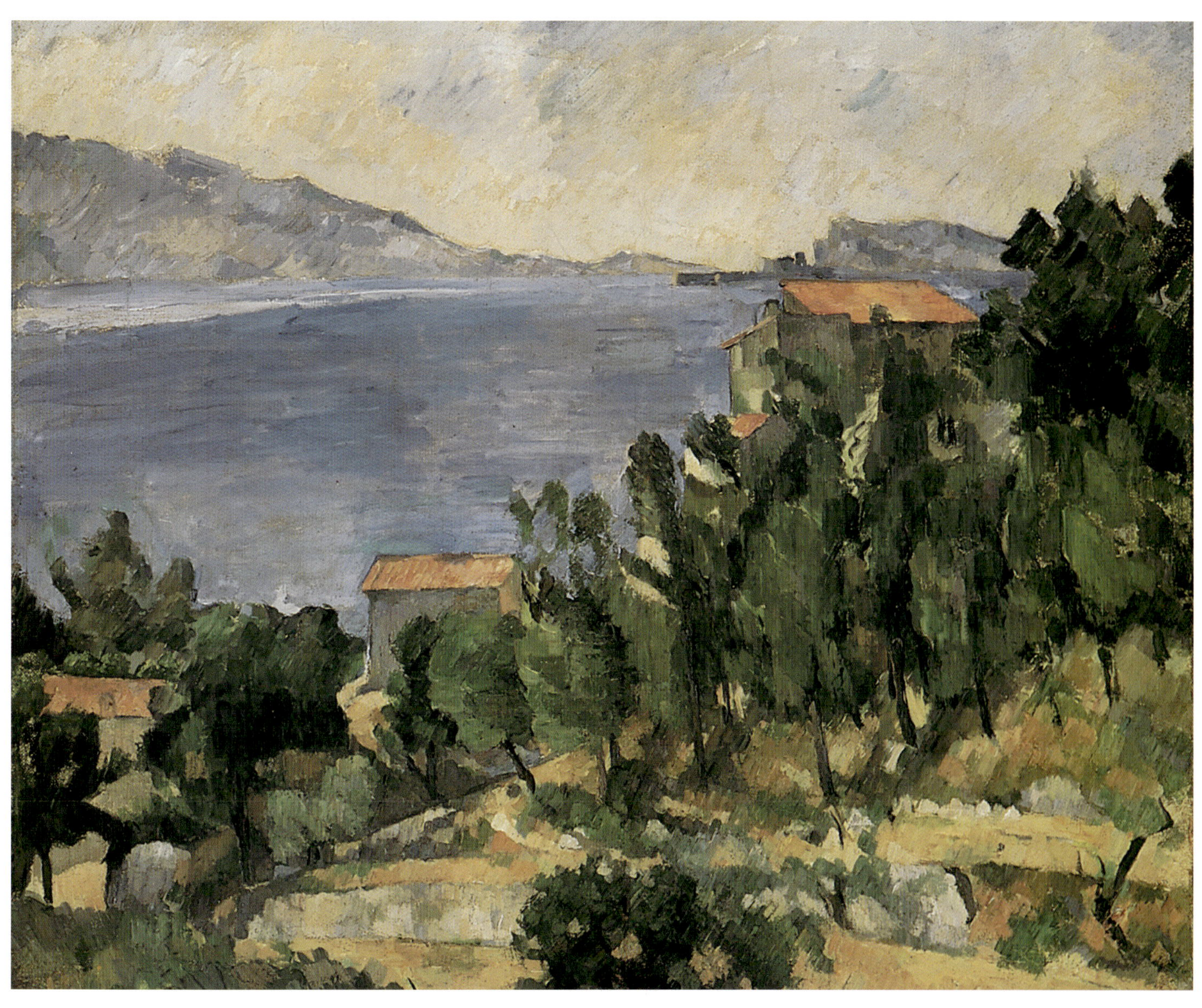

PAUL CÉZANNE (FRENCH, 1839 – 1906)
THE SEA AT L'ÉSTAQUE, 1878-82

oil on canvas, 21 1/4 x 25 5/8" (54 x 65.1 cm.)
Collection Memorial Art Gallery of the University of Rochester, New York
Anonymous gift in tribute to Edward Harris and in memory of
H. R. Stirlin of Switzerland, 69.45
Traveling to Utica, Buffalo, and Rochester
CAT. NO 75

oil on canvas, 25 3/4 x 21 1/2" (65.4 x 54.6 cm.)
Collection Albright-Knox Art Gallery, Buffalo, New York
Fellows for Life Fund, 1926
CAT. NO. 17

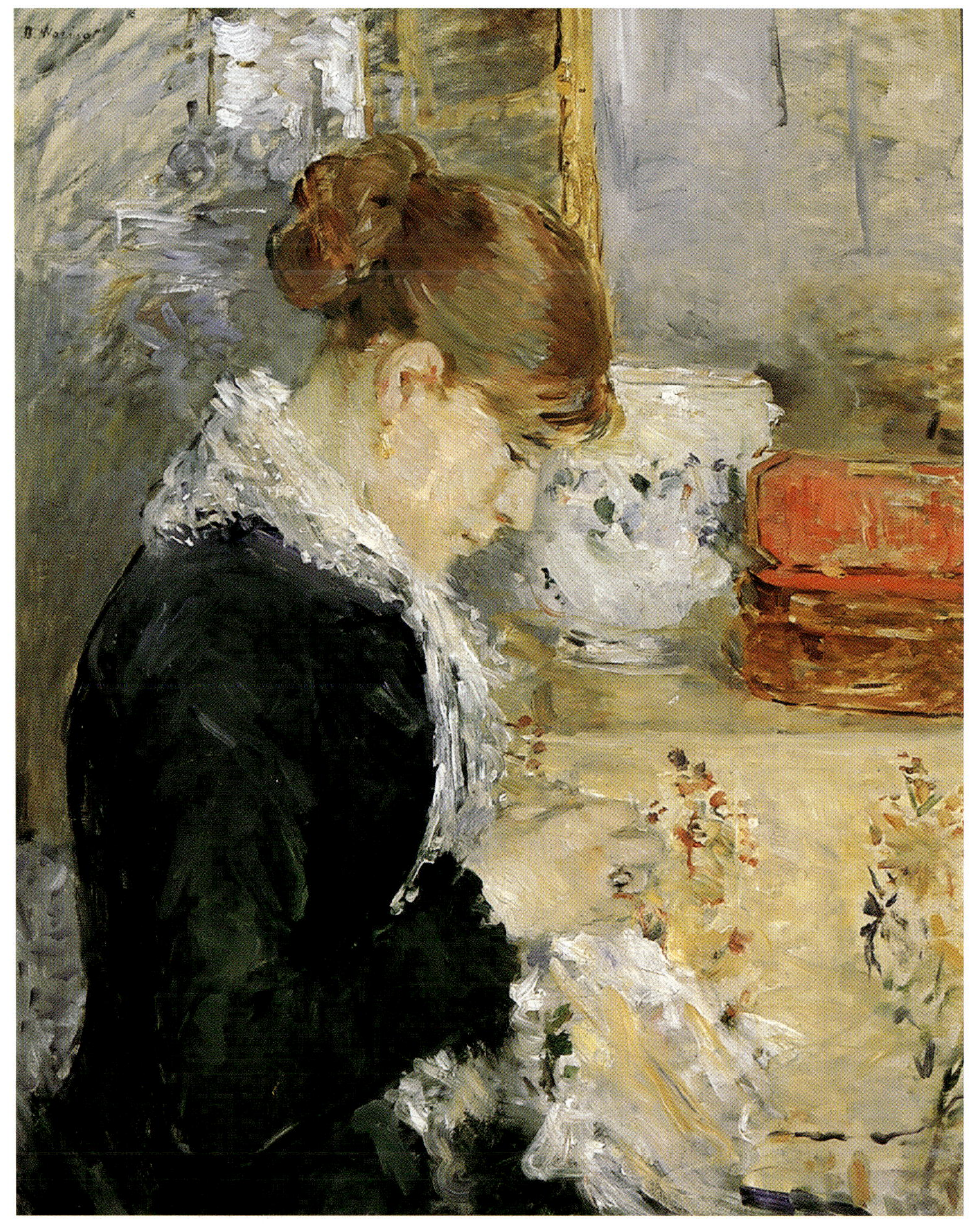

John Singer Sargent (American, 1856 – 1925)
Venetian Bead Stringers, 1880 or 1882

oil on canvas, 26 3/8 x 30 3/4" (67 x 78.1 cm.)
Collection Albright-Knox Art Gallery, Buffalo, New York
Friends of the Albright Art Gallery Fund, 1916
CAT. NO. 23

The son of expatriate Americans, Sargent was born in Florence, Italy, and spent most of his life in Europe and England, yet he is still claimed by the United States as one of its great painters. His bravura brushwork, skillful handling of subtle effects of light, color, and texture, and his daring compositional innovations reflect the influences of his teacher Charles Emile Auguste Carolus-Duran, of Old Master paintings by Frans Hals and Diego Velázquez, and of his contemporaries Édouard Manet and James Abbott McNeill Whistler. In great demand as a portraitist of wealthy Europeans and Americans, he also engaged in mural painting (for example, at the Boston Public Library in Massachusetts). He also created smaller genre scenes, such as this delicate portrayal of young women stringing beads in a shadowy Venetian interior, which was exhibited at the Pan-American Exposition in Buffalo in 1901.

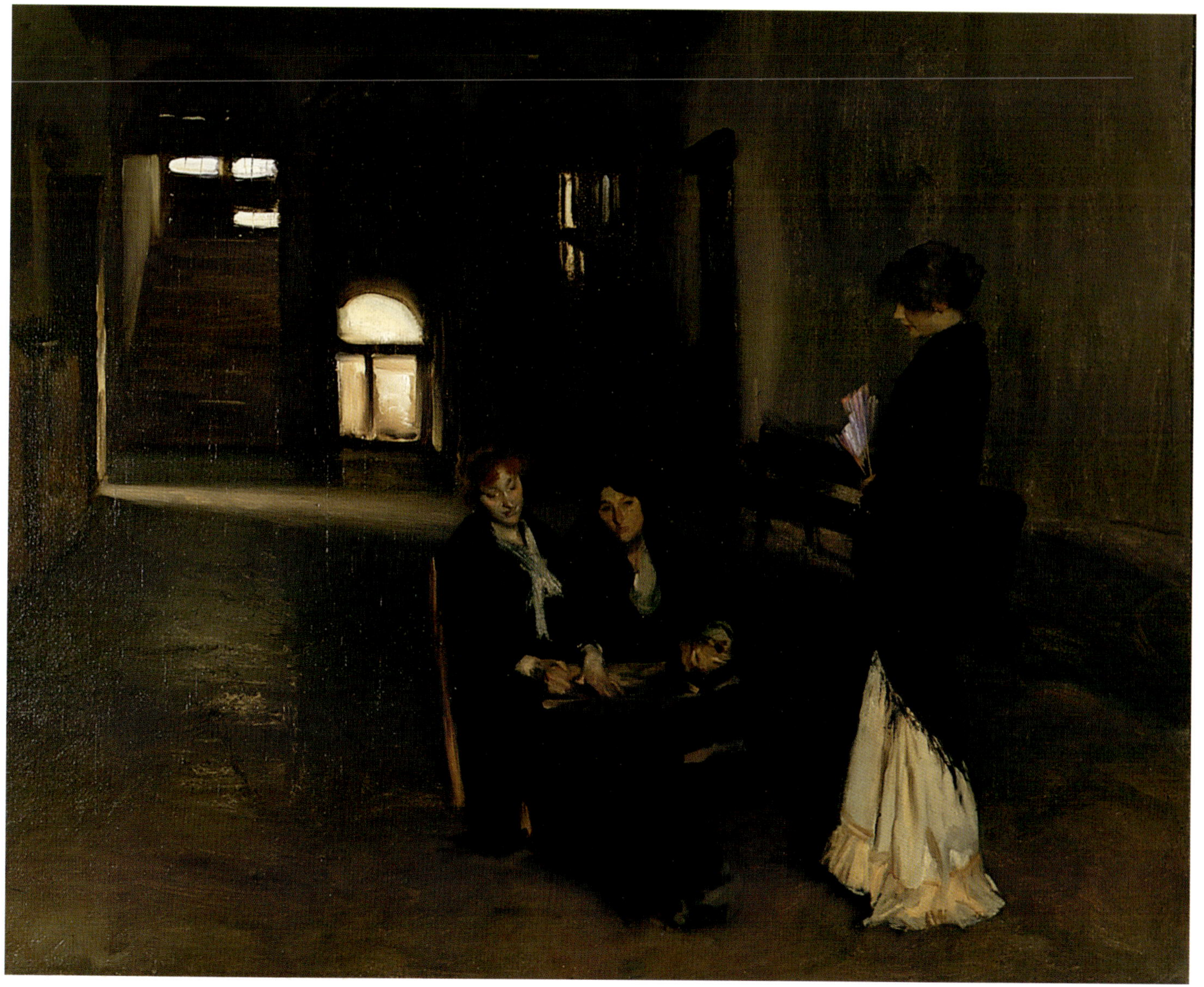

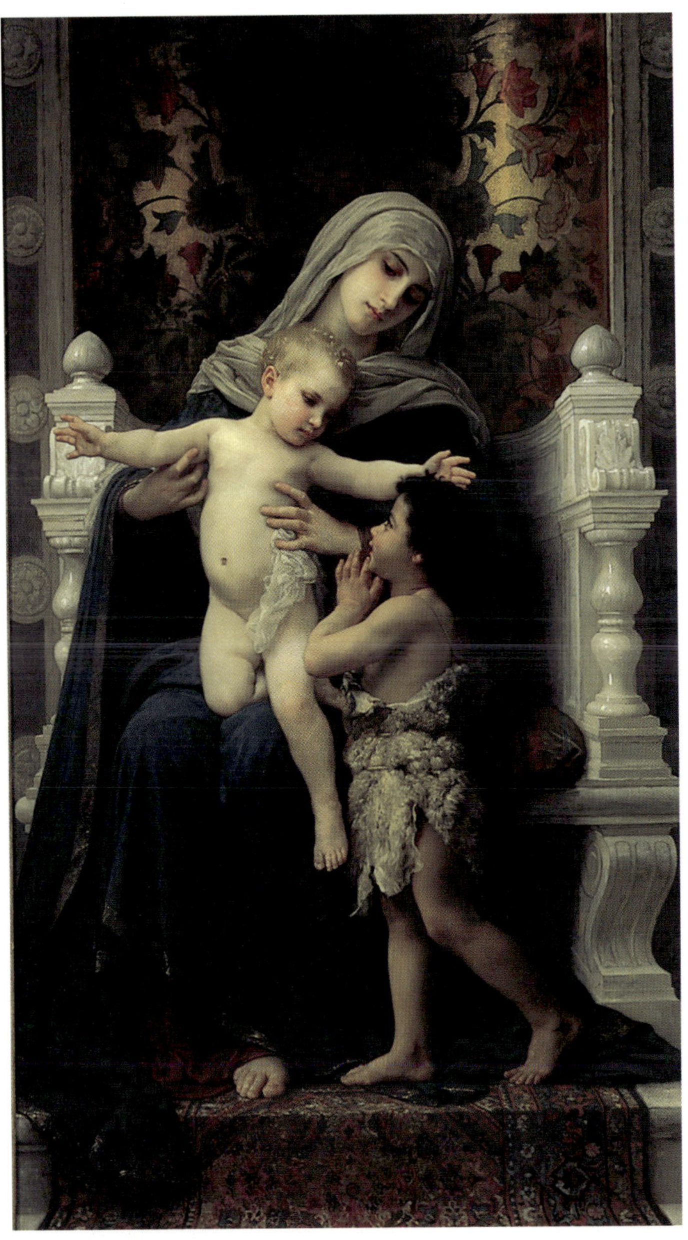

ADOLPHE WILLIAM BOUGUEREAU (FRENCH, 1825 – 1905)
MADONNA AND CHILD WITH ST. JOHN, 1882

oil on canvas, 75 x 43 5/8" (190.5 x 110.8 cm.)
Collection Herbert F. Johnson Museum of Art
Cornell University, Ithaca, New York
Gift of Louis V. Keeler, Class of 1911, and Mrs. Keeler, 60.082
CAT. NO. 52

In the latter part of the nineteenth century, Bouguereau wielded enormous influence within the École des Beaux-Arts and the Académie Julian in Paris. He was widely admired as the greatest artist of the day, attracting pupils such as Henri Matisse. Through his teacher, François Picot, Bouguereau learned the legendary Ingres's techniques of extraordinary draughtsmanship, and his aptitude won for him the École's Prix de Rome, enabling him to study intensively in Italy. Just as the influence of his Italian sojourn may be perceived in his choice of subject – his *Madonna and Child with St. John*, for example, is in keeping with the Renaissance theme of the Madonna enthroned – his academic training may be observed in the marvelous technical skill evident in his careful drawing and painstakingly layered glazes and varnishes.

JOHN H. TWACHTMAN (AMERICAN, 1853 – 1902)
LANDSCAPE, 1882

oil on canvas, 35 x 46" (88.9 x 116.8 cm.)
Collection Munson-Williams-Proctor Arts Institute, Museum of Art,
Utica, New York
Museum Purchase, 58.9
CAT. NO. 93

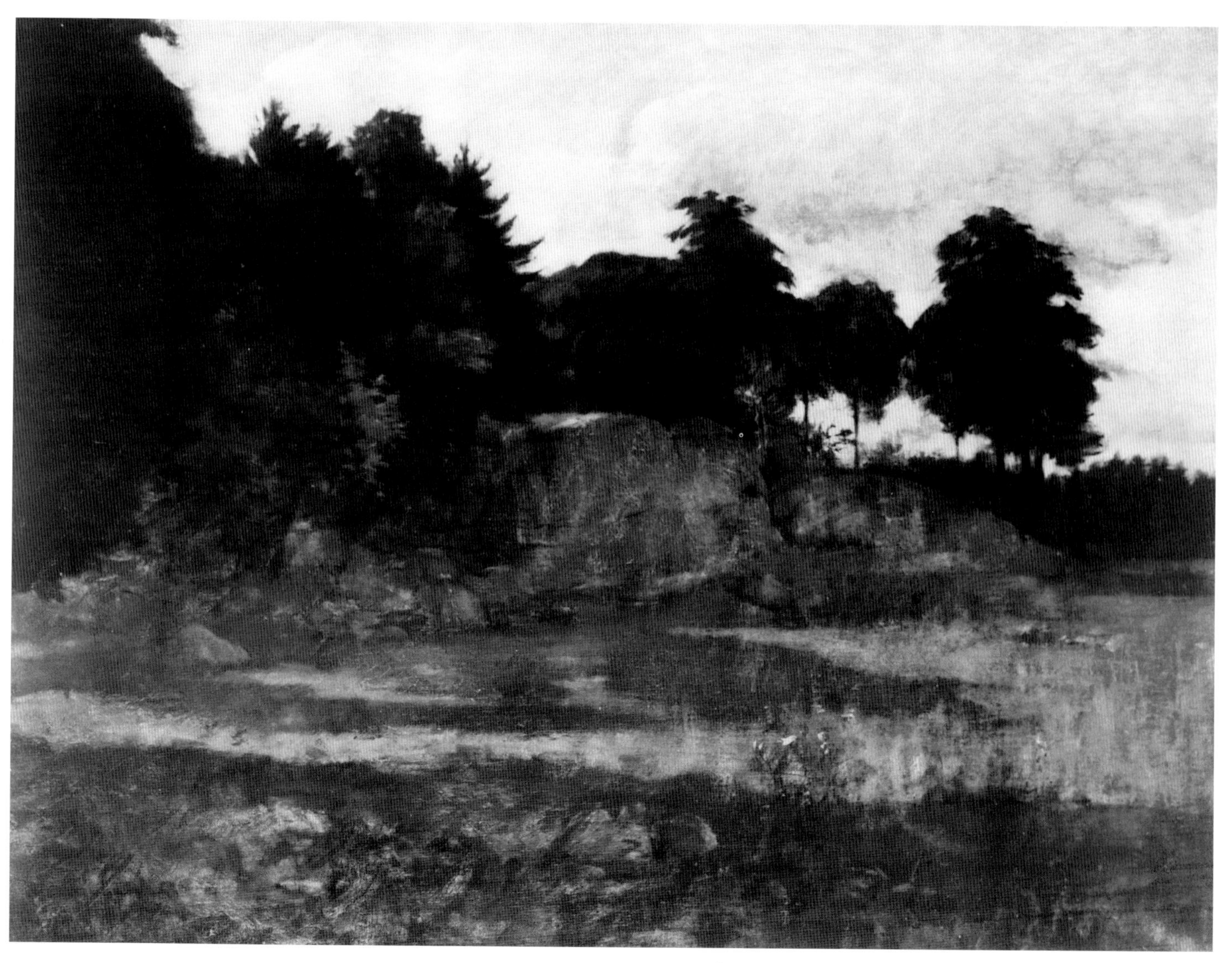

JEAN-LÉON GÉRÔME (FRENCH, 1824 – 1904)
LION IN THE DESERT, CA. 1885

oil on canvas, 27 x 36 3/8" (68.6 x 92.4 cm.)
Collection Albright-Knox Art Gallery, Buffalo, New York
Gift of Patricia Parkinson Neff and Grace de Cernea Reiniger
in memory of their mother, 1972
CAT. NO. 12

When studying this unfinished canvas, one can appreciate Gérôme's technique of building all of his paintings upon a foundation of solid drawing, as the black ink underdrawing remains visible in some areas. During the 1880s, sculptures and paintings of wild animals enjoyed great popularity in France; Gérôme obliged the demand with numerous paintings of lions, animals that he had seen and admired when he traveled in Egypt and the Sinai, and a subject in keeping with his love of the exotic.

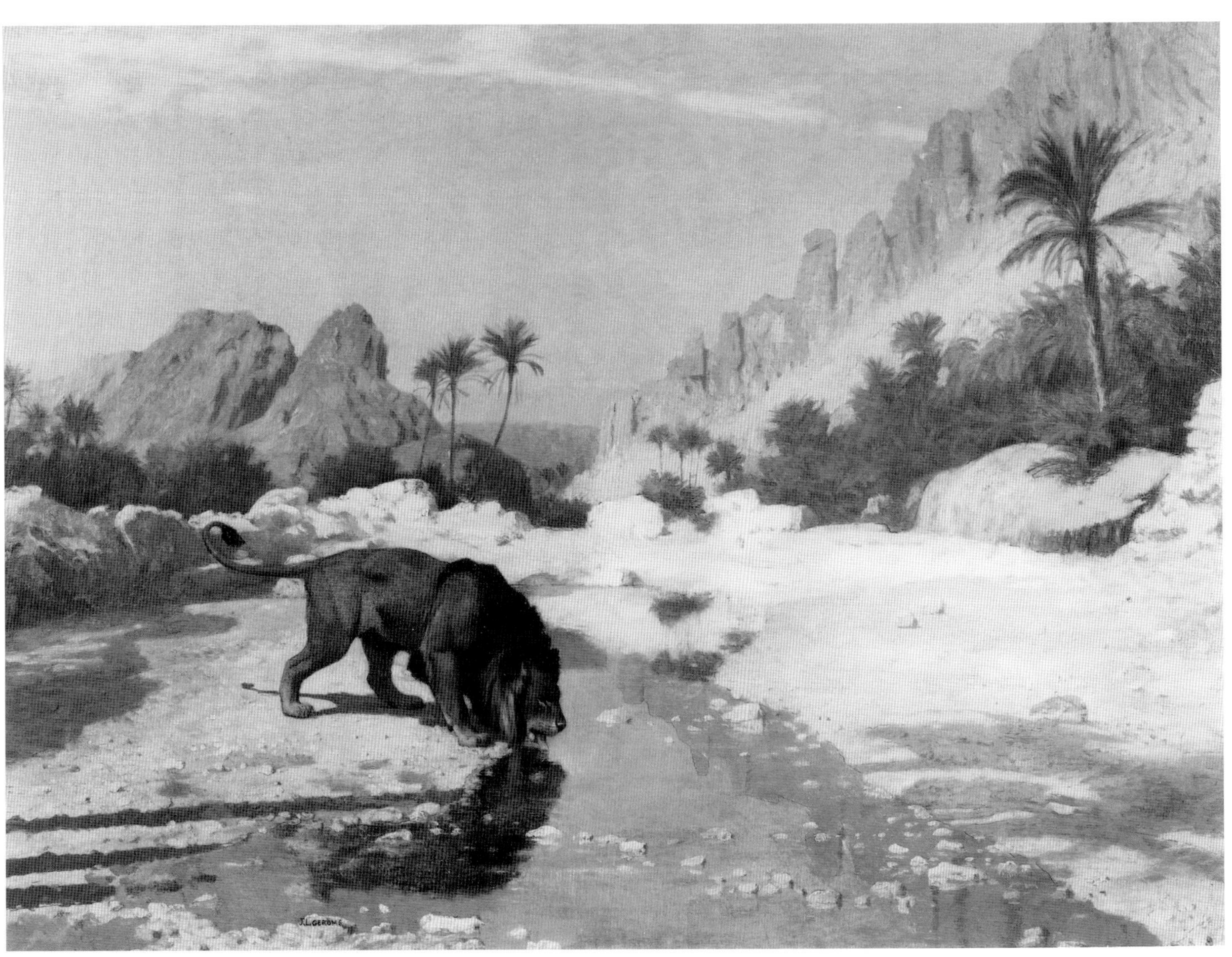

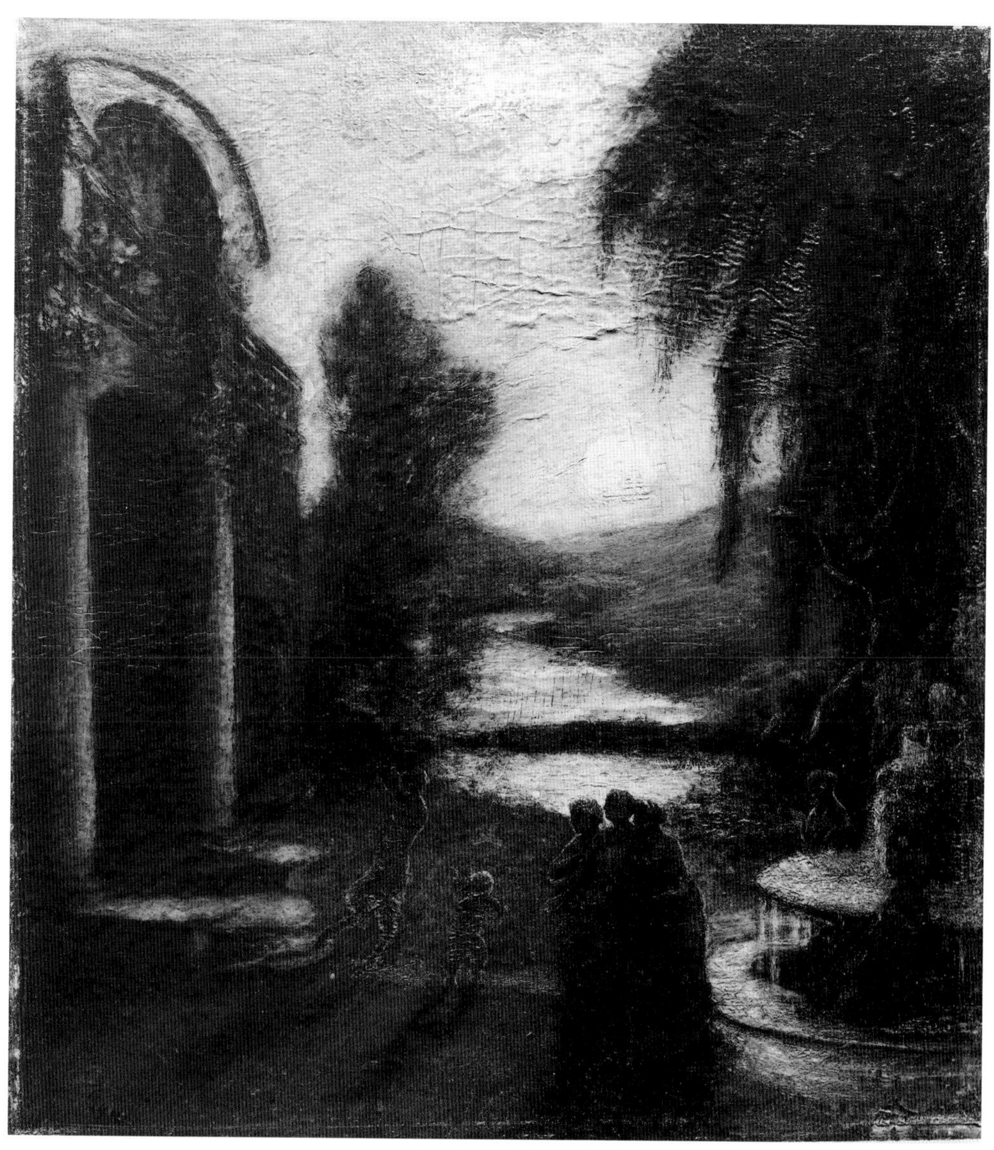

ALBERT PINKHAM RYDER (AMERICAN, 1847 – 1917)
THE TEMPLE OF THE MIND, CA. 1885

oil on wood, 17 3/4 x 16" (45.1 x 40.6 cm.)
Collection Albright-Knox Art Gallery, Buffalo, New York
Gift of R. B. Angus, 1918
Buffalo only
CAT. NO. 22

Ryder's deeply personal, visionary art entered its richest, most mature stage in the 1880s. This painting became one of his best-known works, first exhibited in 1888 at the *First Annual Exhibition of American Paintings* in Chicago and later at other prestigious shows, including the Pan-American Exposition. Inspired by "The Haunted Palace," a darkly Romantic poem by Edgar Allan Poe, Ryder improvised upon Poe's allegorical theme of a deteriorated classical temple representing a troubled mind. As the artist once explained in a letter, the three graces (a metaphor for the "finer attributes of the mind") have been driven from the temple; they await "a weeping love" to join them on the moonlit lawn as a devilish faun triumphantly dances up the temple steps to take possession of his newly won domain.

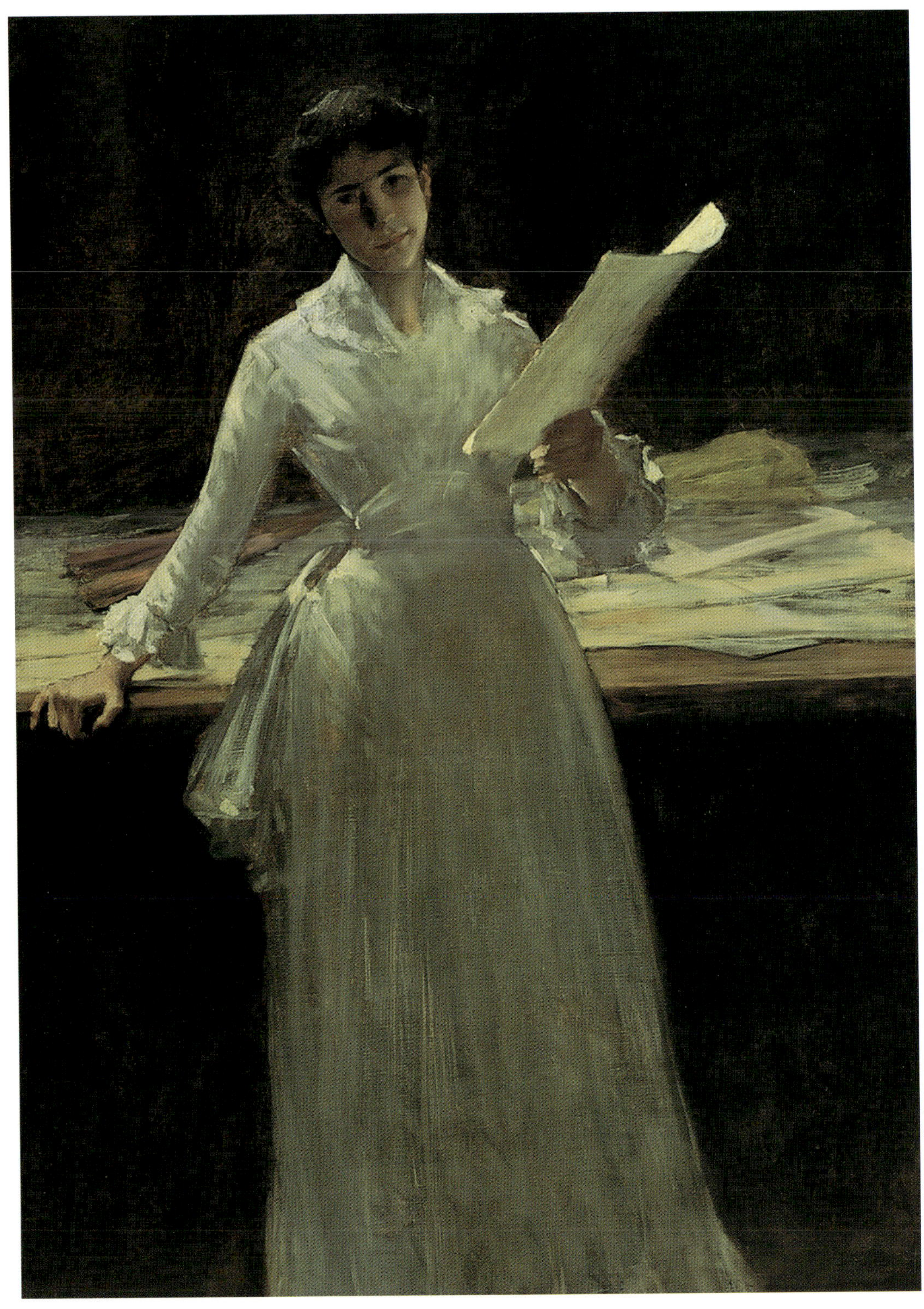

WILLIAM MERRITT CHASE (AMERICAN, 1849 – 1916)
MEMORIES, 1885-86

oil on canvas, 50 1/2 x 37" (128.3 x 94 cm.)
Collection Munson-Williams-Proctor Arts Institute, Museum of Art,
Utica, New York
Museum Purchase, 57.305
CAT. NO. 84

CAMILLE PISSARRO (FRENCH, BORN VIRGIN ISLANDS, 1830 – 1903)
PEASANTS IN THE FIELDS, ERAGNY, 1890

oil on canvas, 25 3/8 x 31 5/8" (64.5 x 80.3 cm.)
Collection Albright-Knox Art Gallery, Buffalo, New York
Gift of A. Conger Goodyear, 1940
CAT. NO. 20

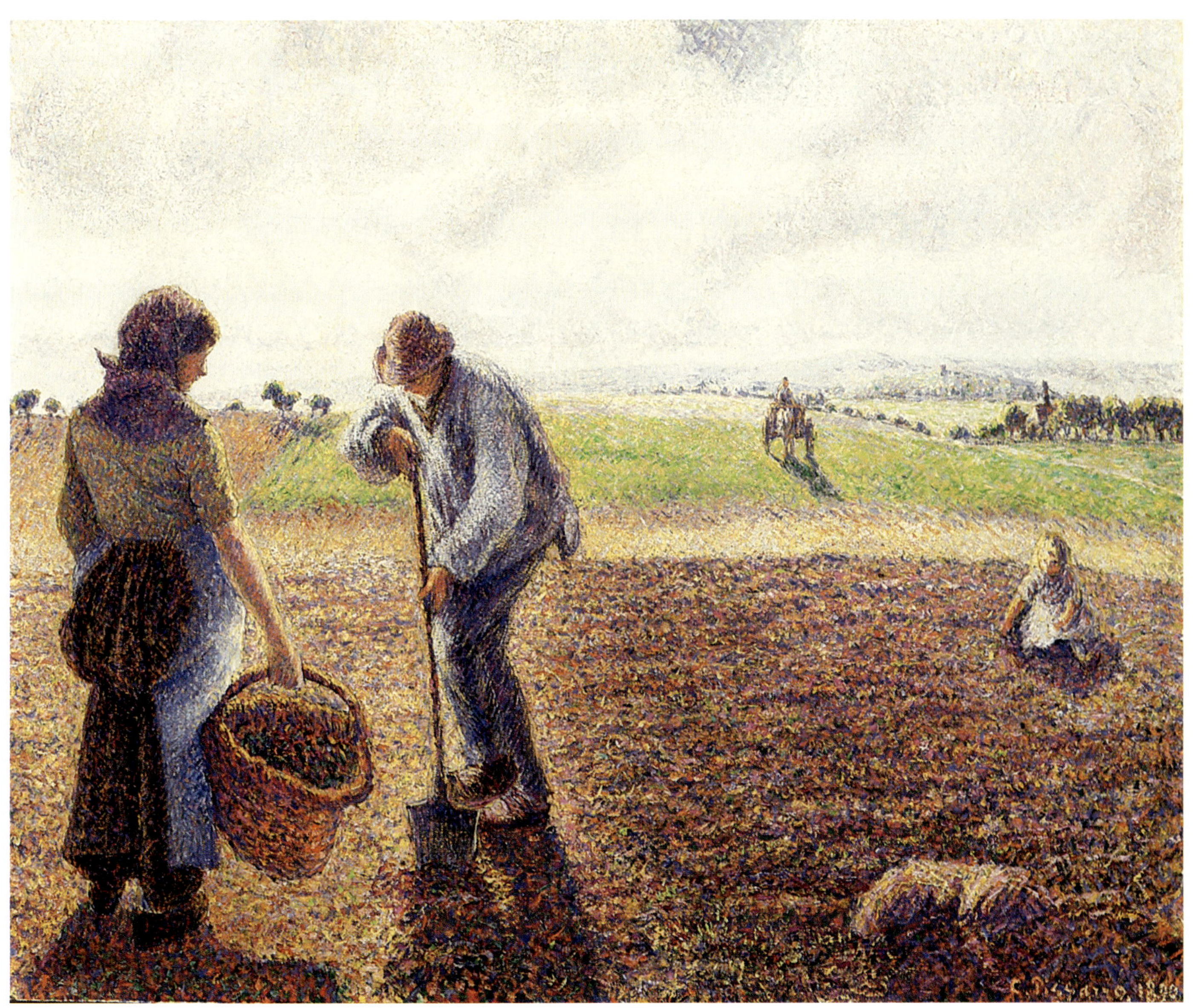

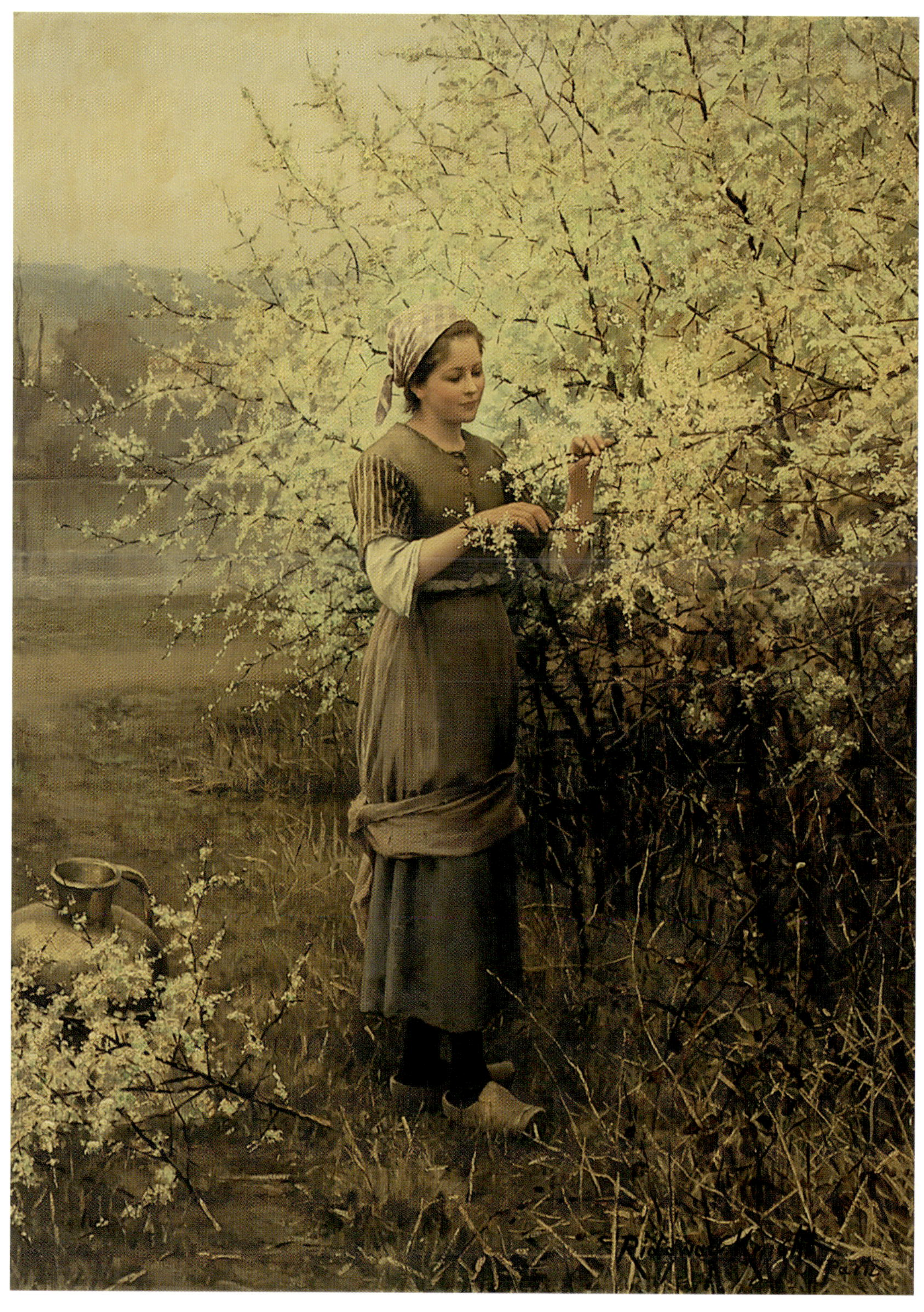

DANIEL RIDGWAY KNIGHT (AMERICAN, 1839 – 1924)

SPRINGTIME, CA. 1890

oil on canvas, 67 1/2 x 50" (171.5 x 127 cm.)
Collection Albright-Knox Art Gallery, Buffalo, New York
Gift of Mrs. Clara A. H. H. Smith in memory of her brother,
Frank Wayland Higgins, 1935
CAT. NO. 14

WALTER LAUNT PALMER (AMERICAN, 1854 – 1932)
AUTUMN MORNING, MIST CLEARING AWAY, 1892

oil on canvas, 38 1/4 x 52 1/4" (97.2 x 132.7 cm.)
Collection Albany Institute of History and Art, New York
Gift of the Estate of Dr. Leonard G. Stanley, 1959
CAT. NO. 2

A classmate of John Singer Sargent when both studied in the atelier of Charles Emile Auguste Carolus-Duran, Palmer shares with Sargent the fluid handling of paint inspired by the example of the seventeenth-century Spanish painter Diego Velázquez and taught by Carolus-Duran. Dappled in shades of brown, green, purple, and pale blue, this quiet, autumnal landscape exudes a contemplative spirit reflective perhaps of Palmer's own state of mind at the time it was painted, as it was begun just before and completed after the death of his first wife. Considered one of Palmer's finest works, *Autumn Morning, Mist Clearing Away* won first prize when it was exhibited at the World's Columbian Exposition in Chicago in 1893.

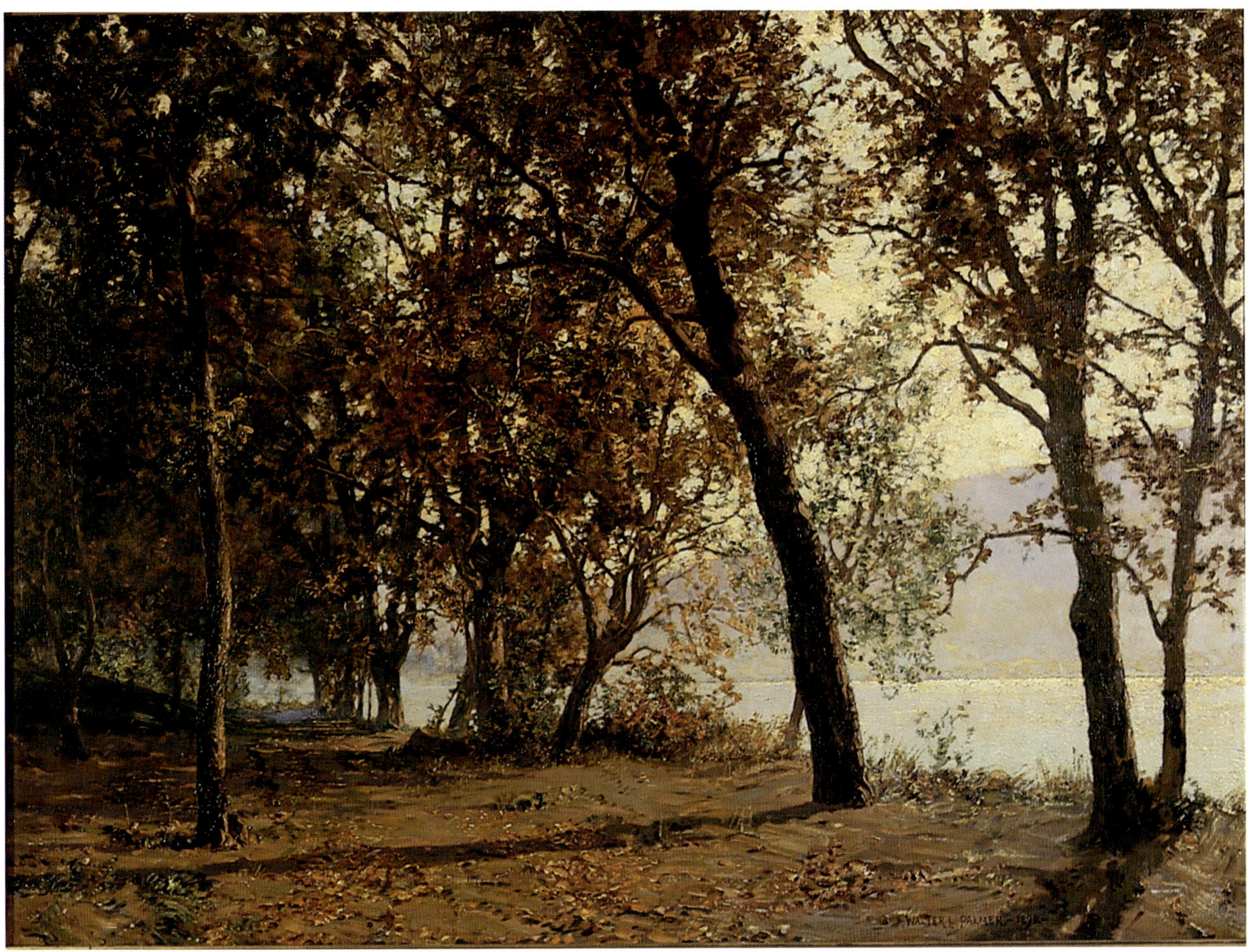

GARI MELCHERS (AMERICAN, 1860 – 1932)
THE WEDDING, CA. 1892

oil on canvas, 43 x 26" (109.2 x 66 cm.)
Collection Albright-Knox Art Gallery, Buffalo, New York
Charles W. Goodyear Fund, 1922
CAT. NO. 16

Like so many young Americans in the last quarter of the nineteenth century, Gari Melchers traveled abroad for his artistic education, first studying at the Royal Academy in Düsseldorf – where he acquired the skills in strong drawing and careful modeling that would come to characterize his work – and later at the Académie Julian in Paris. The subtle, natural interior lighting evident in *The Wedding* also attests to his German training. In 1884, he established a studio in the Dutch town of Egmond aan zee, painting pictures there of the villagers, who were often engaged in religious observances like the simple wedding depicted here.

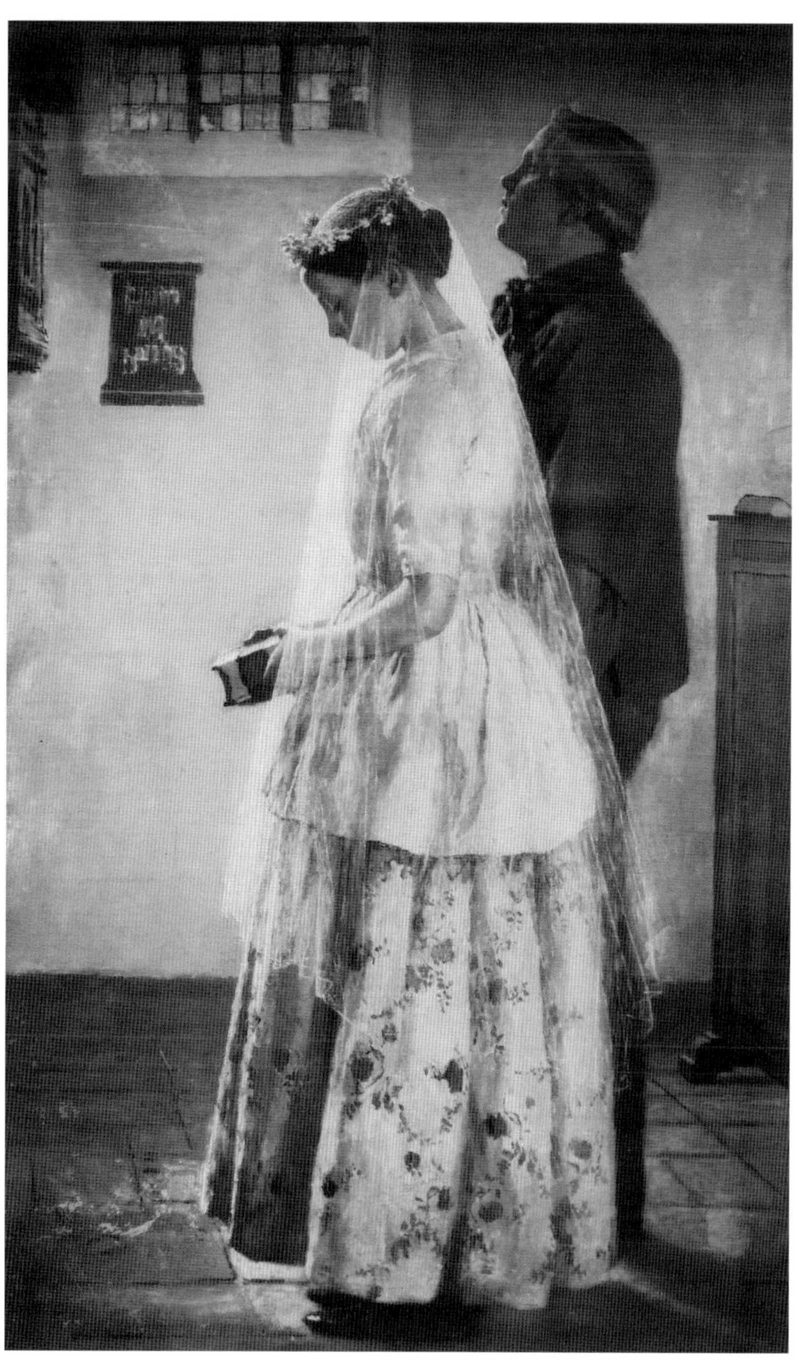

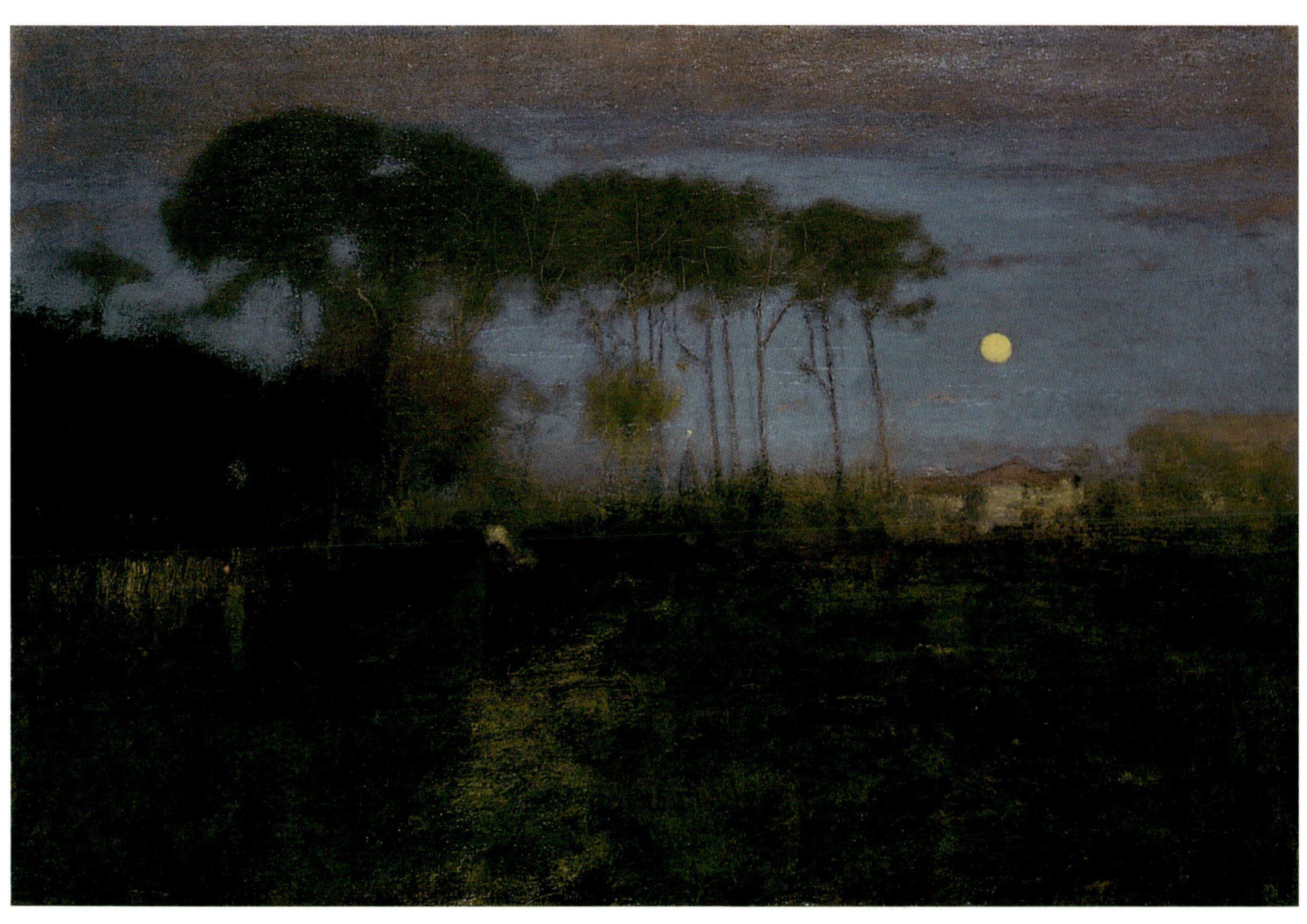

GEORGE INNESS (AMERICAN, 1825 – 1894)
EARLY MOONRISE IN FLORIDA, 1893

oil on canvas, 24 3/8 x 36 1/4" (61.9 x 92.1 cm.)
Collection Memorial Art Gallery of the University of Rochester, New York
George Eastman Collection of the University of Rochester, 36.61
CAT. NO. 77

THEODORE ROBINSON (AMERICAN, 1852 – 1896)
THE BERME ROAD, 1893

oil on canvas, 18 x 22" (45.7 x 55.9 cm.)
Collection Herbert F. Johnson Museum of Art
Cornell University, Ithaca, New York
Purchased through the generosity of the H. A. Metzger, Class of 1921, Bequest, 76.065
CAT. NO. 56

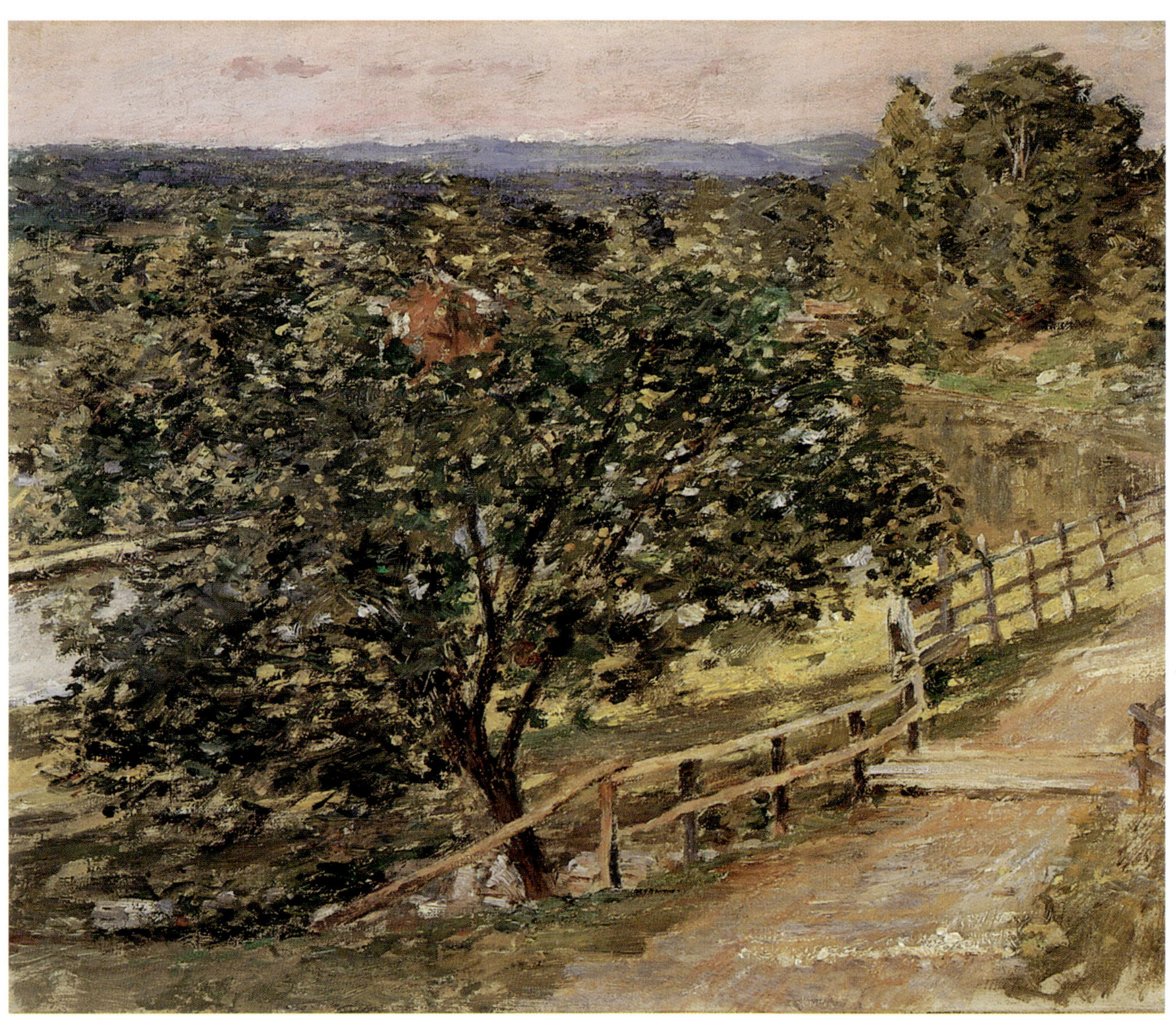

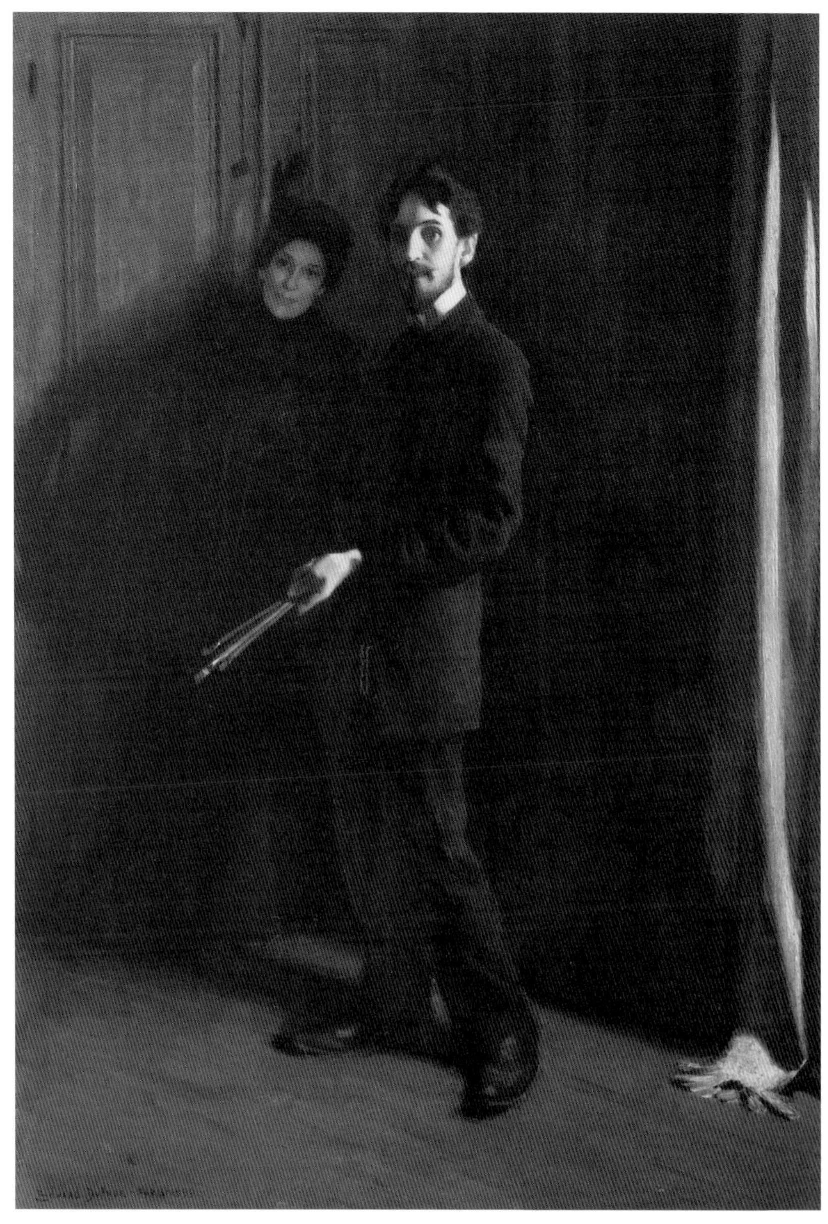

Edward Dufner (American, 1872 – 1957)

In the Studio, 1899

oil on canvas, 28 1/2 x 20" (72.4 x 50.8 cm.)
Collection Albright-Knox Art Gallery, Buffalo, New York
Sherman S. Jewett Fund, 1901
CAT. NO. 9

In the muted tones and atmospheric handling of this painting of a young artist in his Parisian studio, one can readily perceive the influence of James Abbott McNeill Whistler, with whom Dufner studied during his French sojourn from 1898 to 1903. Dufner, a native of Buffalo, had begun his studies at The Buffalo Fine Arts Academy, continued them at the Art Students' League in New York, and culminated them in Paris with Jean-Paul Laurens at the Académie Julian and independently with Whistler. *In the Studio* was exhibited at the Paris Salon in 1900 and, in 1901, on home ground at the Pan-American Exposition, where it won a Bronze Medal. After teaching briefly at The Buffalo Fine Arts Academy upon his return from Europe, Dufner left to accept a post at the Art Students' League in New York, ultimately settling in New Jersey and turning away from his earlier Whistlerian mode of painting to a colorful Impressionist style.

JAMES ABBOTT McNEILL WHISTLER (AMERICAN, 1834 – 1903)
THE SEA, POURVILLE, NO. 2, CA. 1899

oil on wood, 5 3/8 x 9 3/16" (13.7 x 23.3 cm.)
Collection Munson-Williams-Proctor Arts Institute, Museum of Art,
Utica, New York
Museum Purchase with Funds from the Charles E. Merrill Trust, 73.114
CAT. NO. 94

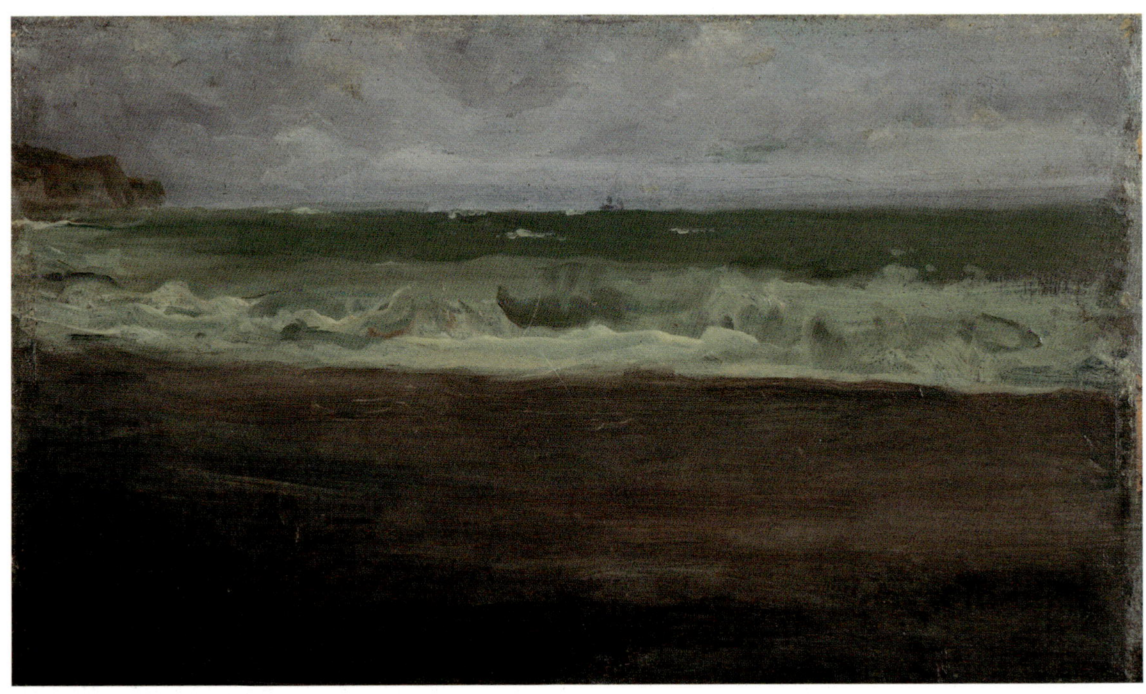

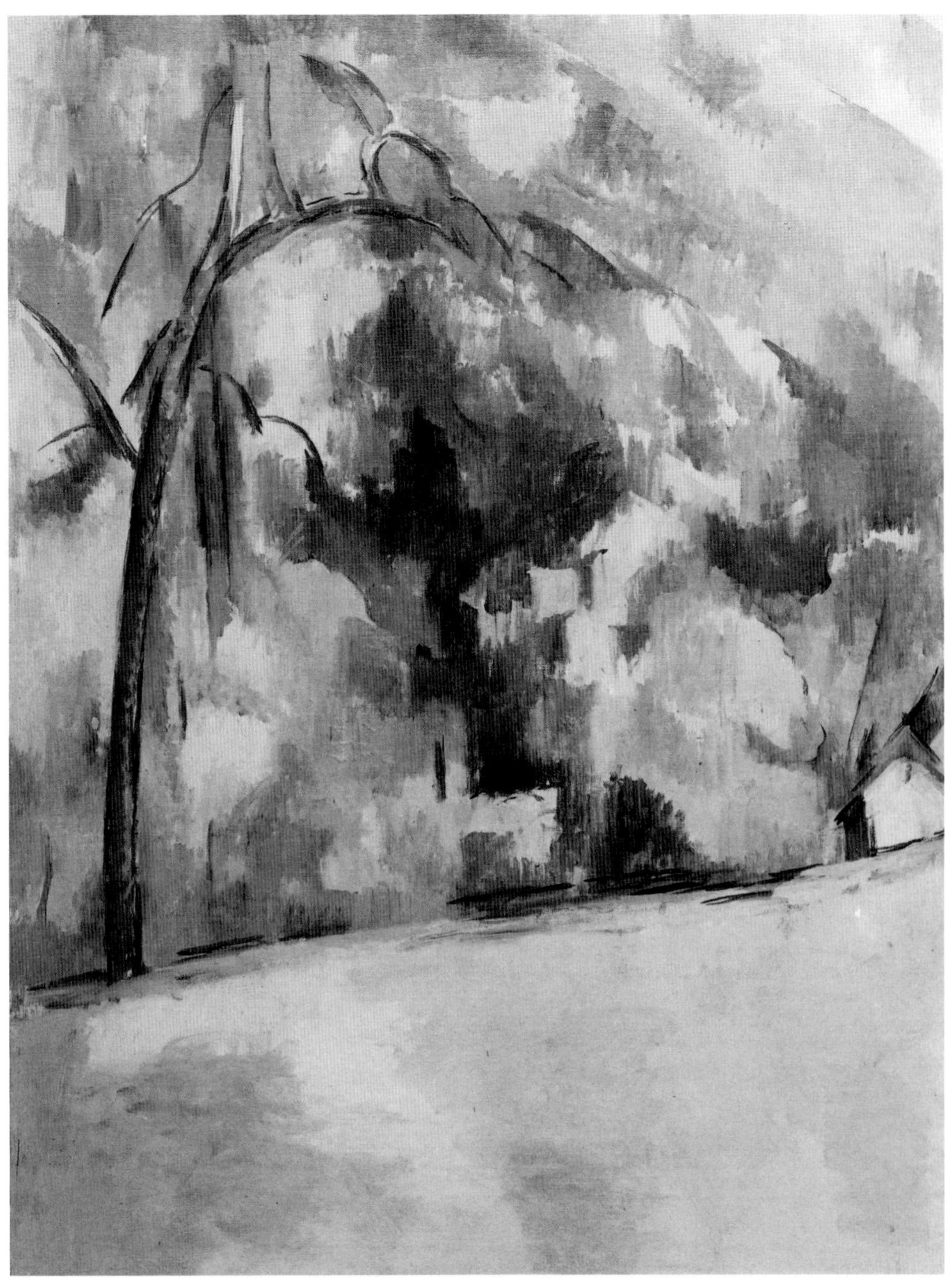

oil on canvas, 32 x 24 7/8" (81.3 x 63.2 cm.)
Collection Albright-Knox Art Gallery, Buffalo, New York
Gift of Mr. and Mrs. Charles A. Ribbel through the Frank E. Ribbel Bequest, 1936
Traveling to Buffalo, Ithaca, Albany, Syracuse, and Rochester
CAT. NO. 5

Morning in Provence exemplifies Cézanne's later works, painted while he was living in seclusion in Aix from 1899 until his death in 1906. Although he continued to develop his means of building images from strokes of color and implying depth through advancing light tones and receding dark tones rather than through linear perspective, he moved away from his earlier, more tightly constructed and heavily painted pictures toward the airy, delicately brushed style evinced in *Morning in Provence*. Indeed, the broad patches of bright, thinly applied color and the loose composition – opened up with areas of pale, exposed canvas – achieve in oil an evanescent effect of shimmering light and air usually associated with watercolor.

WILL HICOK LOW (AMERICAN, 1853 – 1932)
THE TERRACE WALLS, 1901

oil on canvas, 19 1/2 x 25 7/8" (49.5 x 65.7 cm.)
Collection Albany Institute of History and Art, New York
Gift of John Townsend Lansing, 1908
CAT. NO. 1

Low's training at Paris's École Nationale des Beaux-Arts under Jean-Léon Gérôme and Charles Emile Auguste Carolus-Duran imbued him with a taste for classical allegorical figure painting and decoration that prepared him well for a career as one of the most successful decorative artists in the United States. His murals in Albany, for example, at St. Paul's Church, the State Education Building, and the Legislative Library of the State Capital attest to his skills. Low also maintained his European connections, however, visiting his friend, Frederick MacMonnies, at the latter's home in Giverny, France, where the sculptor ran a school from 1905 until 1915. In *The Terrace Walls*, Low recorded his visit with a glittering vision of sunlight playing over MacMonnies's lush garden and terrace walls, the latter topped with decorative sculptures, including a bronze statuette, *Diana*, by MacMonnies's renowned Beaux-Arts teacher, Jean Alexandre Joseph Falguière.

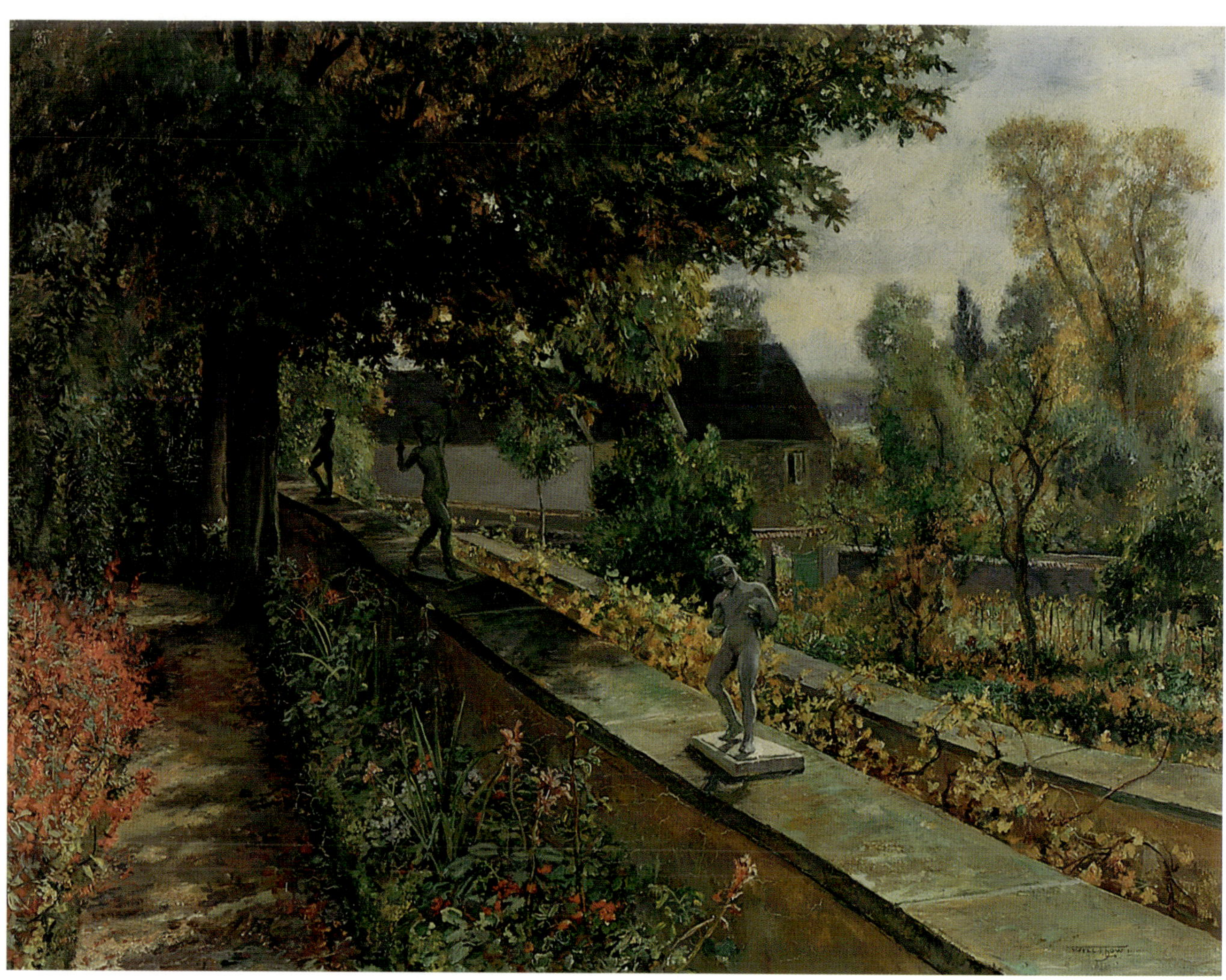

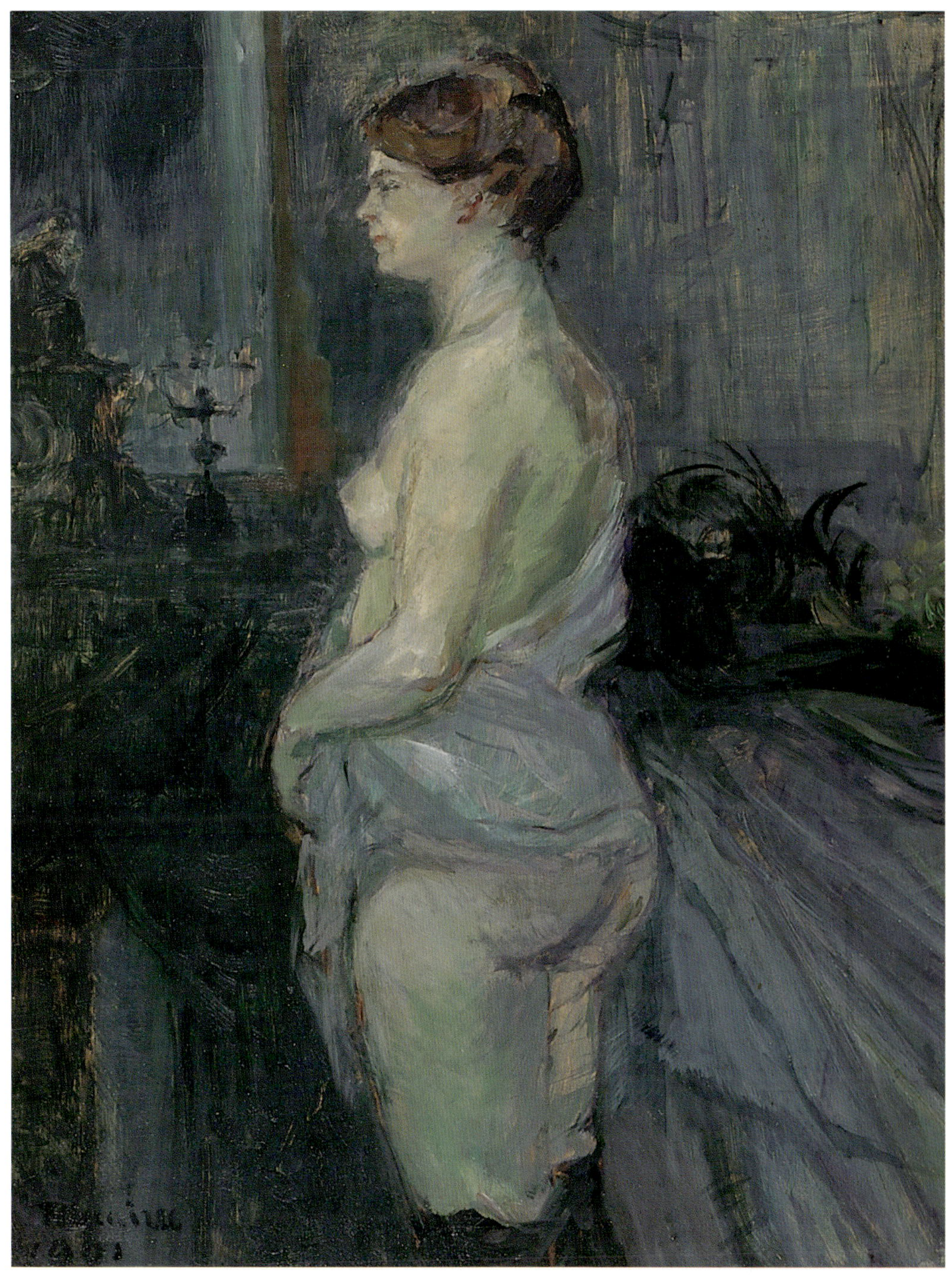

HENRI DE TOULOUSE-LAUTREC (FRENCH, 1864 – 1901)
WOMAN LIFTING HER CHEMISE, 1901

oil on wood panel, 22 x 16 5/8" (55.9 x 42.2 cm.)
Collection Albright-Knox Art Gallery, Buffalo, New York
Gift of A. Conger Goodyear, 1956
CAT. NO. 25

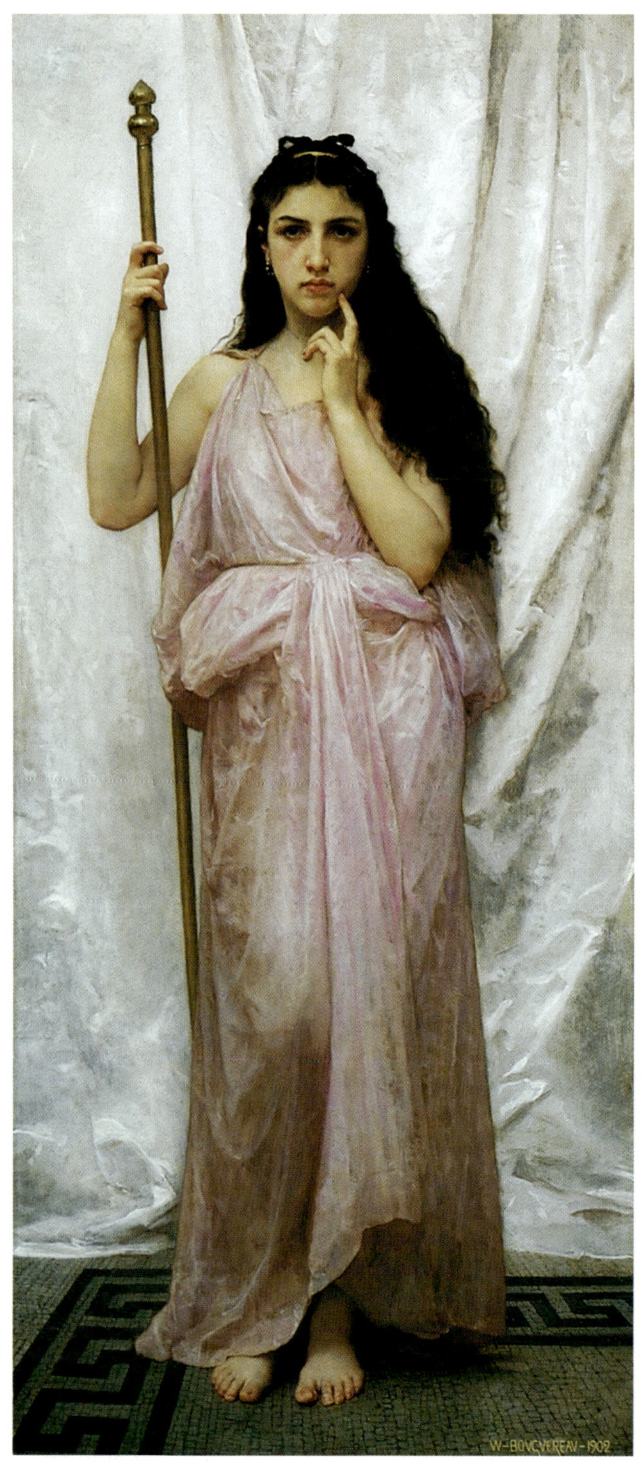

ADOLPHE WILLIAM BOUGUEREAU (FRENCH, 1825 – 1905)
YOUNG PRIESTESS, 1902

oil on canvas, 71 1/4 x 32" (181 x 81.3 cm.)
Collection Memorial Art Gallery of the University of Rochester, New York
Gift of Paul T. White in memory of Josephine Kryl White, 73.1
CAT. NO. 74

THOMAS EAKINS (AMERICAN, 1844 – 1916)
MUSIC, 1904

oil on canvas, 39 3/4 x 49 3/4" (101 x 126.4 cm.)
Collection Albright-Knox Art Gallery, Buffalo, New York
George Cary, Edmund Hayes, and James G. Forsyth Funds, 1955
CAT. NO. 10

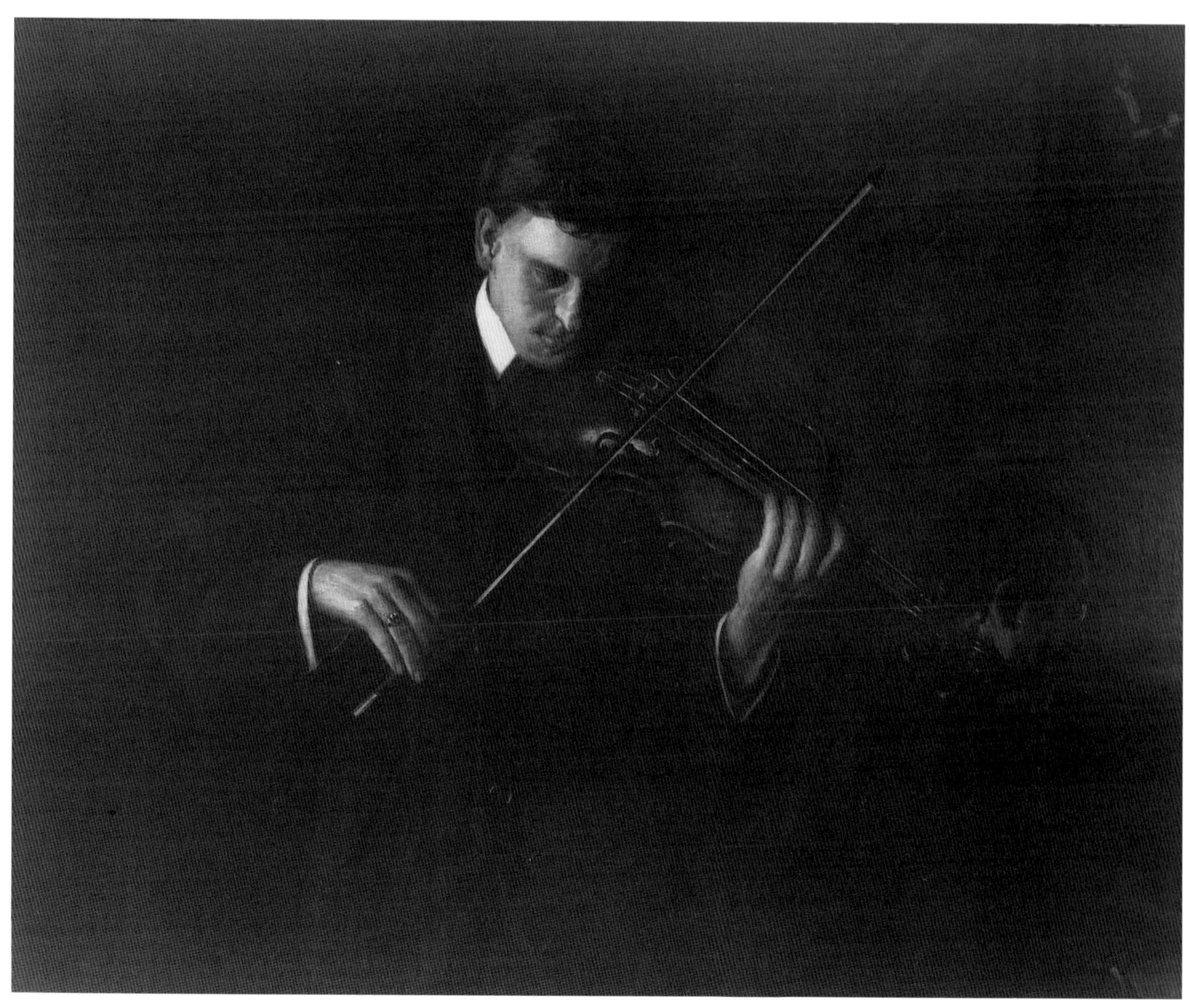

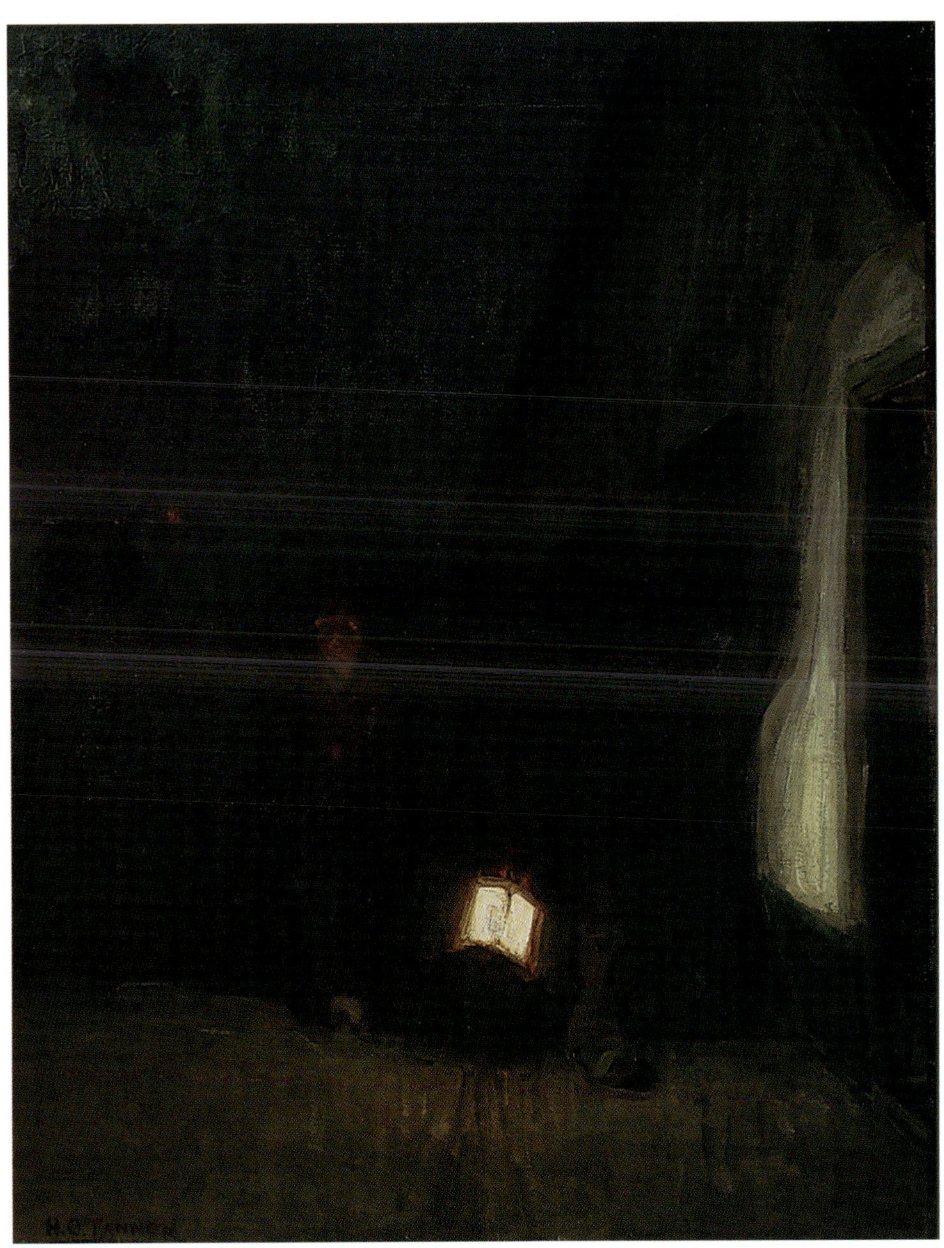

HENRY OSSAWA TANNER (AMERICAN, 1859 – 1937)
RETURN OF THE FISHERMAN, CA. 1905

oil on canvas, 26 1/4 x 19 3/4" (66.7 x 50.2 cm.)
Collection Herbert F. Johnson Museum of Art
Cornell University, Ithaca, New York
Gift of Mrs. Stephen W. Jacobs, 79.029.001
CAT. NO. 57

While the white male bastion of art in the late nineteenth century in many ways remained resistant to women who wished to
pursue a professional career, it was nearly impervious to people of color. Tanner, son of an African Methodist Episcopal Church
bishop in Philadelphia, nevertheless persisted in his efforts to compete at the highest levels and succeeded, studying first with
Thomas Eakins at the Pennsylvania Academy in Philadelphia and then with Benjamin Constant at the Académie Julian in Paris.
Although he retained ties with leaders of the African-American community in the United States, such as Booker T. Washington and
W.E.B. Dubois, Tanner found French society less racked by racial prejudice and thus settled in Paris. He eventually won interna-
tional acclaim for his broadly painted biblical images, landscapes, and genre scenes like *Return of the Fisherman*, a hauntingly
lantern-lit night scene set in the Calais district of northwest France. Tanner considered this to be one of his best small works.

EVERETT SHINN (AMERICAN, 1873 – 1953)
THEATER BOX, 1906

oil on canvas, 16 1/8 x 20 1/8" (41 x 51.1 cm.)
Collection Albright-Knox Art Gallery, Buffalo, New York
Gift of T. Edward Hanley, 1937
CAT. NO. 24

Shinn, like several of his Ashcan School colleagues, began his career as a newspaper illustrator in Philadelphia and later moved to New York City, where he began to portray the life of the city streets with gritty realism. A trip to Paris proved a major turning point in his career, however, for it was there that he became fascinated with the theater and began painting the Parisian nightlife in a manner reminiscent of the French artist Edgar Degas. *Theater Box*, though painted after his return to the United States and shown at the seminal exhibition of The Eight at the Macbeth Gallery in 1908, shares Degas's typical skewed vantage point and theatrical lighting, its subject signaling Shinn's drift away from the Ashcan School's social philosophy and towards an increasing involvement with the theater world.

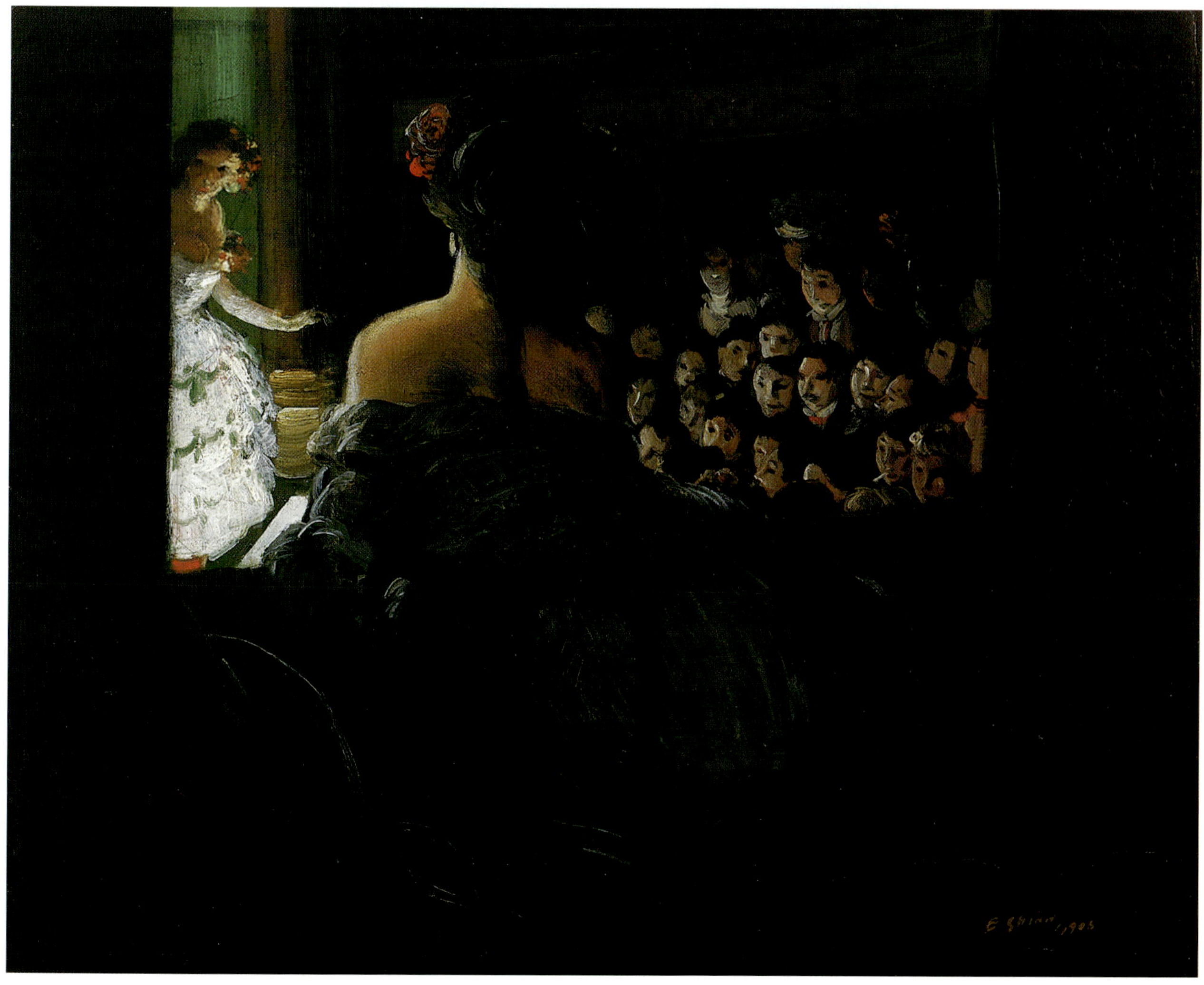

The Trees represents Derain's work at the height of his brief Fauve period. Fauve, meaning "wild beast," was the name given to a group of artists including Derain, Maurice Vlaminck, Henri Matisse, and Georges Braque when they shocked the critics of the 1904 Salon d'Automne exhibition in Paris with their wildly colored canvases. Derain painted these undulating trees – a popular theme among the Fauves – following a summer spent with Matisse at Collioure, where he developed his characteristic rectangular brushstroke, juxtaposition of contrasting colors, and agitated color and linear rhythms.

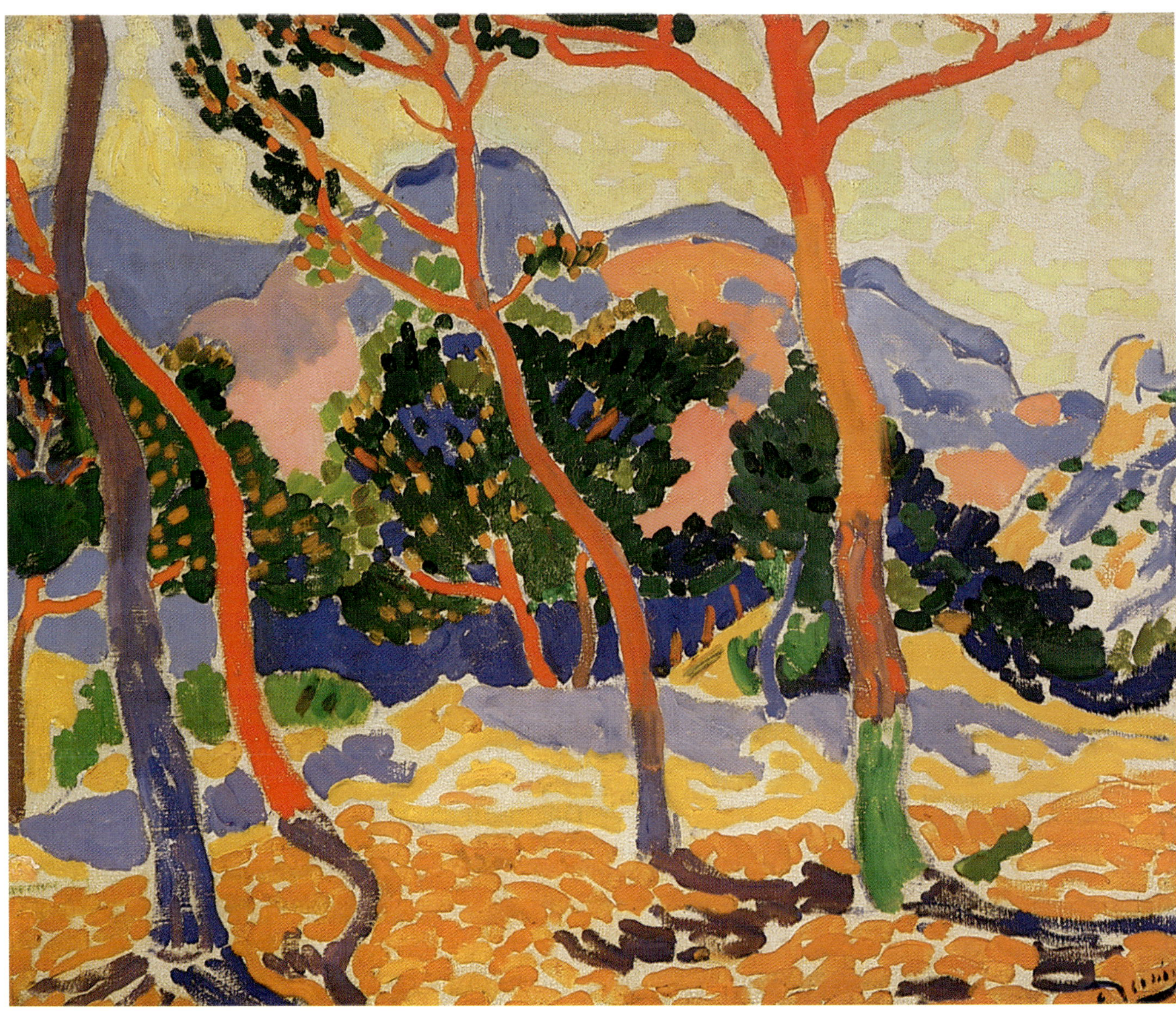

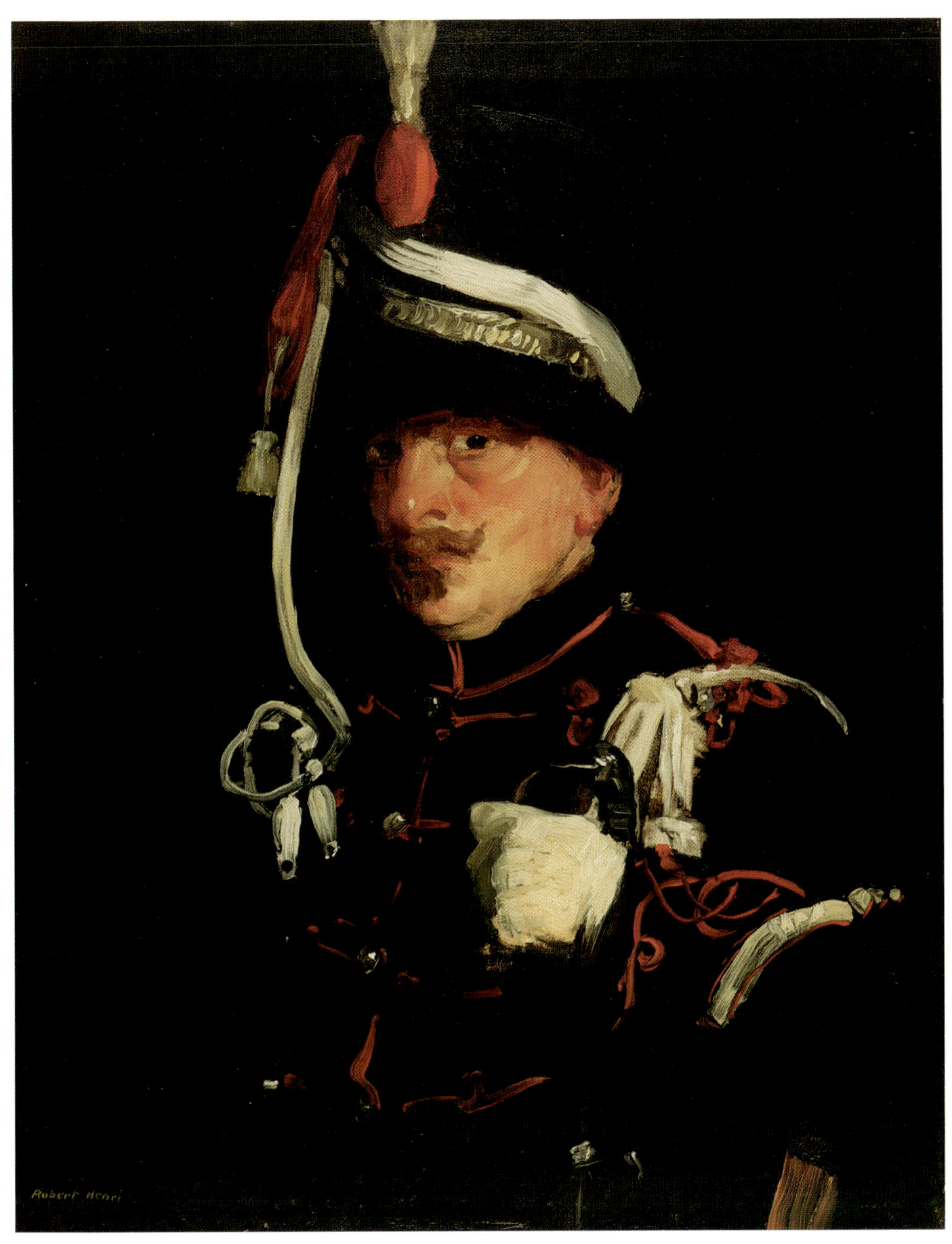

ROBERT HENRI (AMERICAN, 1865 – 1929)
DUTCH SOLDIER, 1907

oil on canvas, 32 5/8 x 26 1/8" (82.9 x 66.4 cm.)
Collection Munson-Williams-Proctor Arts Institute, Museum of Art,
Utica, New York
Museum Purchase, 58.8
CAT. NO. 88

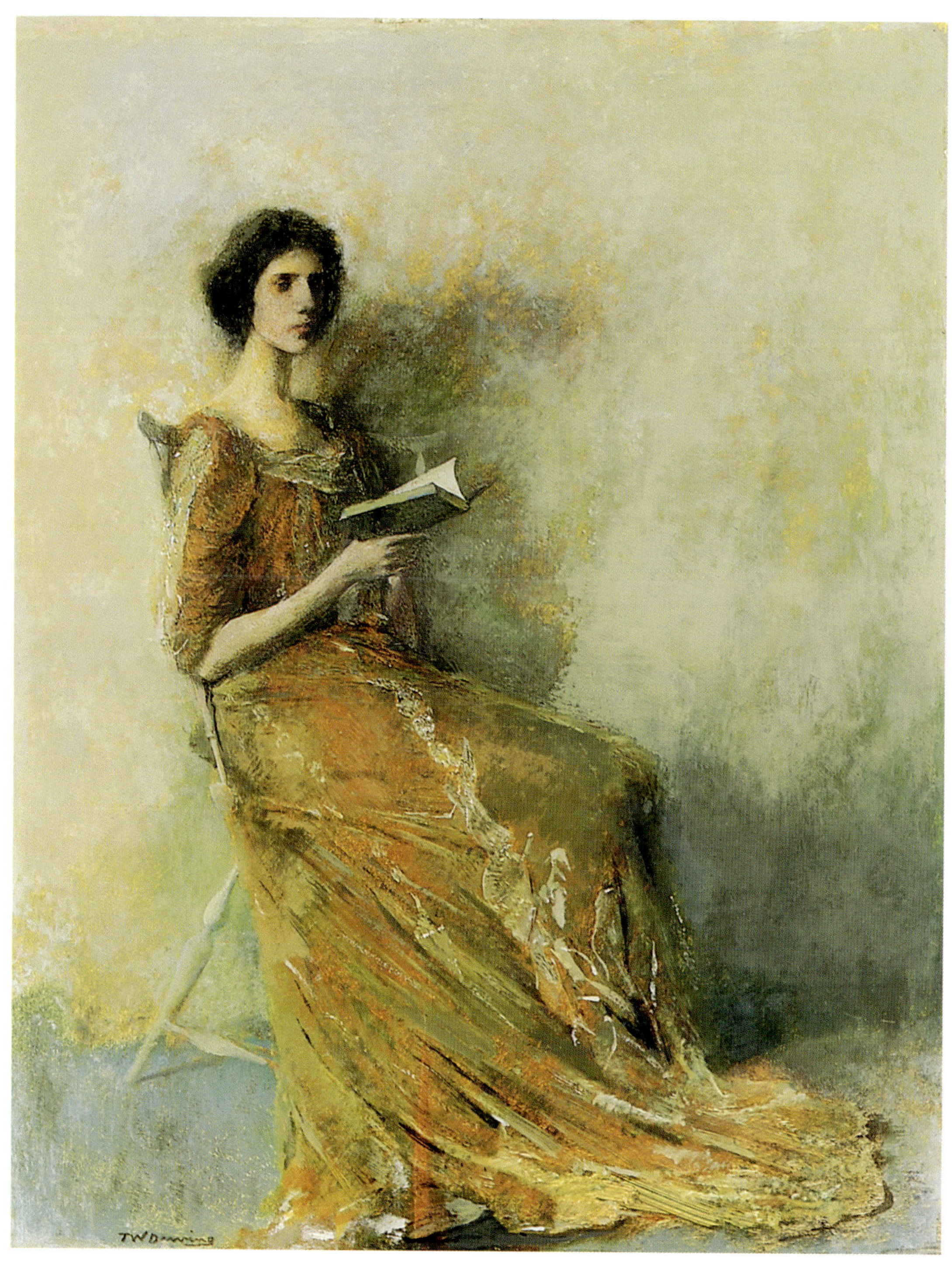

THOMAS WILMER DEWING (AMERICAN, 1851 – 1938)
PORTRAIT IN A BROWN DRESS, CA. 1908

oil on wood panel, 20 x 15 1/2" (50.8 x 39.4 cm.)
Collection Memorial Art Gallery of the University of Rochester, New York
Gift of Mr. and Mrs. Alexander Millar Lindsay, III, in memory of
Jesse Williams and Grace Curtice Lindsay and their daughter,
Carolyn Lindsay White, 57.79
CAT. NO. 76

GEORGE LUKS (AMERICAN, 1867 – 1933)
ROUNDHOUSE AT HIGH BRIDGE, 1909-10

oil on canvas, 30 3/8 x 36 1/4" (77.2 x 92.1 cm.)
Collection Munson-Williams-Proctor Arts Institute, Museum of Art,
Utica, New York
Museum Purchase, 50.17
CAT. NO. 89

Brash in personality as well as in artistic style, Luks, of all the Ashcan School painters, perhaps identified most closely with the residents of the teeming tenements and bustling streets of New York. Like the poet Walt Whitman, he reveled in the vitality of the rapidly developing nation, viewing its people and its industry with optimism and pride. Even when he turned from his usual subject of urban humanity to paint the industrial environment itself, he conveyed a sense of earthy romanticism underlying his realism. In *Roundhouse at High Bridge*, in which soft gray plumes of factory smoke merge into the delicately tinted mauve and blue-gray sky, Luks created a nearly abstract, visual poetry worthy of Whistler.

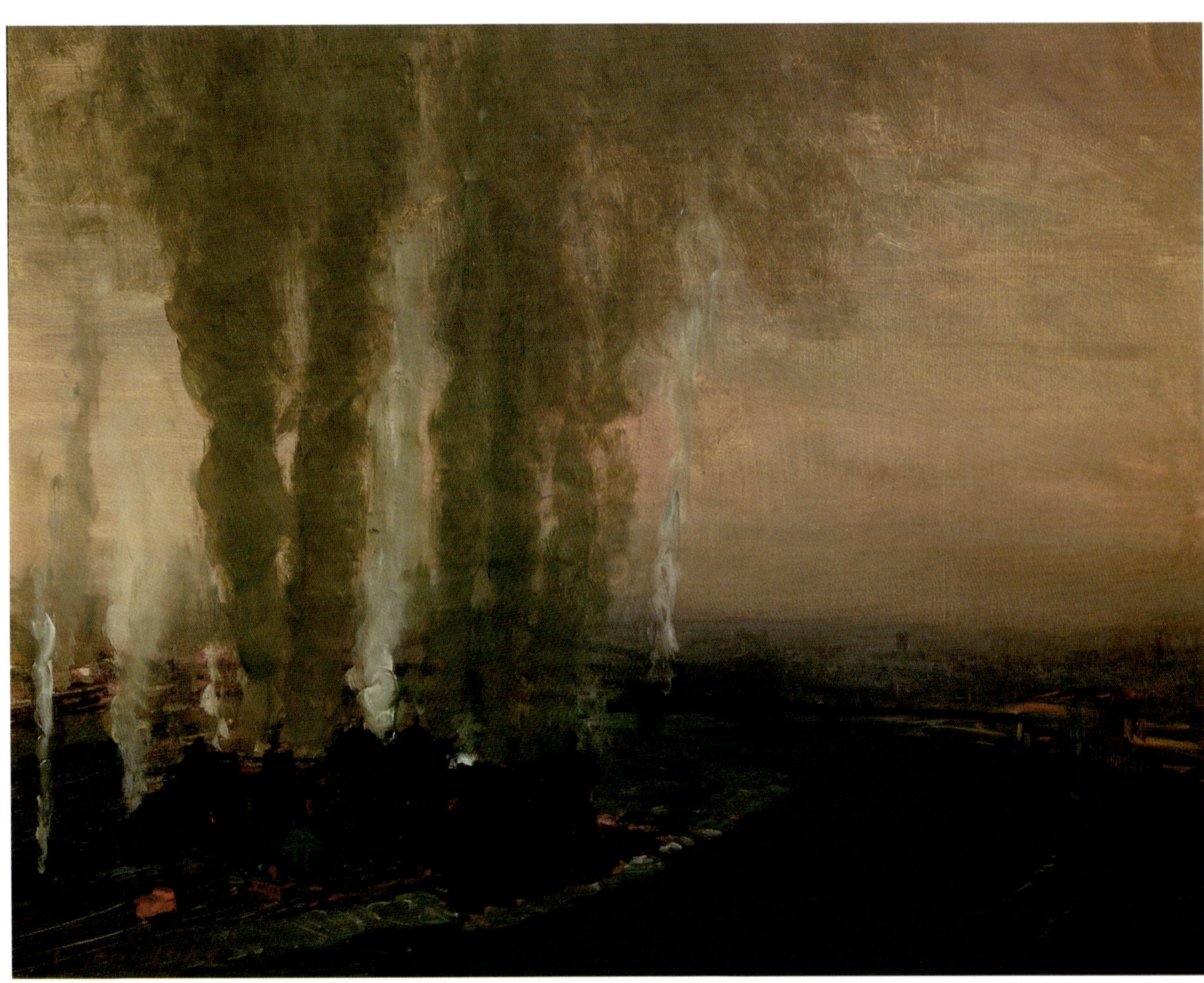

oil on canvas, 36 x 39" (91.4 x 99.1 cm.)
Collection Memorial Art Gallery of the University of Rochester, New York
Gift of Emily Sibley Watson, 13.7
CAT. NO. 79

A founding member of the American Impressionist group The Ten in 1897, Metcalf had previously studied academic painting under Gustave-Rodolphe Boulanger and Jules-Joseph Lefebvre at the Académie Julian in Paris during his stay in France from 1883 to 1888. In the summers of those years, he had been among the first Americans to paint at Giverny, where the famous French Impressionist painter Claude Monet made his home. Upon his return to the United States, Metcalf turned his Impressionist vision to those areas in New England still most untouched by the changes of modern life, such as Cornish, New Hampshire, where he spent considerable time painting from 1909 to 1911. Included in the 1913 invitational *Inaugural Exhibition of Paintings by American Artists* at the Memorial Art Gallery in Rochester, *The Golden Carnival*, with its idyllic country landscape unmarred by human intrusion, characterizes his work during his Cornish period.

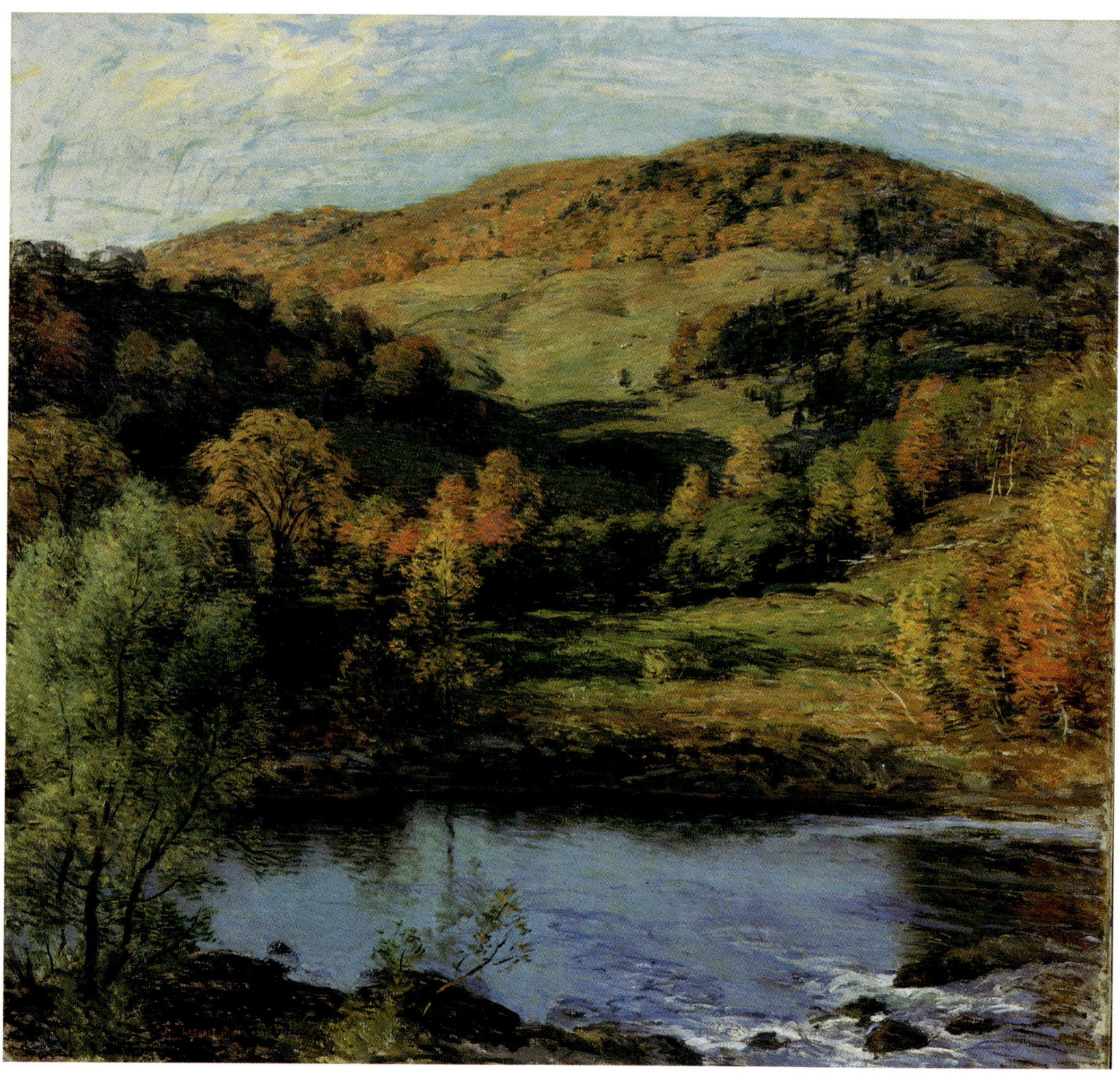

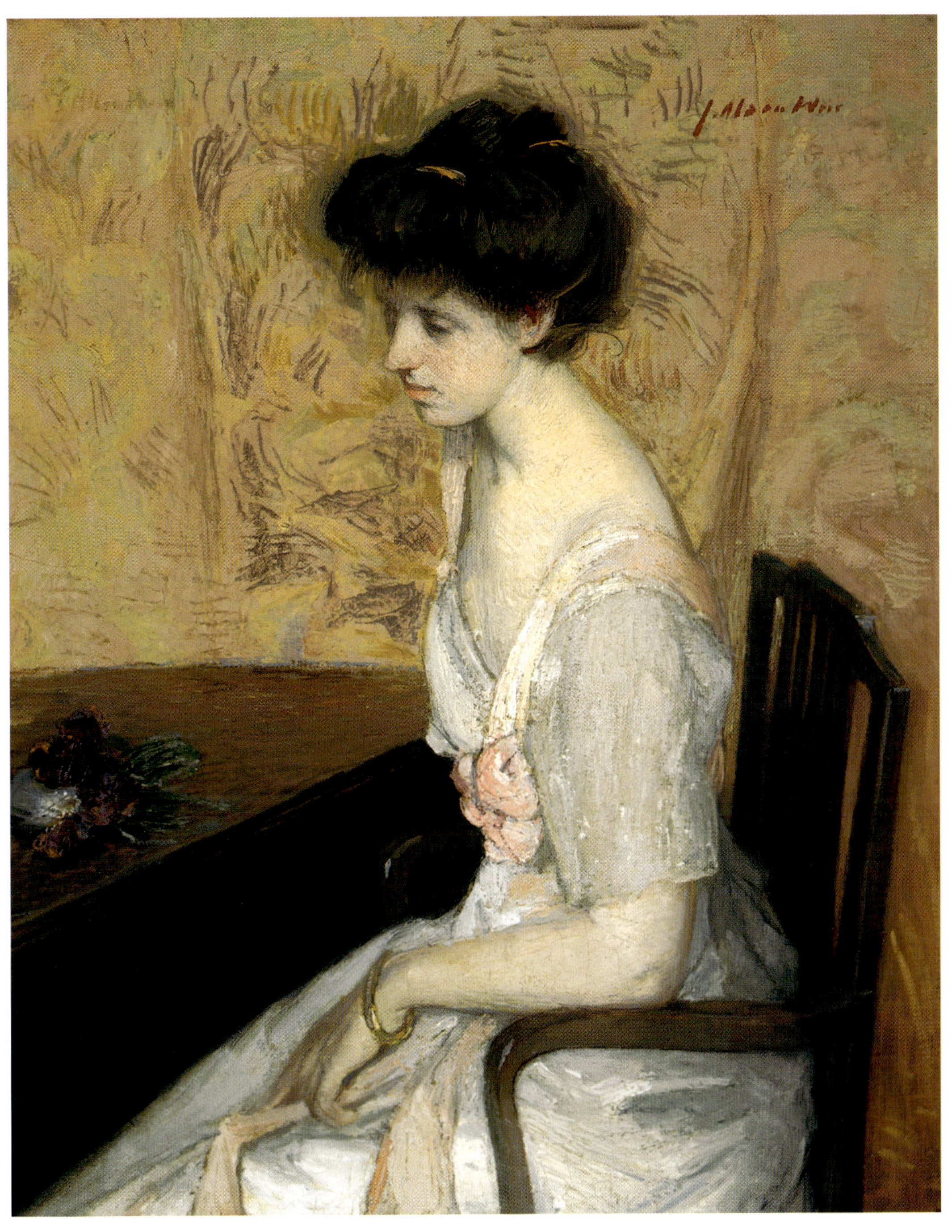

JULIAN ALDEN WEIR (AMERICAN, 1852 – 1919)
PORTRAIT OF A WOMAN, 1910

oil on canvas, 39 5/8 x 32 1/4" (100.6 x 81.9 cm.)
Collection Everson Museum of Art, Syracuse, New York
Museum Purchase, Friends of American Art Fund, 1913
CAT. NO. 38

oil on canvas, 32 x 26" (81.3 x 66 cm.)
Collection Munson-Williams-Proctor Arts Institute, Museum of Art,
Utica, New York
Museum Purchase, 58.87
CAT. NO. 92

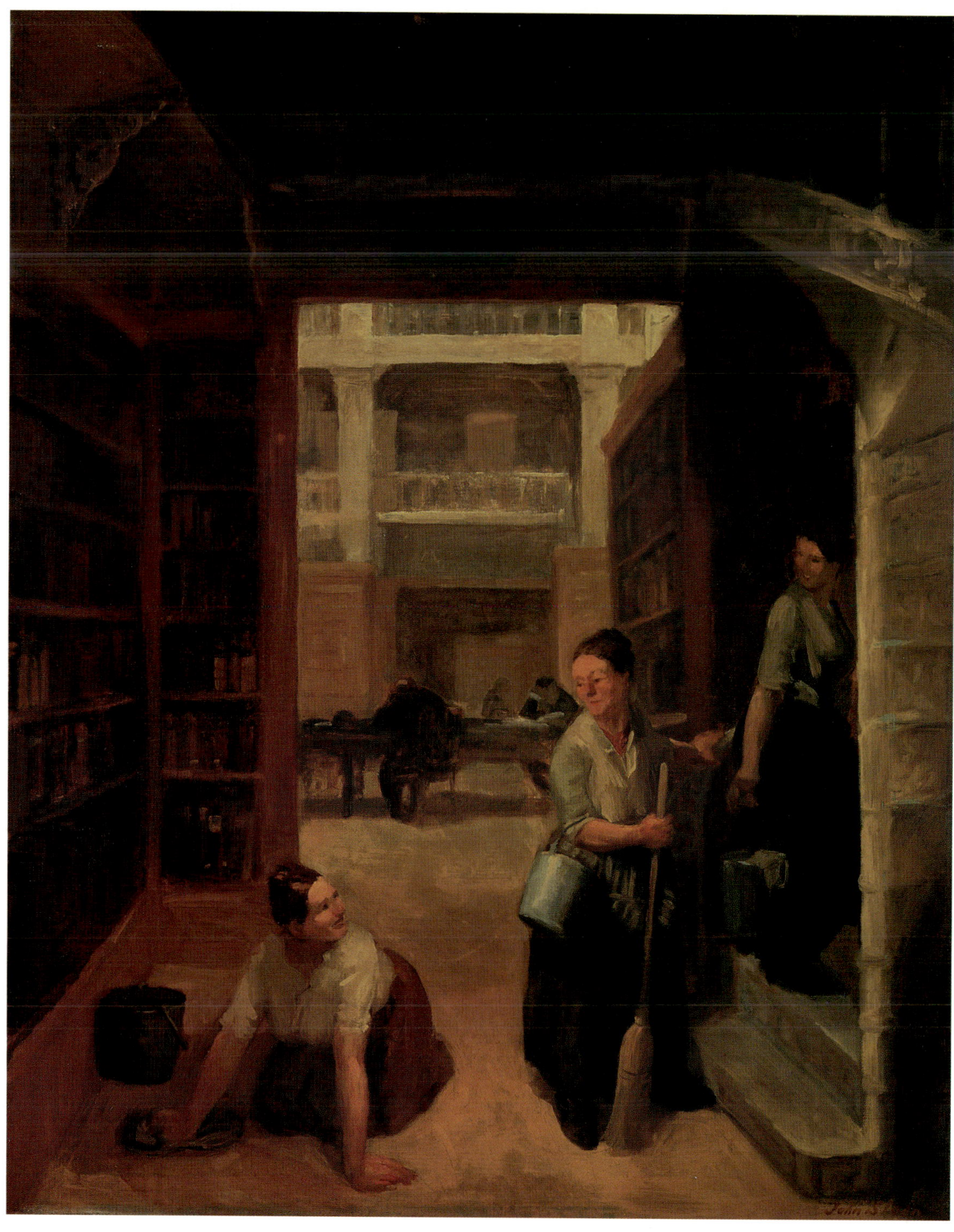

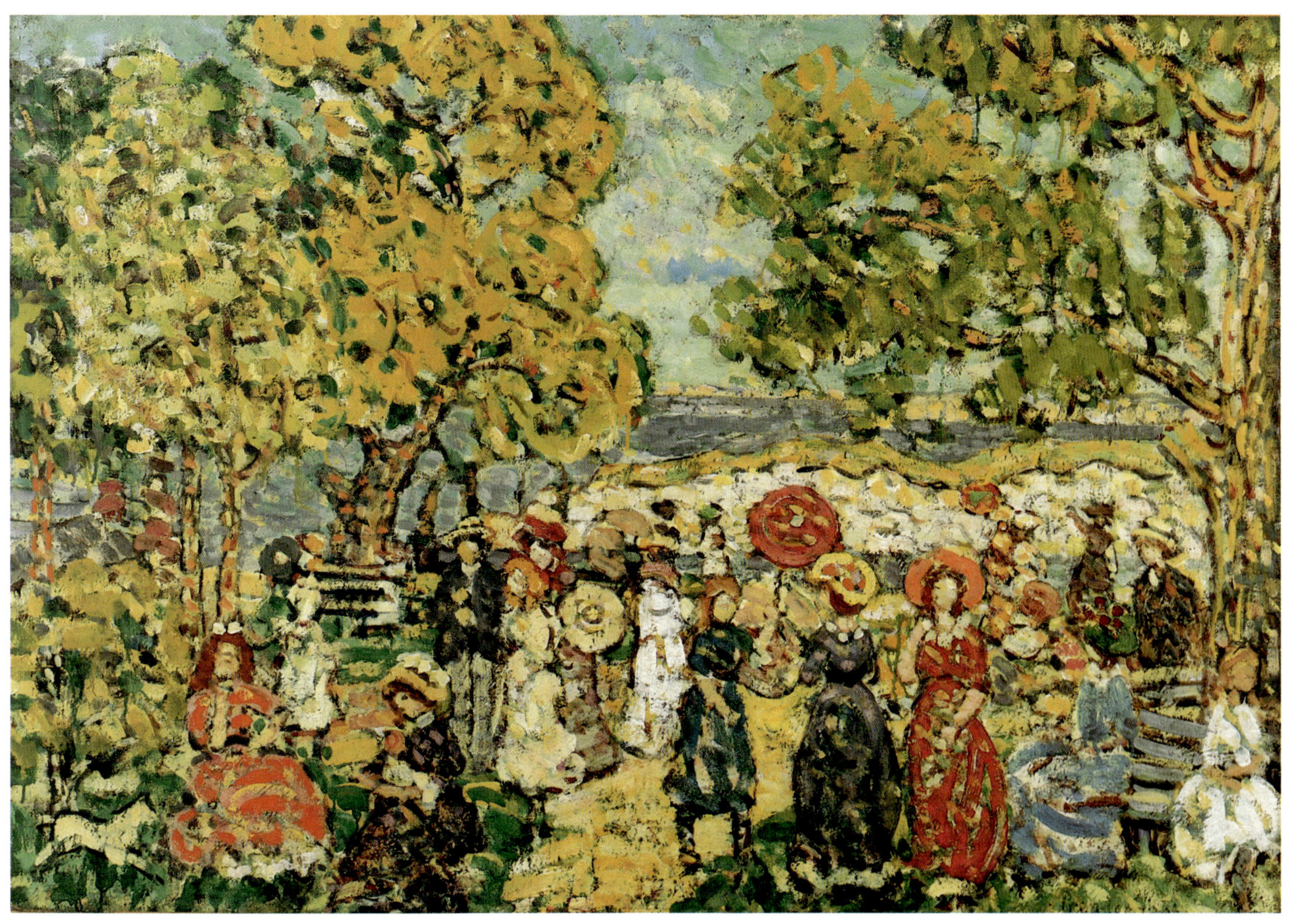

MAURICE B. PRENDERGAST (AMERICAN, BORN NEWFOUNDLAND, 1858 – 1924)
LANDSCAPE WITH FIGURES, CA. 1910-12

oil on canvas, 29 3/4 x 42 3/4" (75.6 x 108.6 cm.)
Collection Munson-Williams-Proctor Arts Institute, Museum of Art,
Utica, New York
Edward W. Root Bequest, 57.212
CAT. NO. 90

Prendergast's paintings were critically singled out from those of the rest of The Eight when exhibited at the Macbeth Gallery
in 1908 as the most radical and closely related to contemporary European movements. Unlike the urban realism pursued by most
of his peers in The Eight, Prendergast's style drew from his appreciation for the work of Paul Cézanne, Henri Matisse, and Pierre
Bonnard, among others. His work featured a festive panoply of strollers to be found in city streets and parks and vacationers at
popular resorts such as Salem Willows, on the Massachusetts coast, where this landscape was most likely painted. *Landscape with
Figures*, with its elaborately carved frame by Maurice's brother Charles, was shown at the famous New York Armory Show in 1913
and was immediately purchased by Edward Wales Root, an insightful collector who later became an important consultant in the
development of the Munson-Williams-Proctor's collection.

PIERRE-AUGUSTE RENOIR (FRENCH, 1841 – 1919)
THE POND AT CHAVILLE (ÉTANG DE CHAVILLE), 1911

oil on canvas, 18 3/16 x 22" (46.2 x 55.9 cm.)
Collection Memorial Art Gallery of the University of Rochester, New York
Gift of Dr. and Mrs. James H. Lockhart, Jr., 91.87
CAT. NO. 80

Young women immersed in nature, as seen in this painting, remained a favorite theme for the French Impressionist artist Renoir throughout his career. His signature, feathery brushstroke and pastel colors lightened and softened even further in his later paintings; the looser handling evolved naturally from his earlier style but also suggested the impact that crippling arthritis had on his art.

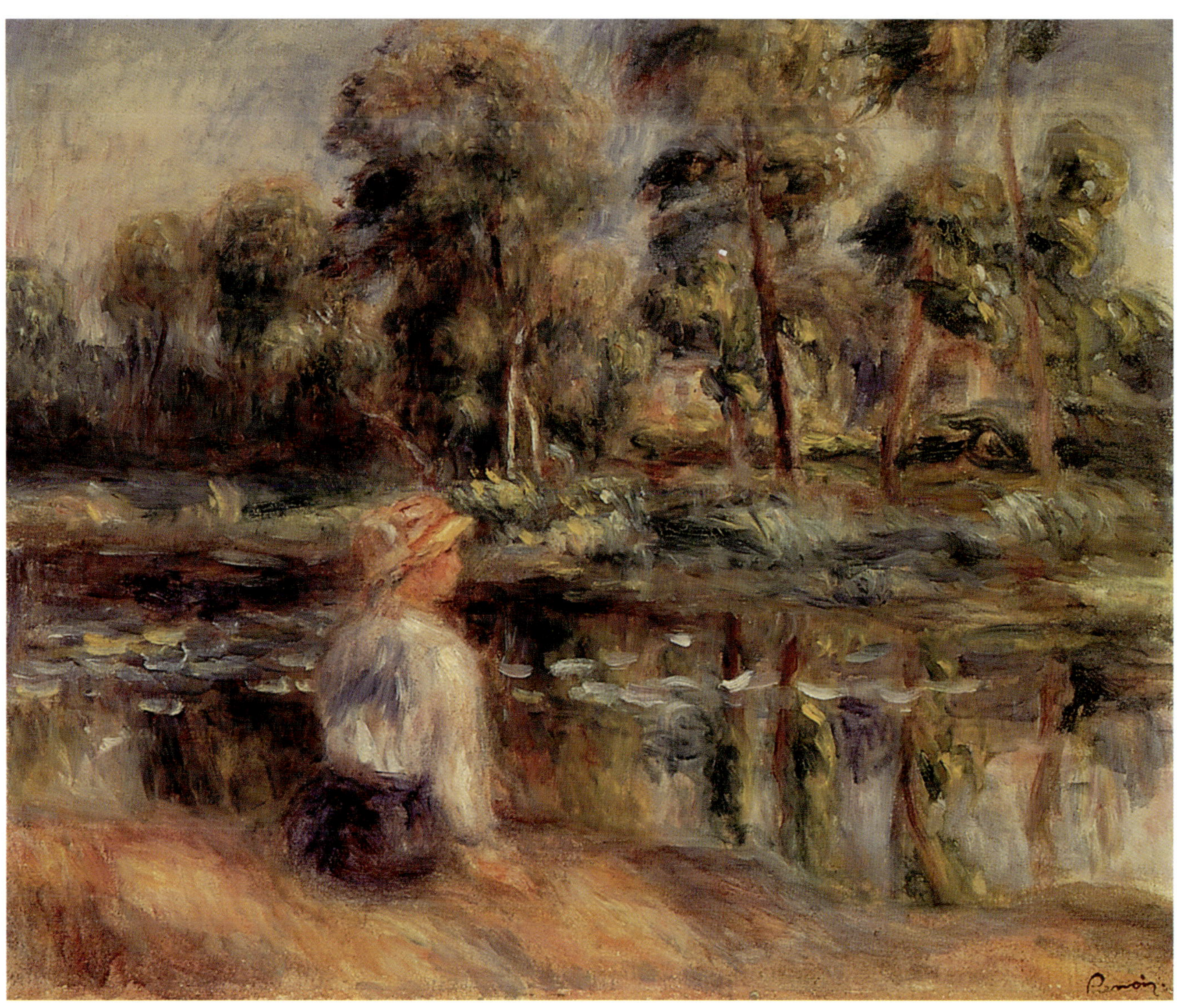

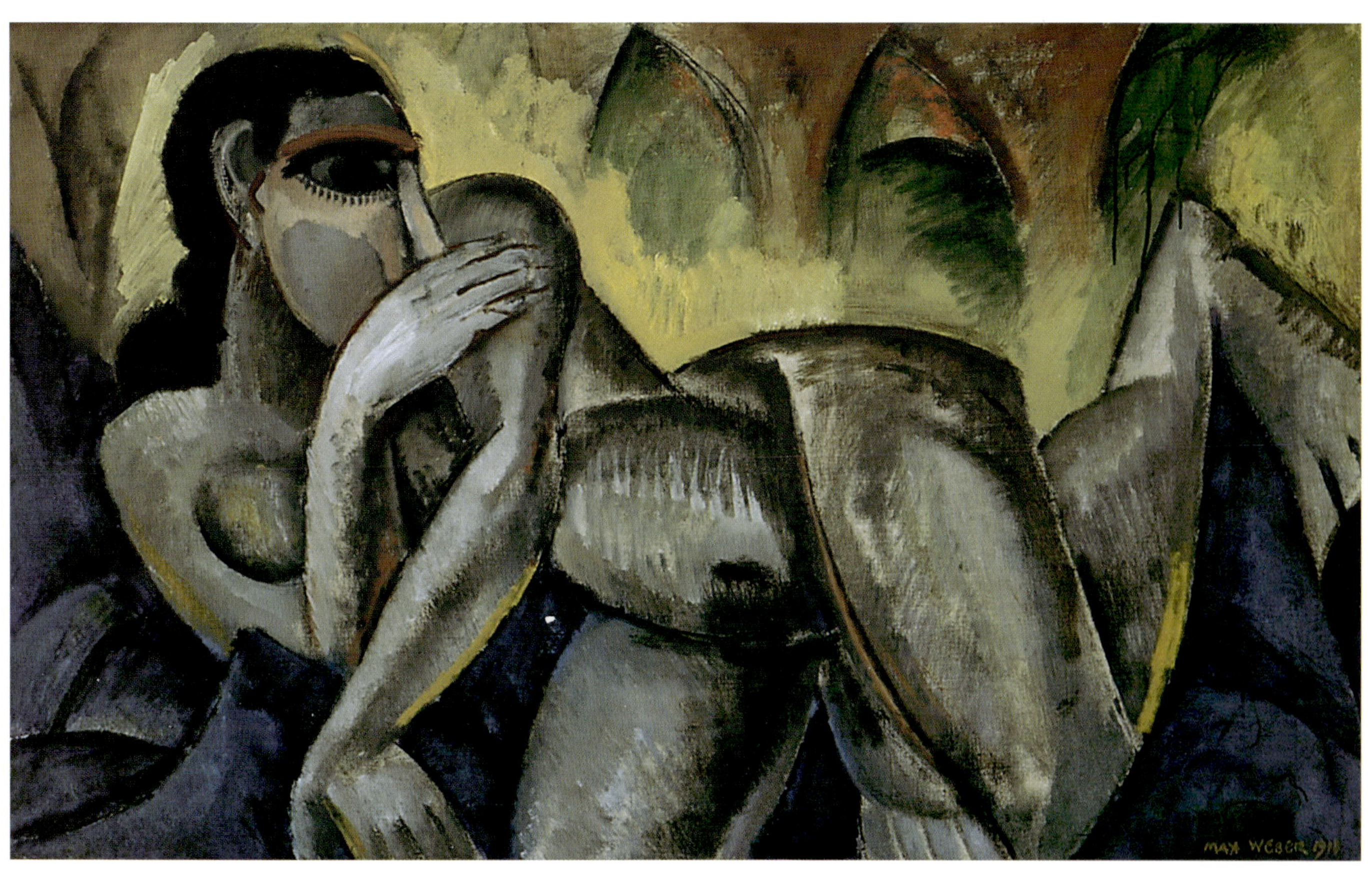

MAX WEBER (AMERICAN, BORN RUSSIA, 1881 – 1961)
FIGURE STUDY, 1911

oil on canvas, 24 x 40 1/2" (61 x 102.8 cm.)
Collection Albright-Knox Art Gallery, Buffalo, New York
Charles W. Goodyear Fund, 1959
CAT. NO. 27

FREDERICK CHILDE HASSAM (AMERICAN, 1859 – 1935)
ROCKS AND SEA, ISLES OF SHOALS, 1912

oil on canvas, 23 1/4 x 25" (59.1 x 63.5 cm.)
Collection Herbert F. Johnson Museum of Art
Cornell University, Ithaca, New York
Gift of Lois Birrell Morrill, Hotel School Class of 1949, 84.074
CAT. NO. 55

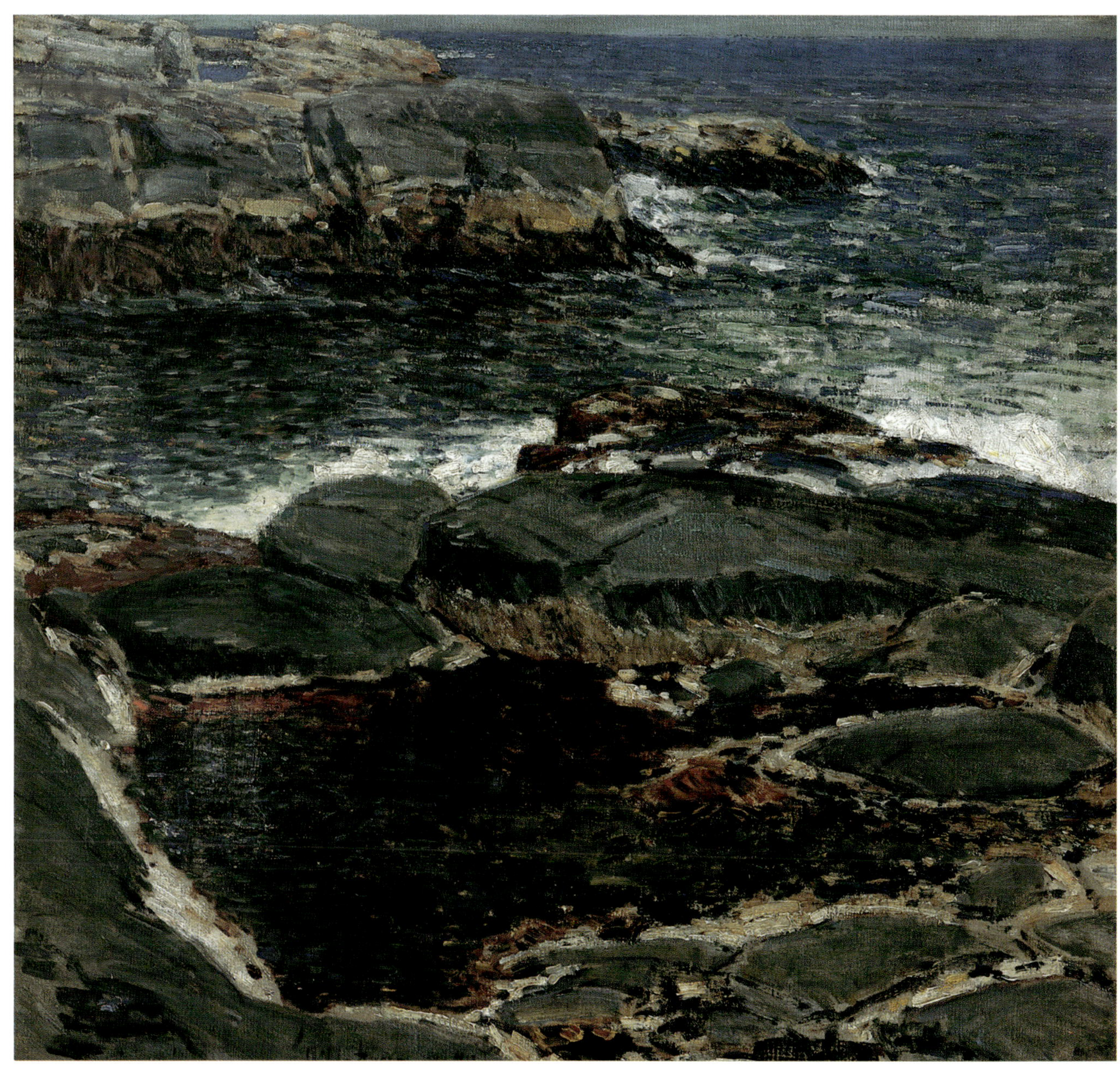

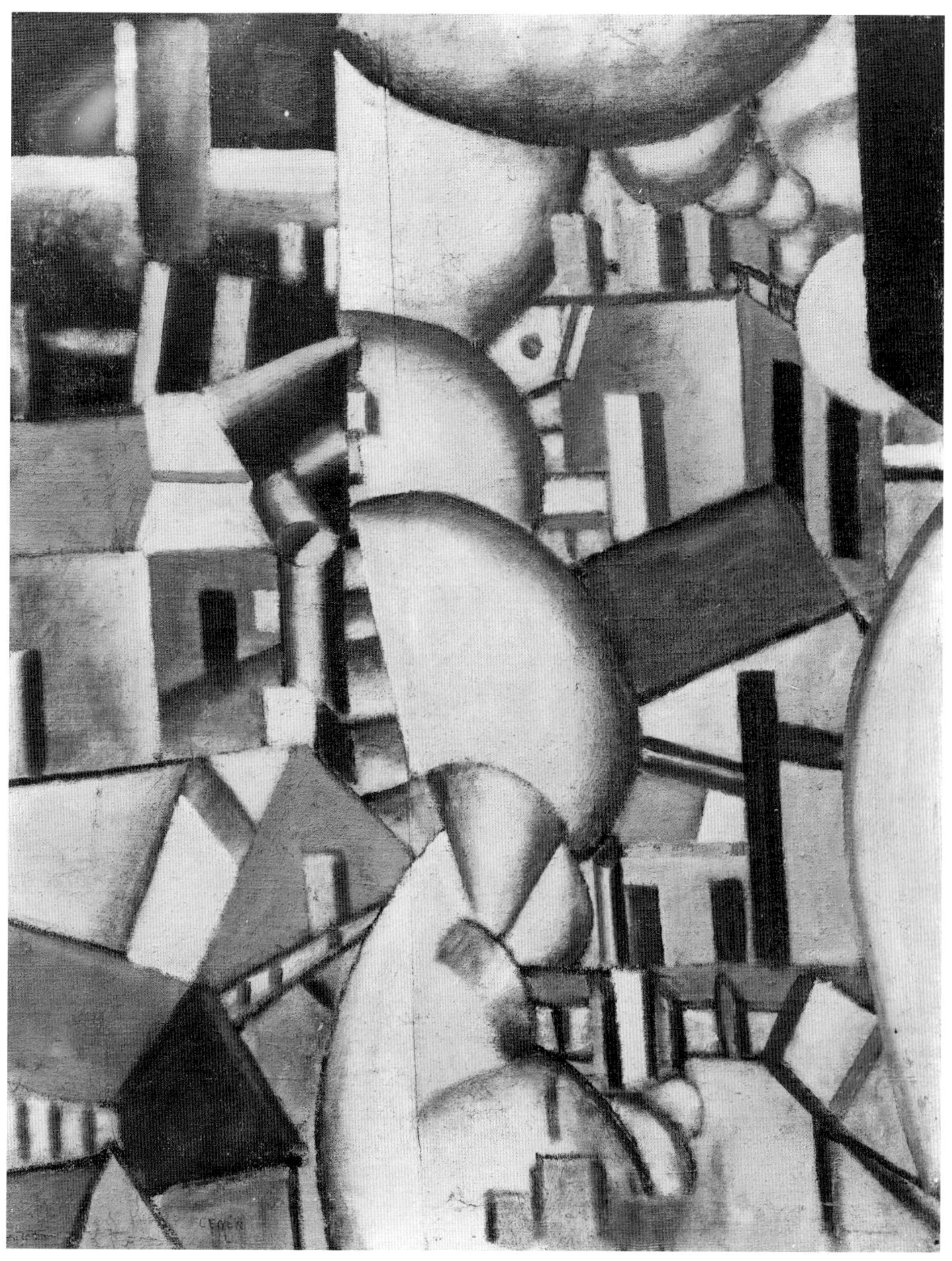

FERNAND LÉGER (FRENCH, 1881 – 1955)
SMOKE, 1912

oil on canvas, 36 1/4 x 28 3/4" (92.1 x 73 cm.)
Collection Albright-Knox Art Gallery, Buffalo, New York
Room of Contemporary Art Fund, 1940
CAT. NO. 15

FRANCIS PICABIA (FRENCH, 1879 – 1953)
FIGURE TRISTE, 1912

oil on canvas, 46 1/2 x 47" (118.1 x 119.4 cm.)
Collection Albright-Knox Art Gallery, Buffalo, New York
Gift of The Seymour H. Knox Foundation, Inc., 1968
CAT. NO. 19

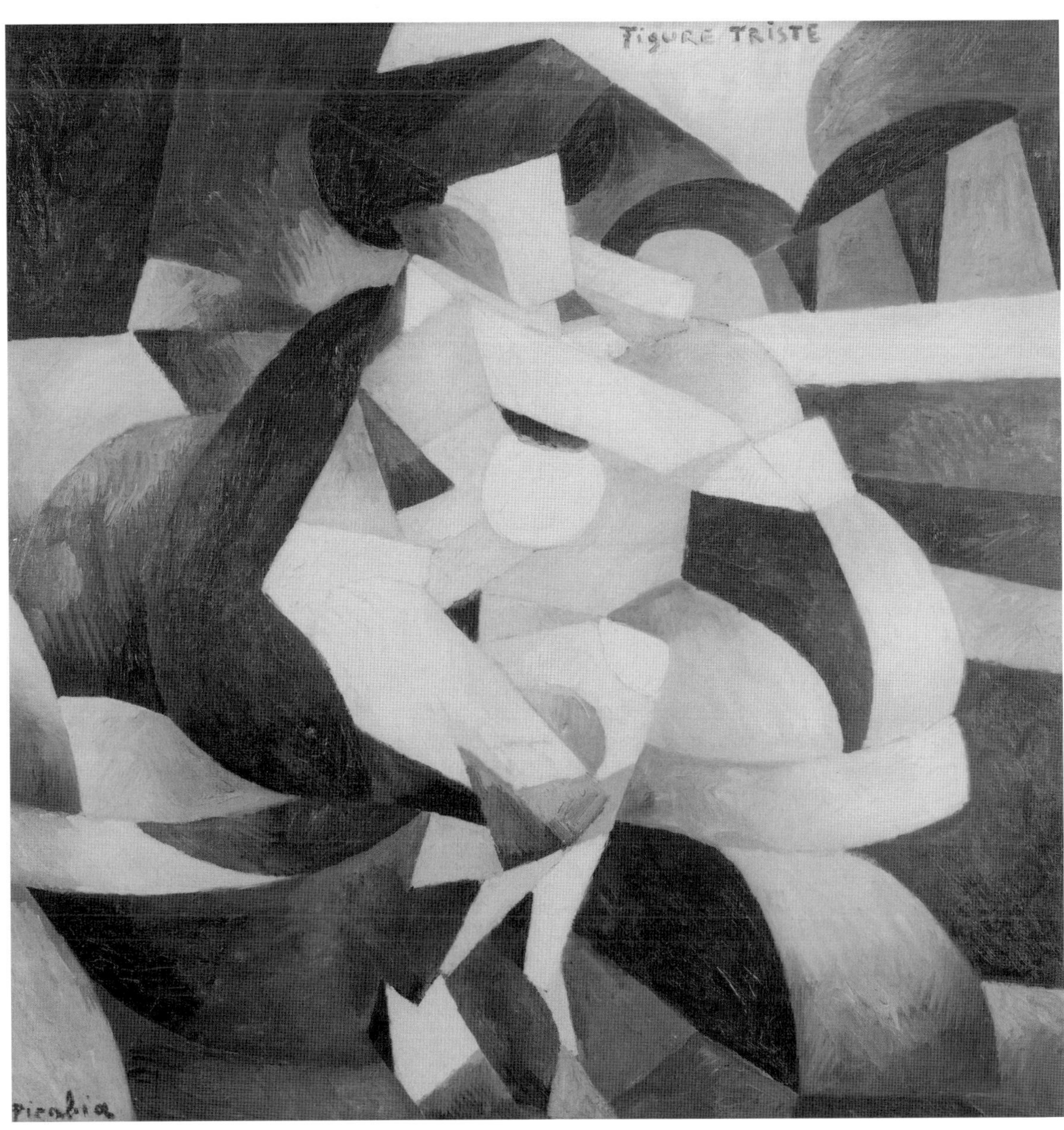

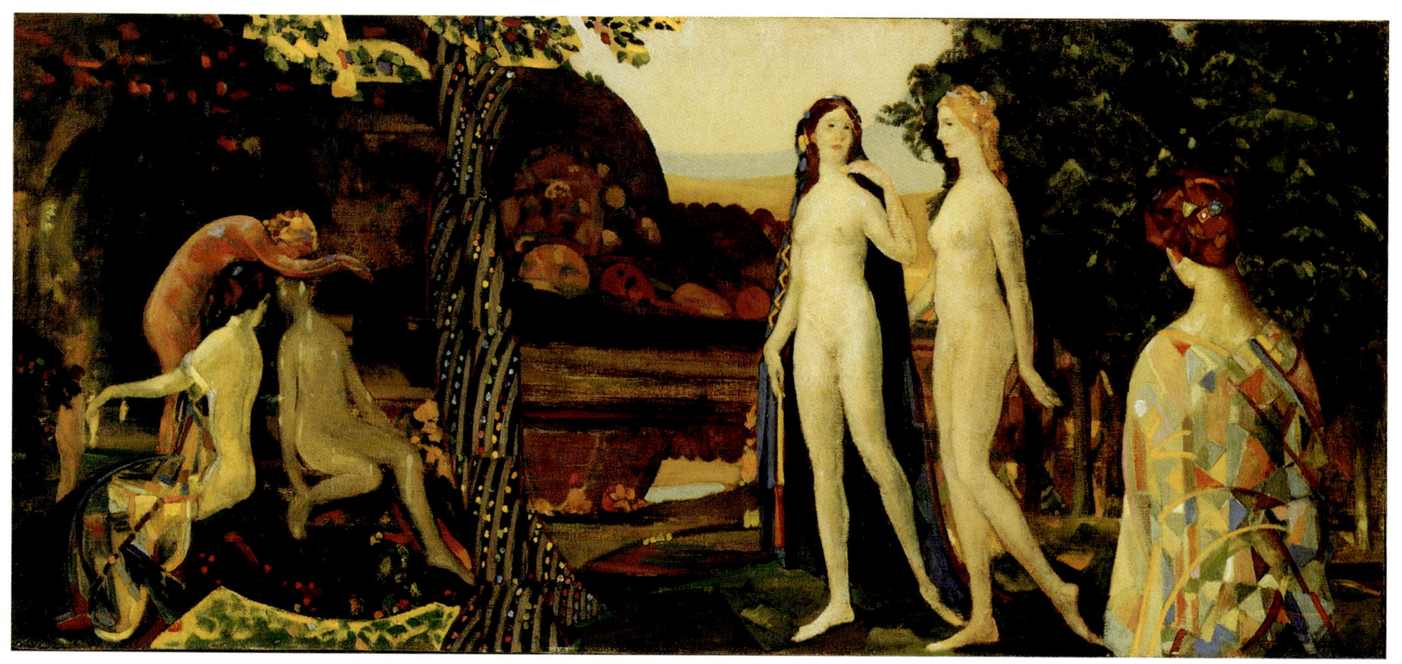

ARTHUR B. DAVIES (AMERICAN, 1862 – 1928)
JEWEL-BEARING TREE OF AMITY, CA. 1912

oil on canvas, 18 1/4 x 40 3/8" (46.4 x 102.6 cm.)
Collection Munson-Williams-Proctor Arts Institute, Museum of Art,
Utica, New York
Museum Purchase, 56.5
CAT. NO. 85

Like most of Davies's paintings, *Jewel-Bearing Tree of Amity* resists precise interpretation of its meaning. Nancy Miller has
pointed out in her essay for the Munson-Williams-Proctor's collection catalogue that the jewel-encrusted tree with its
entwining trunks may derive from an image of magical trees described in *The Golden Bough*, James G. Frazer's study of
myth from which Davies often gleaned inspiration. The theme of graceful women, sometimes unclothed and engaged in
vague activities within an idealized natural setting, is central to Davies's work, however, and the enigmas that his mysterious compositions pose reveal a Symbolist bent toward poetic evocation. While the general subject of *Jewel-Bearing Tree of
Amity* relates to the work Davies produced prior to 1913, the bright, abstract patterns decorating the women's clothes and
the tree suggest the influence of European modernism, to which Davies most certainly would have been exposed during his
involvement with organizing the groundbreaking 1913 Armory Show.

ROGER DE LA FRESNAYE (FRENCH, 1885 – 1925)
STILL LIFE WITH THREE HANDLES, CA. 1912

oil on canvas, 18 x 24" (45.7 x 61 cm.)
Collection Albright-Knox Art Gallery, Buffalo, New York
Gift of A. Conger Goodyear, 1943
CAT. NO. 11

Among the French Cubist painters, de la Fresnaye remained the closest in style to Paul Cézanne, whose work he greatly respected. Several of Cézanne's techniques – the tilted tabletop, flattened volumes, and merging of forms connected by shared strokes of color – appear in de la Fresnaye's *Still Life with Three Handles*. Unlike Picasso and Braque, he never broke down the forms of the objects he depicted.

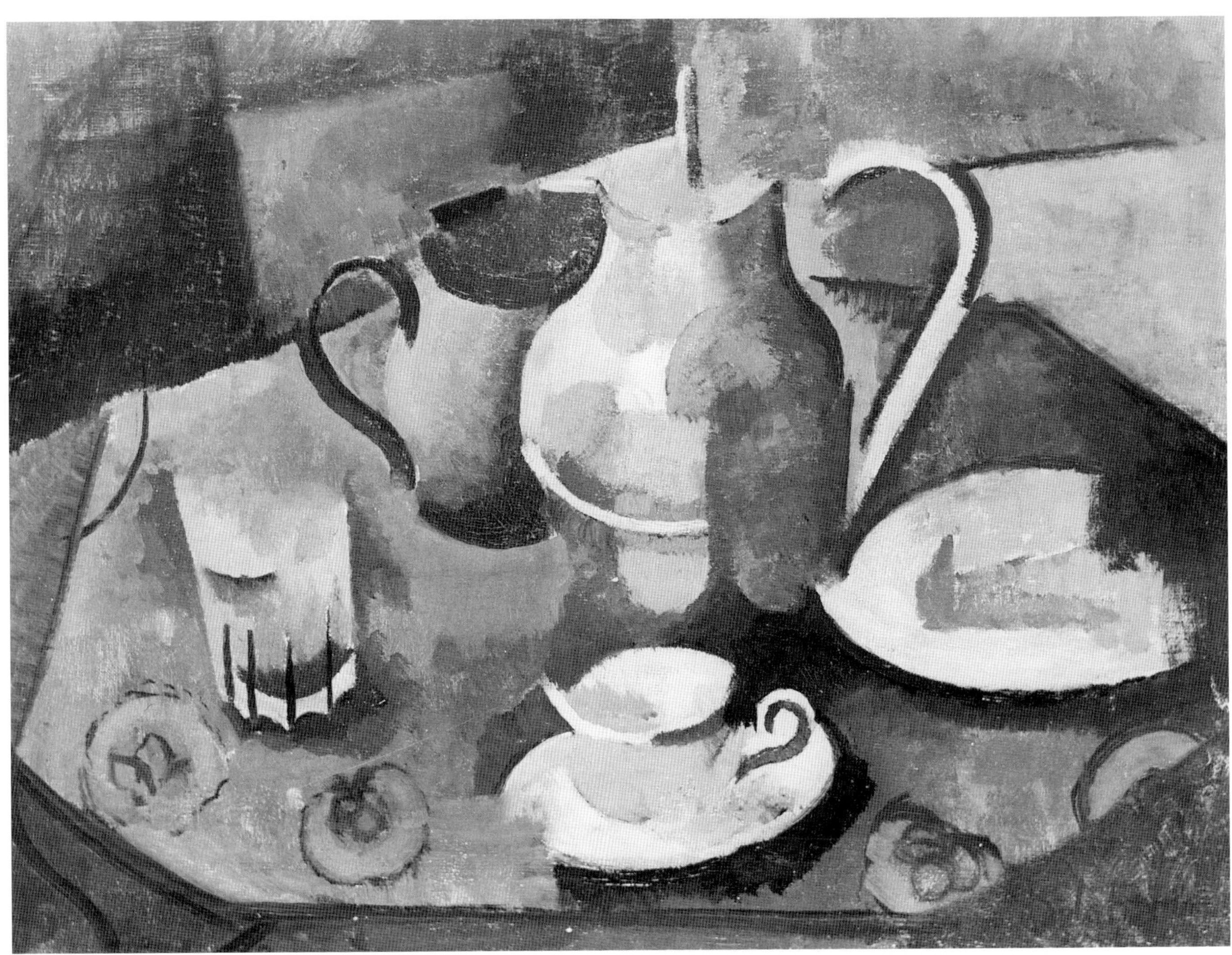

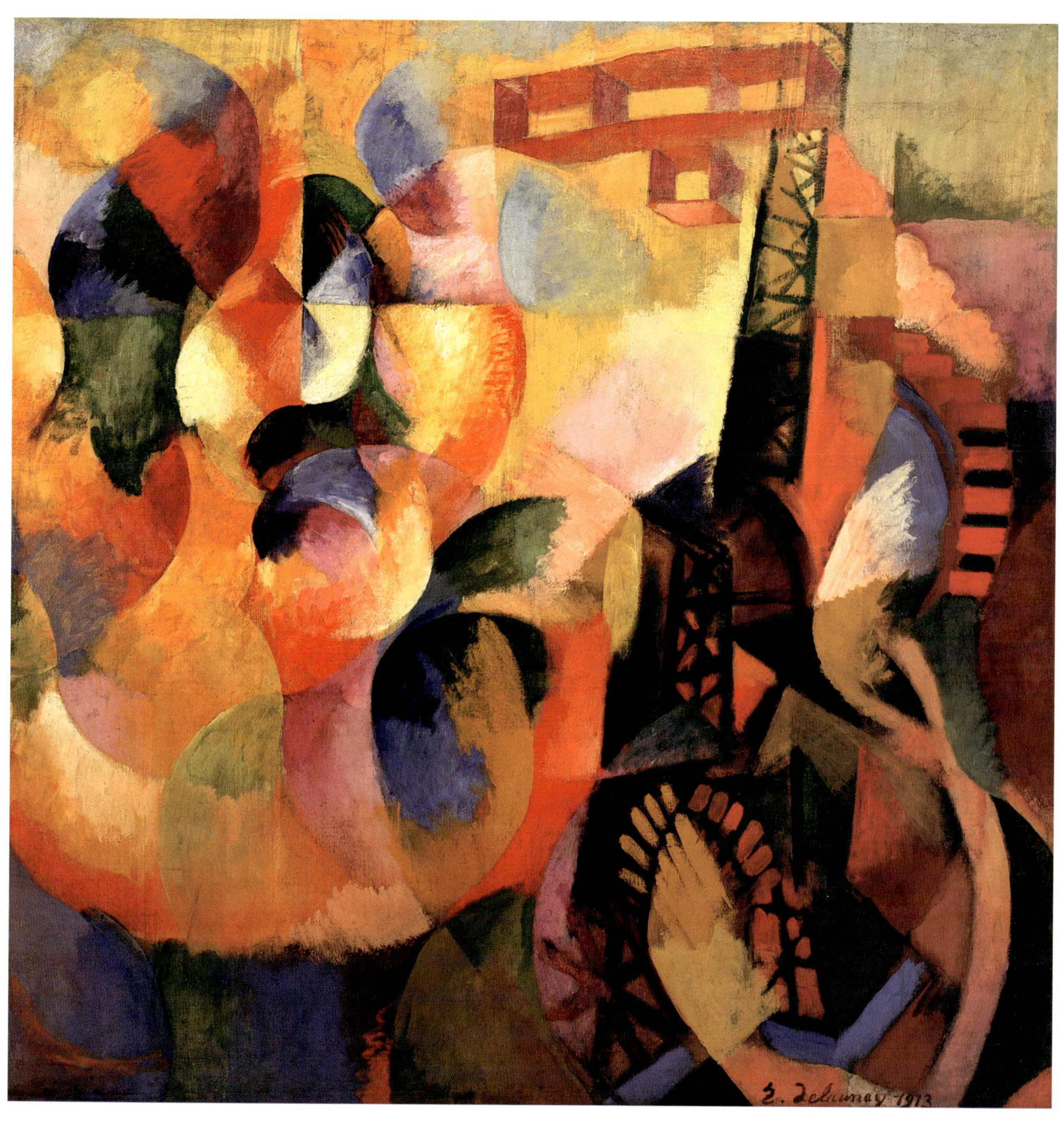

ROBERT DELAUNAY (FRENCH, 1885 – 1941)

SUN, TOWER, AIRPLANE, 1913

oil on canvas, 52 x 51 5/8" (132.1 x 131.1 cm.)
Collection Albright-Knox Art Gallery, Buffalo, New York
A. Conger Goodyear Fund, 1964
CAT. NO. 7

MORGAN RUSSELL (**AMERICAN, 1886 – 1953**)
COSMIC SYNCHROMY, 1913-14

oil on canvas, 16 1/4 x 13 1/8" (41.3 x 33.3 cm.)
Collection Munson-Williams-Proctor Arts Institute, Museum of Art,
Utica, New York
Museum Purchase, 57.26
CAT. NO. 91

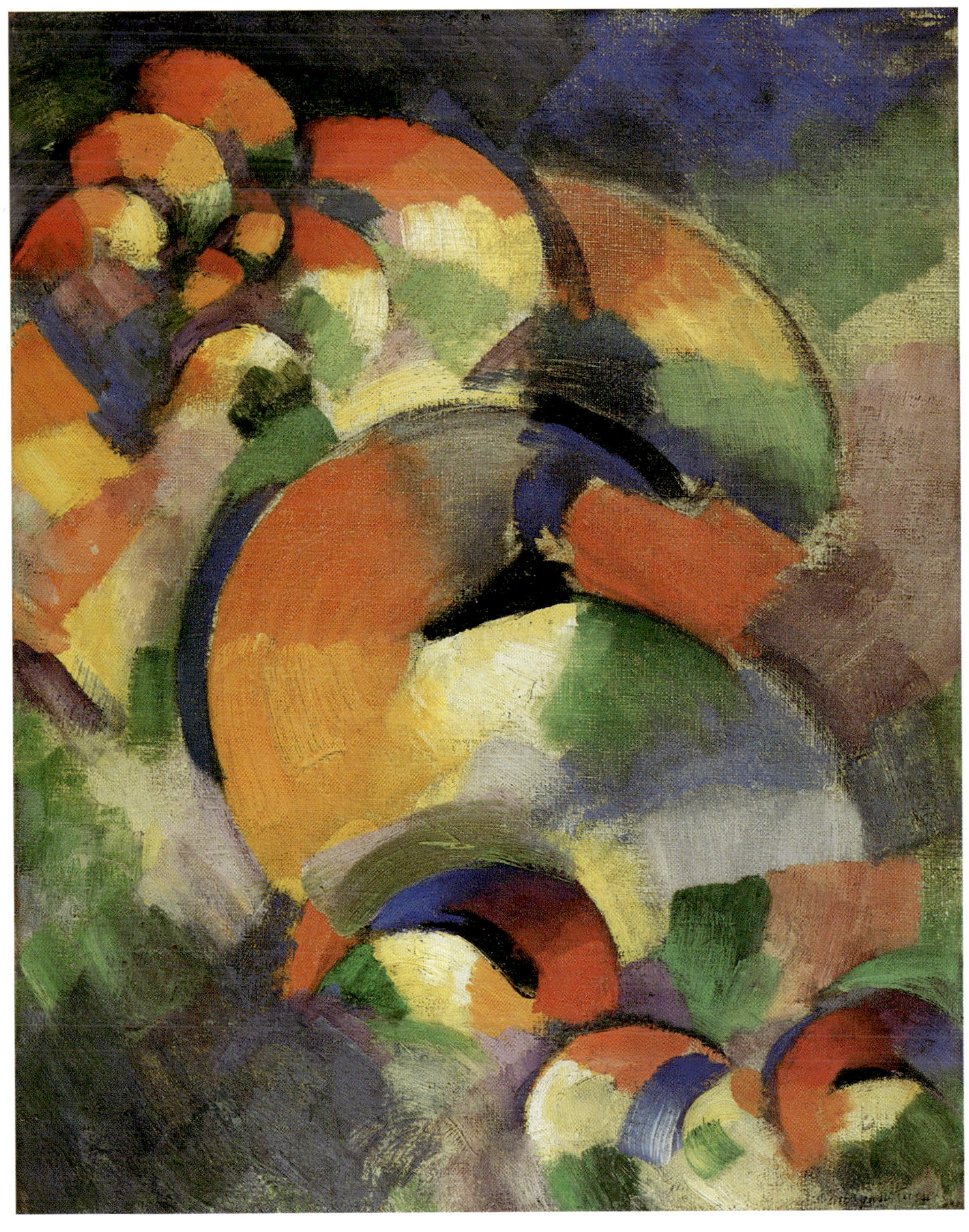

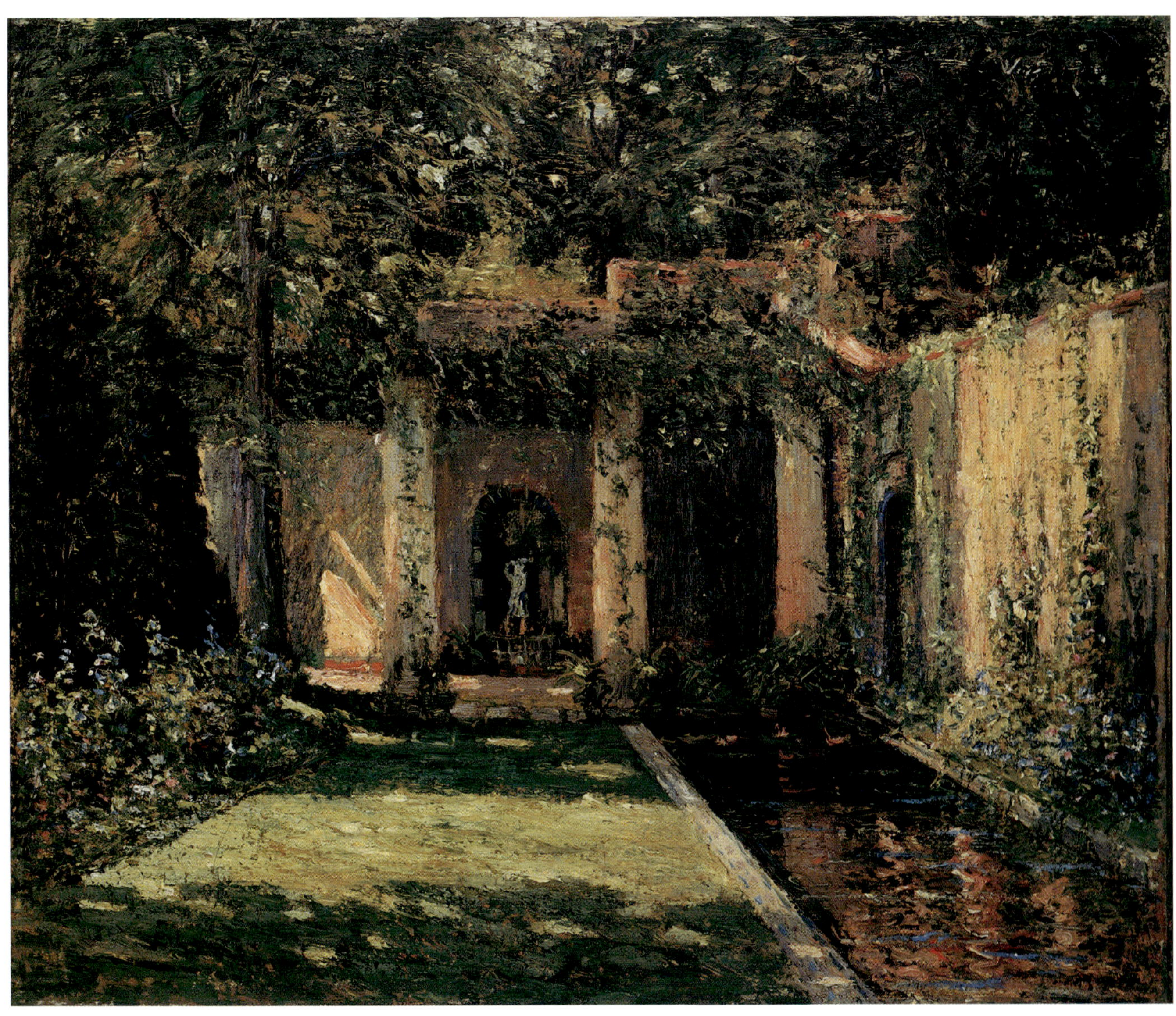

ERNEST LAWSON (AMERICAN, 1873 – 1939)
THE GARDEN, 1914

oil on canvas, 20 x 24" (50.8 x 61cm.)
Collection Memorial Art Gallery of the University of Rochester, New York
Gift of the Estate of Emily and James Sibley Watson, 51.36
CAT. NO. 78

Lawson's initiation to Impressionism occurred when he studied with American Impressionists John Twachtman and Julian Alden Weir, who conducted a school in Cos Cob, Connecticut, where they taught plein-air painting. His commitment to the style deepened further as a result of his sojourn in France from 1893 to 1896, during which he formed a friendship with the French Impressionist painter Alfred Sisley. Lawson was perhaps best known as the member of The Eight whose urban landscapes bridged the gap between American Impressionism and American Realism. He also occasionally painted more idyllic landscapes as in the case of this glittering image of wealthy businessman H.H. Rogers's garden in Tuxedo Park, New York, a canvas that supports the description of Lawson's later technique as painting with "crushed jewels."

MARSDEN HARTLEY (AMERICAN, 1877 – 1943)
PAINTING NO. 46, 1914-15

oil on canvas, 39 1/4 x 32" (99.7 x 81.3 cm.)
Collection Albright-Knox Art Gallery, Buffalo, New York
Philip Kirwen Fund, 1956
CAT. NO. 13

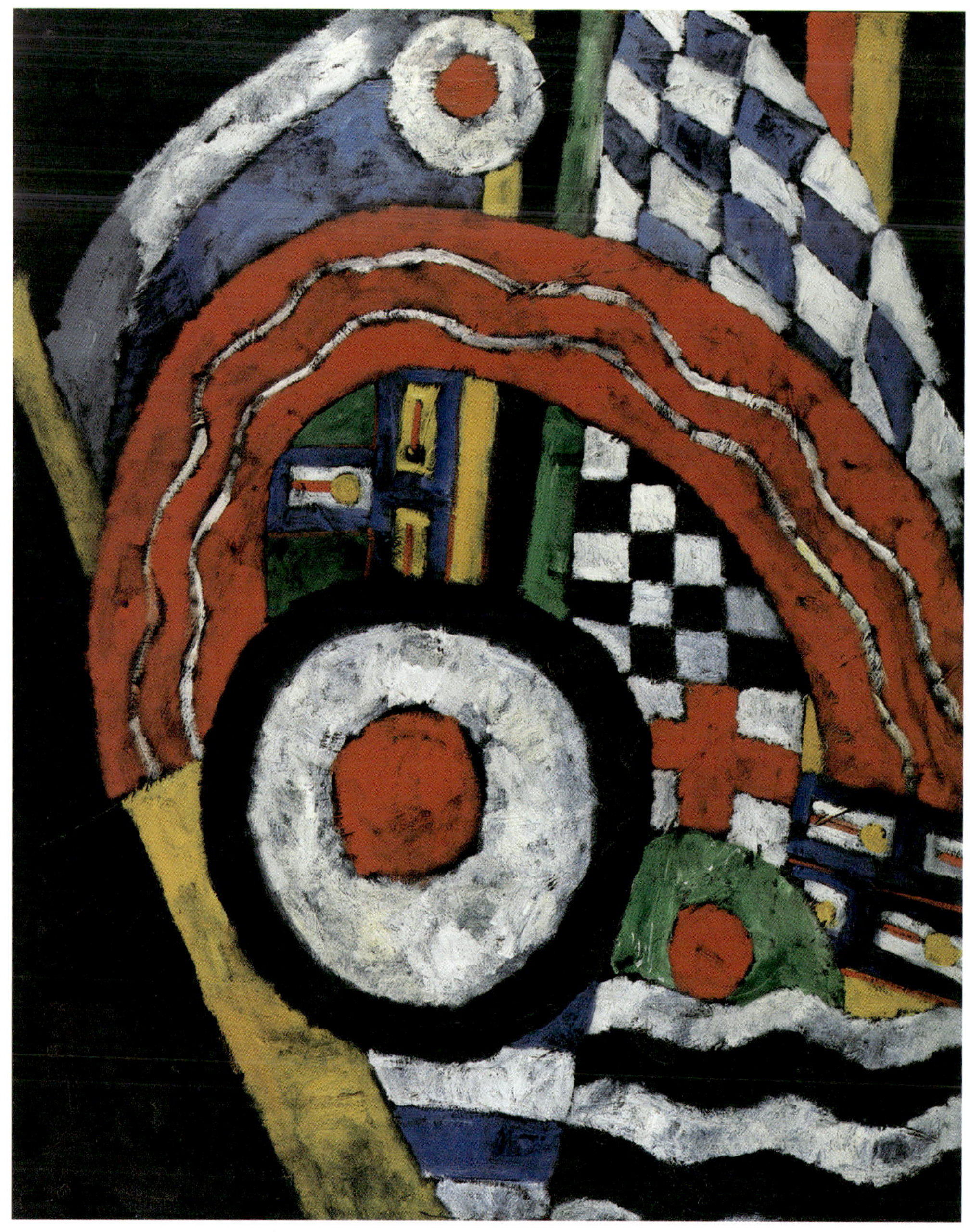

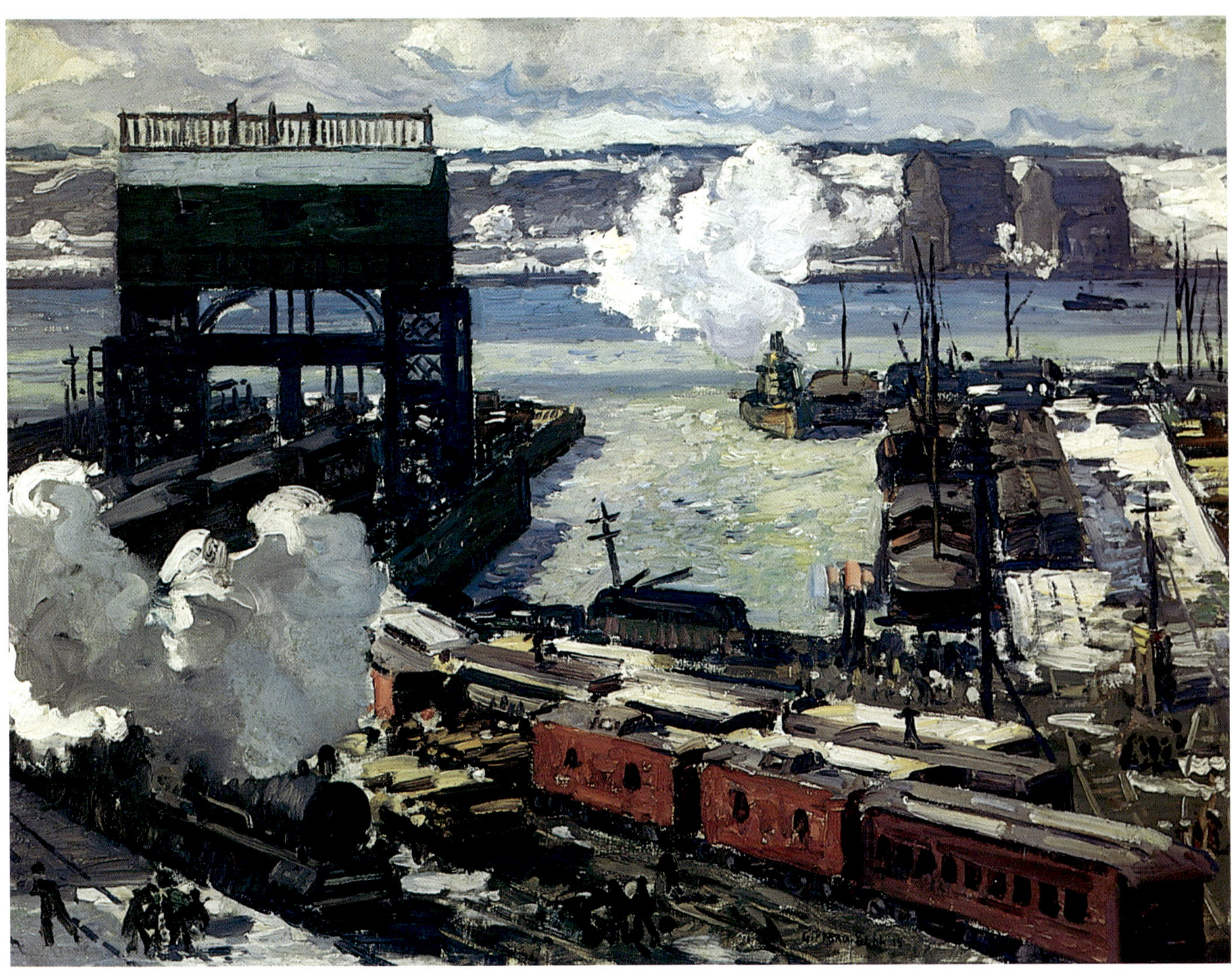

GIFFORD BEAL (AMERICAN, 1879 – 1956)
FREIGHT YARDS, 1915

oil on canvas, 35 1/4 x 47 1/2" (89.5 x 120.7 cm.)
Collection Everson Museum of Art, Syracuse, New York
Museum Purchase, Friends of American Art Fund, 1915
CAT. NO. 37

A member of the generation of realists following the original Ashcan School group, Beal painted a variety of subjects ranging from seafarers and circus scenes to urban landscapes that reflected an optimistic response to the power and picturesque qualities of the industrial environment. Beal, a devoted student of William Merritt Chase with whom he studied from 1891 to 1900, incorporated Chase's spontaneous, dashing brushwork into his own style, although he often reigned it in to achieve a tighter modeling of form. *Freight Yards* demonstrates the capacity of Beal's forceful brushwork to charge his painting with a muscular vitality fitting to the industrial scene.

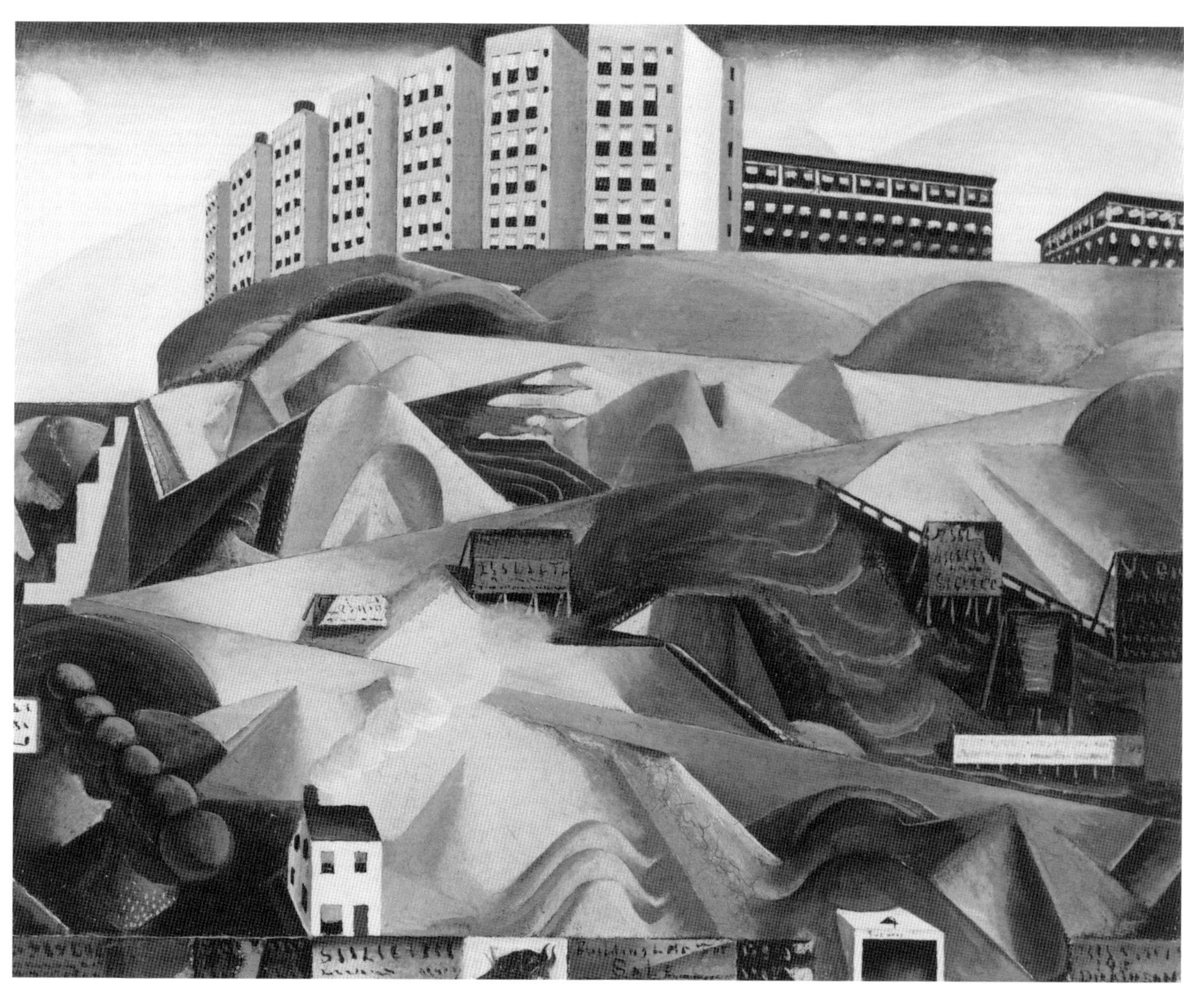

PRESTON DICKINSON (AMERICAN, 1891 – 1930)
FORT GEORGE HILL, 1915

oil on canvas, 14 x 17" (35.6 x 43.2 cm.)
Collection Munson-Williams-Proctor Arts Institute, Museum of Art,
Utica, New York
Edward W. Root Bequest, 57.132
CAT. NO. 87

MAN RAY (AMERICAN, 1890 – 1976)
SYMPHONY ORCHESTRA, 1916

oil on canvas, 52 x 36" (132.1 x 91.4 cm.)
Collection Albright-Knox Art Gallery, Buffalo, New York
George B. and Jenny R. Mathews Fund, 1970
CAT. NO. 21

Symphony Orchestra dates from the period of Man Ray's early artistic maturity when he was experimenting
with the collage-like abstraction of Synthetic Cubism and the mechanistic Cubism of Francis Picabia and
Marcel Duchamp. He met the latter in 1915, thus beginning what would become a life-long friendship. The
artistic wit and experimental approach to materials that would blossom in Man Ray's later Dadaist works
appear in the jazzy, syncopated rhythms of color and composition, the clever visual references to various
instruments (for example, the keyboard-like design on the lower left and the suggestions of the necks of
stringed instruments in the upper parts of the canvas), and the use of aluminum paint in some areas. The
humorous, painted suture that covers a repair in the upper right corner of the canvas (presumably added by
the artist himself), in particular, demonstrates the Dadaist sensibility that he would develop fully after his
permanent move to France in 1921.

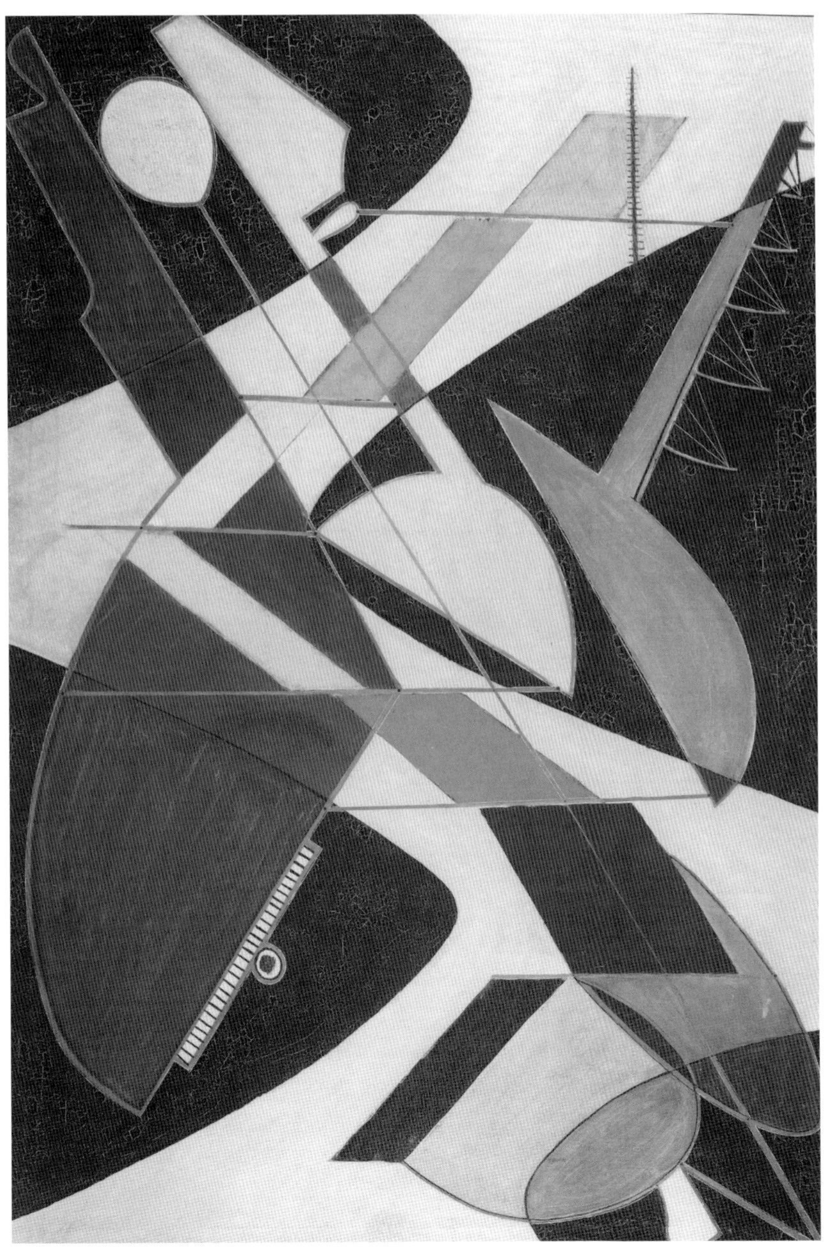

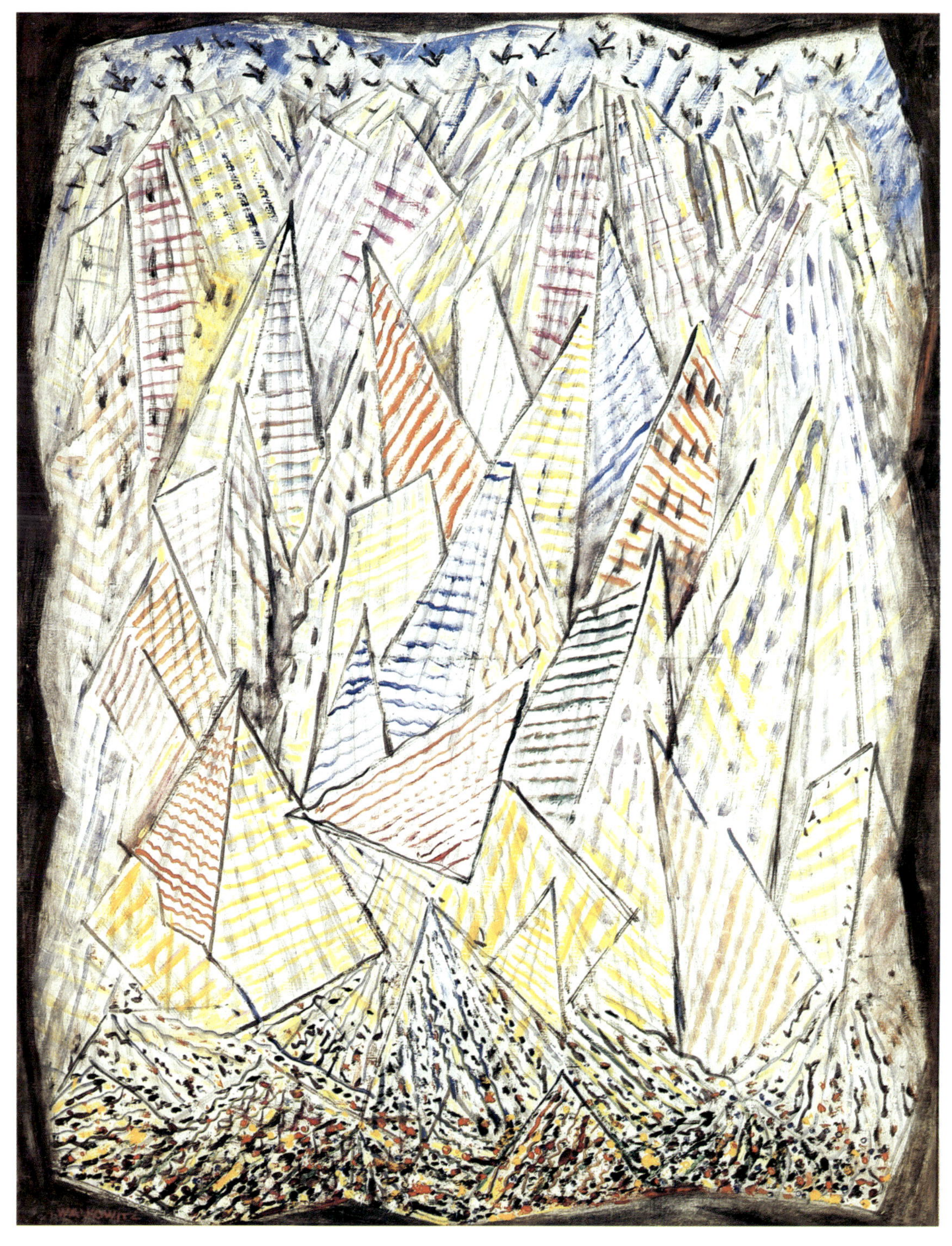

ABRAHAM WALKOWITZ (AMERICAN, BORN RUSSIA, 1878 – 1965)
IMPROVISATION OF NEW YORK CITY, CA. 1916

oil on canvas, 44 x 33" (111.7 x 83.8 cm.)
Collection Albright-Knox Art Gallery, Buffalo, New York
George B. and Jenny R. Mathews,
Elisabeth H. Gates, and Edmund Hayes Funds, 1979
CAT. NO. 26

GEORGIA O'KEEFFE (AMERICAN, 1887 – 1986)
BLACK SPOT NO. 3, 1919

oil on canvas, 24 x 16" (61 x 40.6 cm.)
Collection Albright-Knox Art Gallery, Buffalo, New York
George B. and Jenny R. Mathews and Charles Clifton Funds, 1973
Buffalo only
CAT. NO. 18

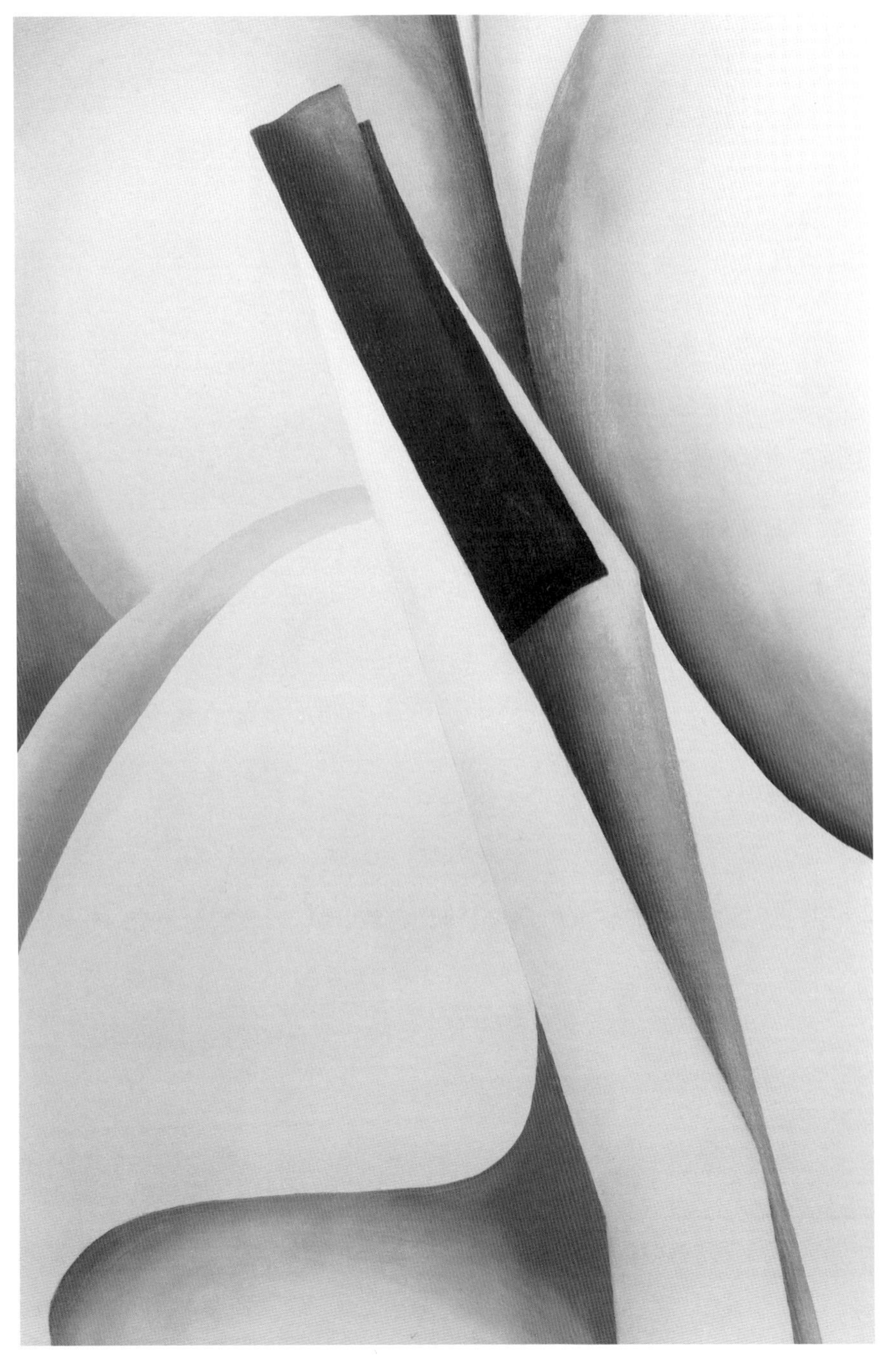

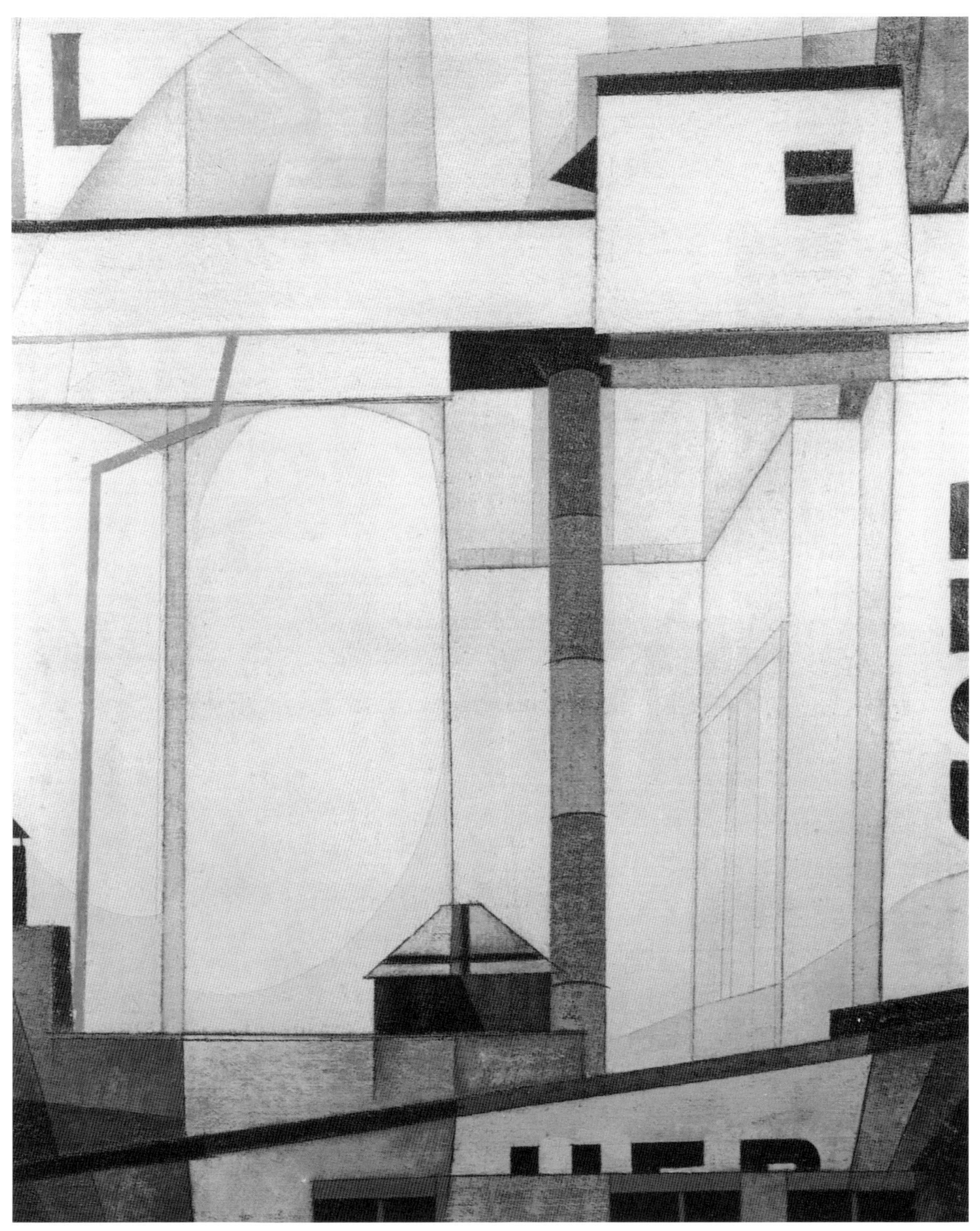

CHARLES DEMUTH (AMERICAN, 1883 – 1935)
NOSPMAS. M. EGIAP NOSPMAS. M., 1921

oil on canvas, 24 x 20 1/4" (61 x 51.4 cm.)
Collection Munson-Williams-Proctor Arts Institute, Museum of Art,
Utica, New York
Museum Purchase, 68.29
CAT. NO. 86

WILLIAM GLACKENS (AMERICAN, 1870 – 1938)
THE WATER SLIDE, N.D.

oil on canvas, 29 1/2 x 24 1/2" (74.9 x 62.2 cm.)
Collection Herbert F. Johnson Museum of Art
Cornell University, Ithaca, New York
On loan from Willard Straight Hall, Cornell University, LOAN 56.071
CAT. NO. 54

Glackens, like his peers in The Eight – John Sloan, Everett Shinn, and George Luks – began his career as a newspaper illustrator and studied with Thomas Anshutz at the Pennsylvania Academy in Philadelphia. He thus obtained a strong grounding in the urban realism associated with the Ashcan School. Nevertheless, his frequent travels in Europe and attraction to French Impressionism eventually led him toward a more lighthearted Impressionism reminiscent of the feathery, pastel paintings of Pierre-Auguste Renoir's late career. Between 1911 and 1916, Glackens spent his summers at Bellport, Long Island, where he painted numerous scenes, similar to *Water Slide*, of vacationers enjoying the pleasures of the seashore.

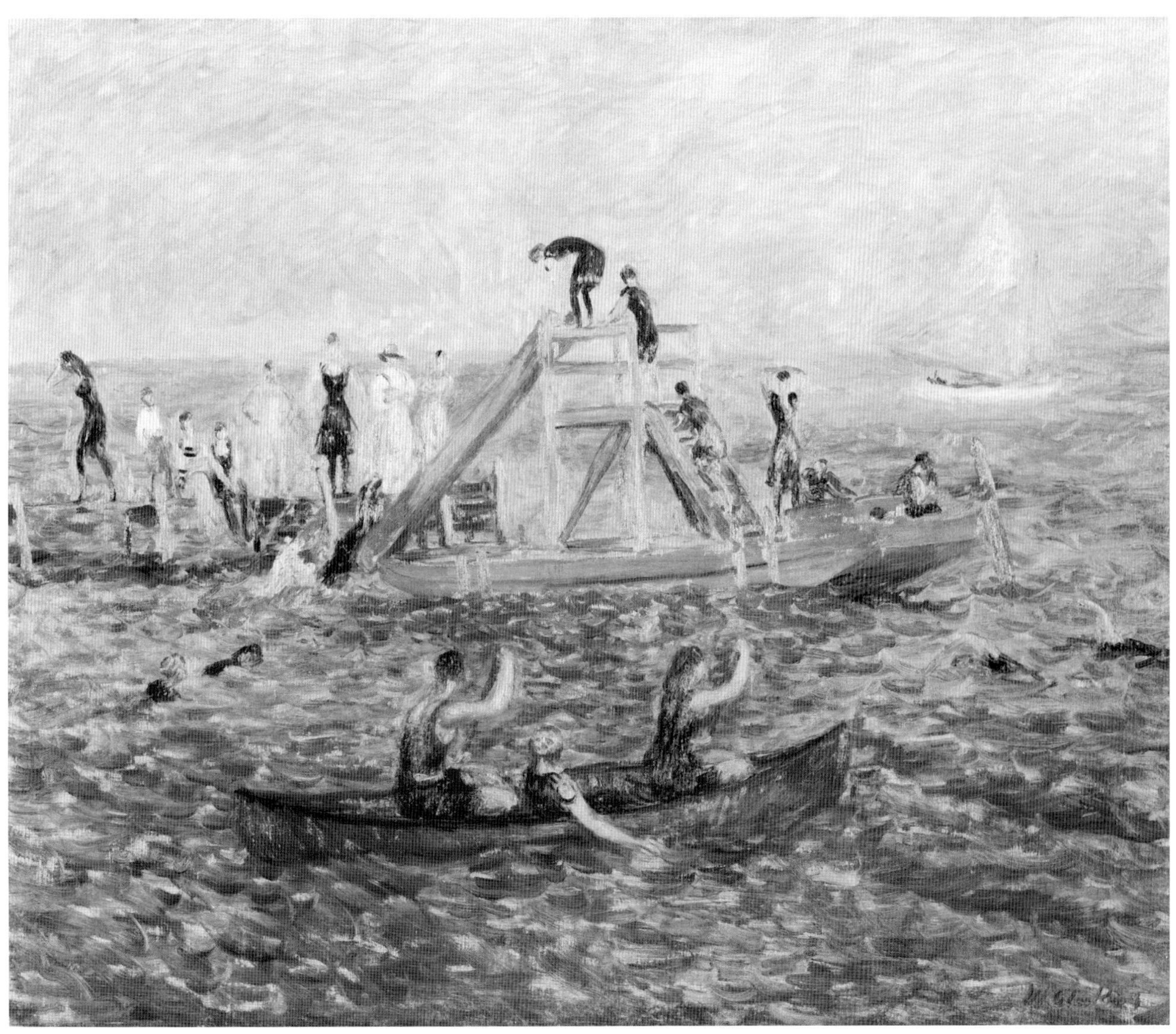

SCULPTURE

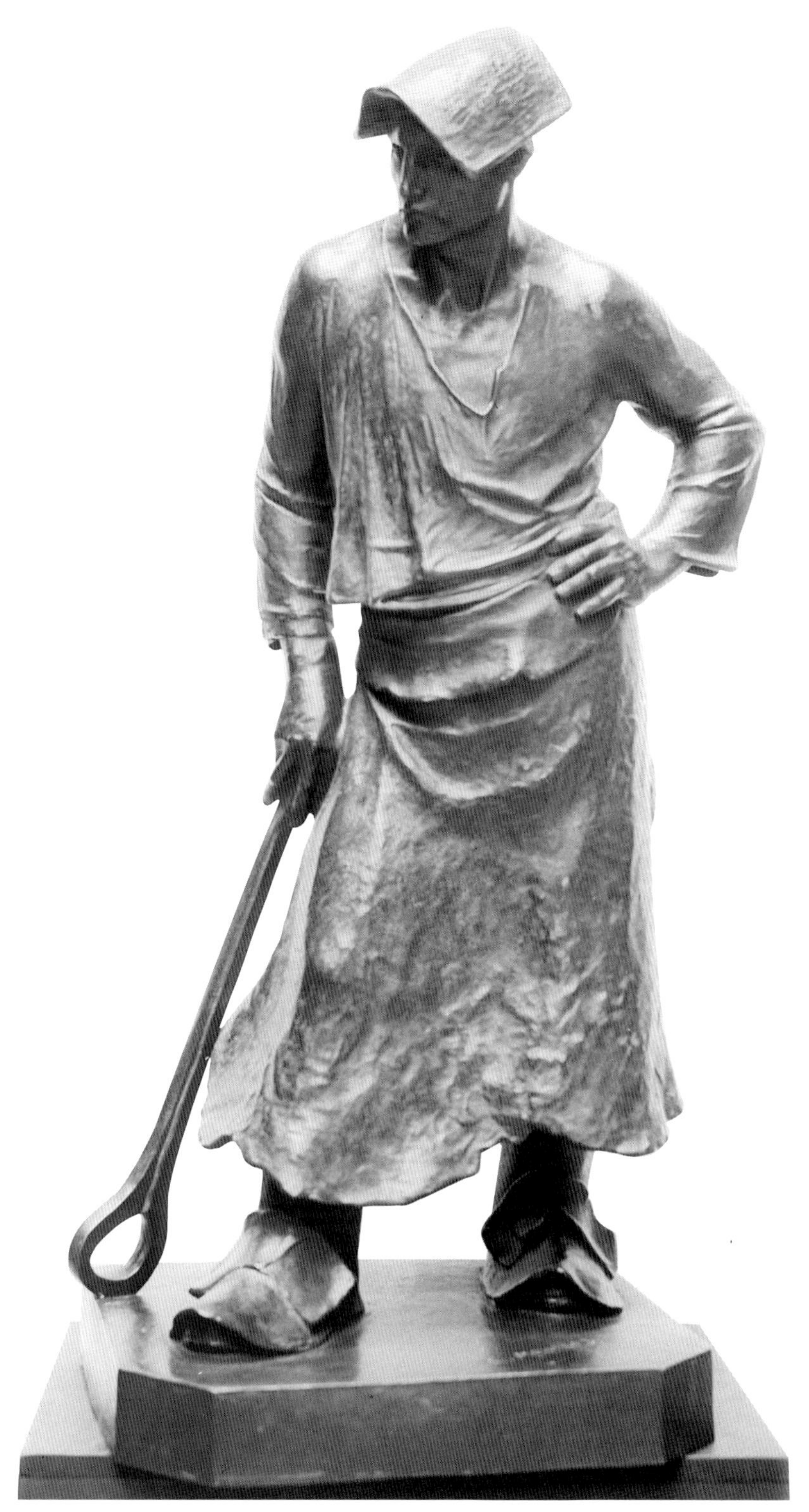

CONSTANTIN MEUNIER (BELGIAN, 1831 – 1905)
THE HAMMERMAN, 1885

bronze, 46 1/2 x 21 1/2 x 13" (118.1 x 54.6 x 33 cm.) [including base]
Collection Albright-Knox Art Gallery, Buffalo, New York
Charles W. Goodyear Fund, 1913
CAT. NO. 29

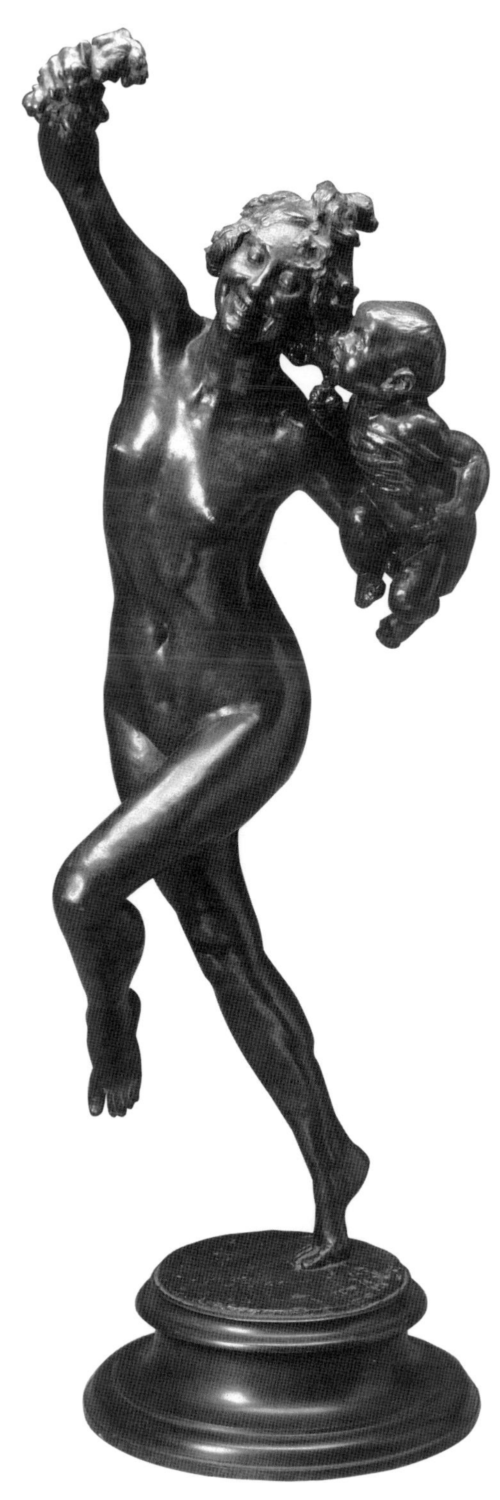

bronze, 33 3/4 x 11" (85.7 x 27.9 cm.)
Collection Memorial Art Gallery of the University of Rochester, New York
Gift of Lawrence R. Klepper and Michelle P. Klepper
and General Acquisition Funds, 86.17
CAT. NO. 81

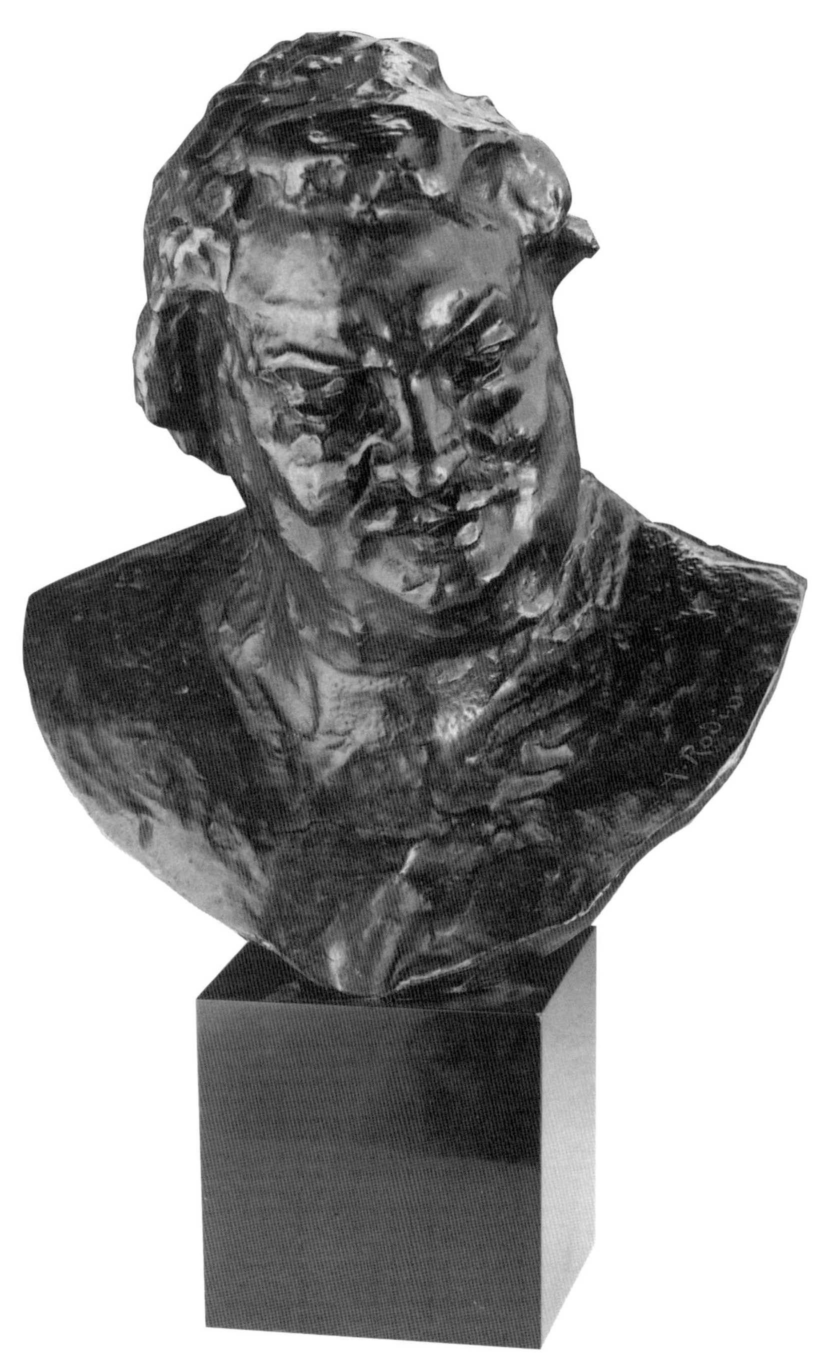

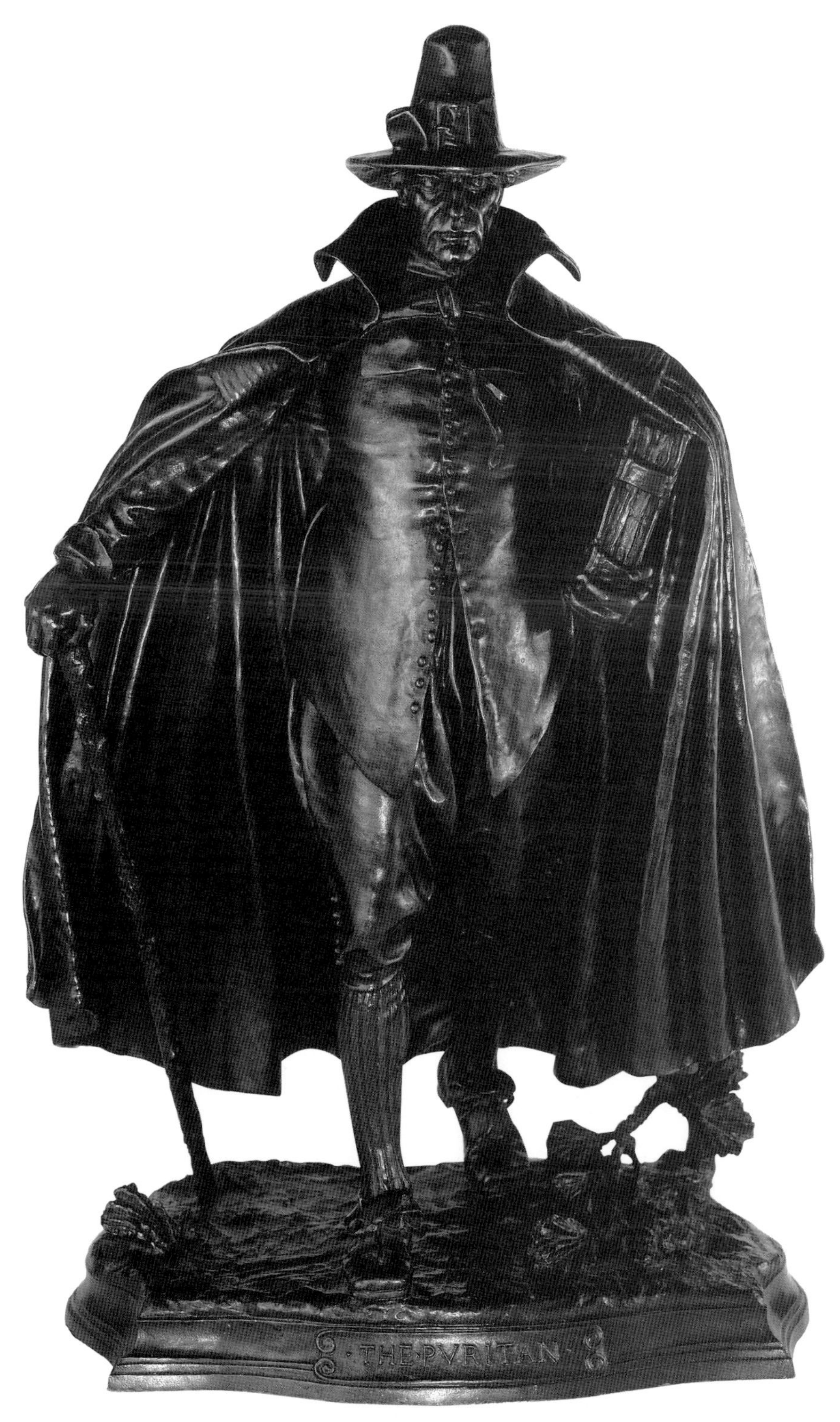

AUGUSTUS SAINT-GAUDENS (AMERICAN, 1848 – 1907)
THE PURITAN, 1899

bronze, 30 3/4 x 20 x 11 1/2" (78.1 x 50.8 x 29.2 cm.)
Collection Herbert F. Johnson Museum of Art
Cornell University, Ithaca, New York
Museum Acquisition Purchase Fund, 72.083
CAT. NO. 59

HENRI MATISSE (FRENCH, 1869 – 1954)
RECLINING NUDE I, 1907

bronze, 13 11/16 x 19 3/4 x 11" (34.8 x 50.2 x 27.9 cm.)
Collection Albright-Knox Art Gallery, Buffalo, New York
Room of Contemporary Art Fund, 1945
CAT. NO. 28

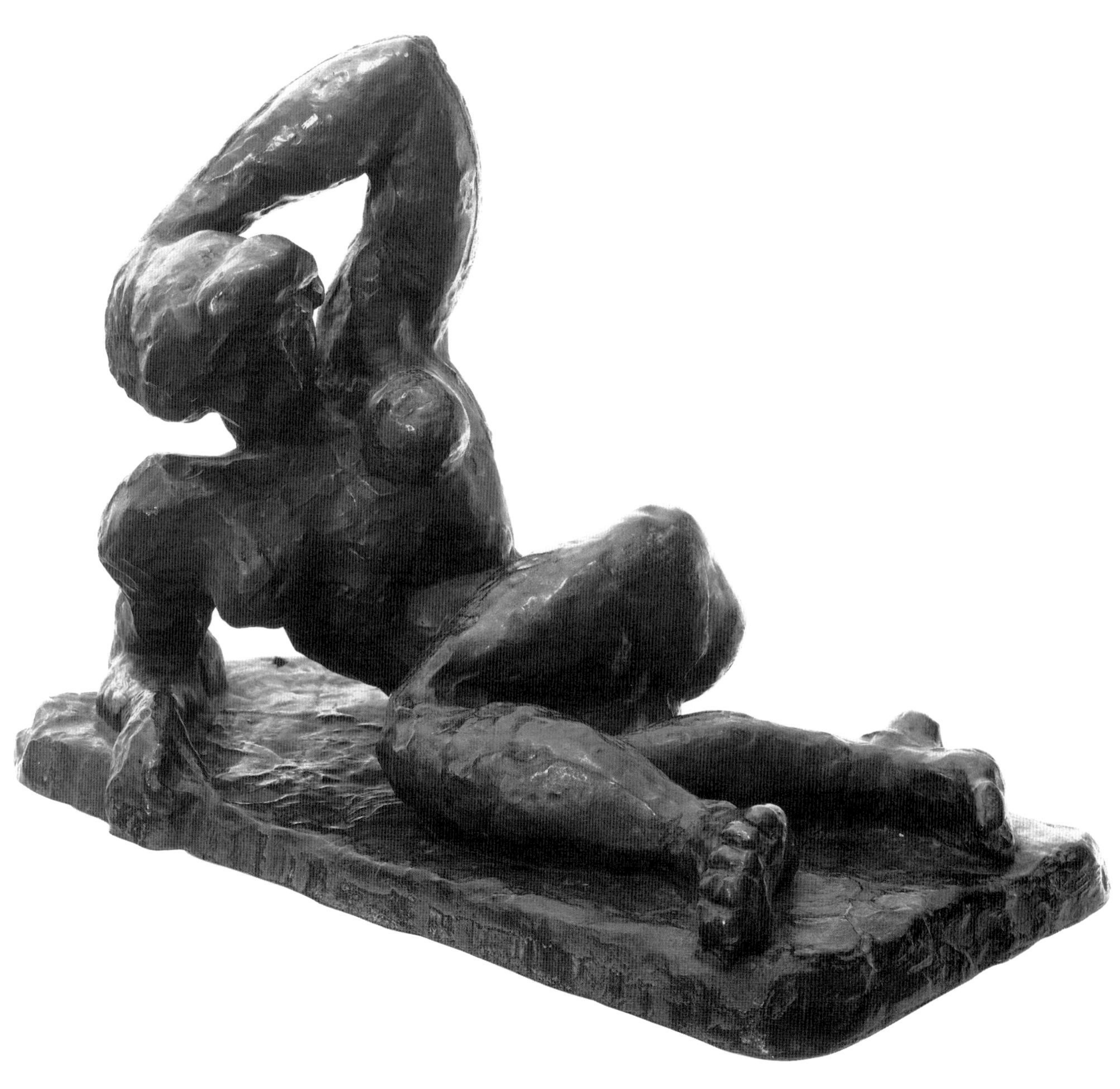

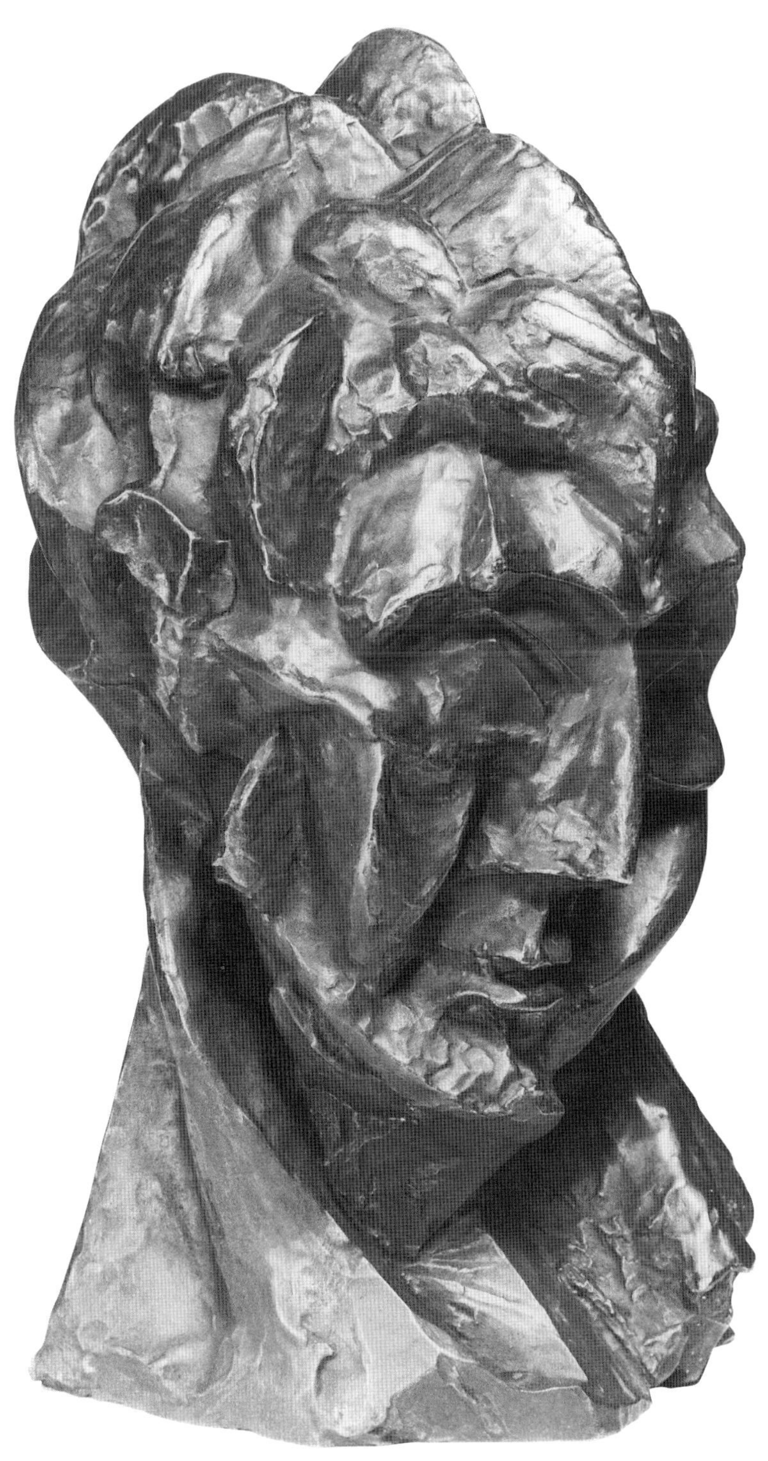

bronze, 16 1/4 x 10 3/8 x 10 3/4" (41.3 x 26.4 x 27.3 cm.)
Collection Albright-Knox Art Gallery, Buffalo, New York
Edmund Hayes Fund, 1948
CAT. NO. 30

ALICE MORGAN WRIGHT (AMERICAN, 1881 – 1975)
TROJAN WOMEN, 1927

bronze, 23 x 12 x 22" (58.4 x 30.5 x 55.9 cm.)
Collection Albany Institute of History and Art, New York
Gift of Mrs. Clark Fleming, 1978
CAT. NO. 4

Alice Morgan Wright, a native of Albany, New York, was among the first American modernist sculptors to draw on the example of Rodin's expressive figures, in some instances extending his figural exaggerations into greater abstraction. She incorporated elements of French Cubist and Italian Futurist sculpture into some of her own works as well, yet her overall production remained varied throughout her career, alternating between abstraction and a more conventional naturalism. While women had begun to make headway in entering and competing in the field of sculpture as early as the 1860s, when a group of American female sculptors dubbed "the White Marmorean Flock" established themselves in Italy, they still encountered serious obstacles to success in the twentieth century. Wright's choice of subject matter reflected not only her awareness of women's artistic struggles but also her involvement with issues of women's rights and humanitarian concerns in general. She remains among those who made a significant contribution to the advancement of modern sculpture in early twentieth-century America.

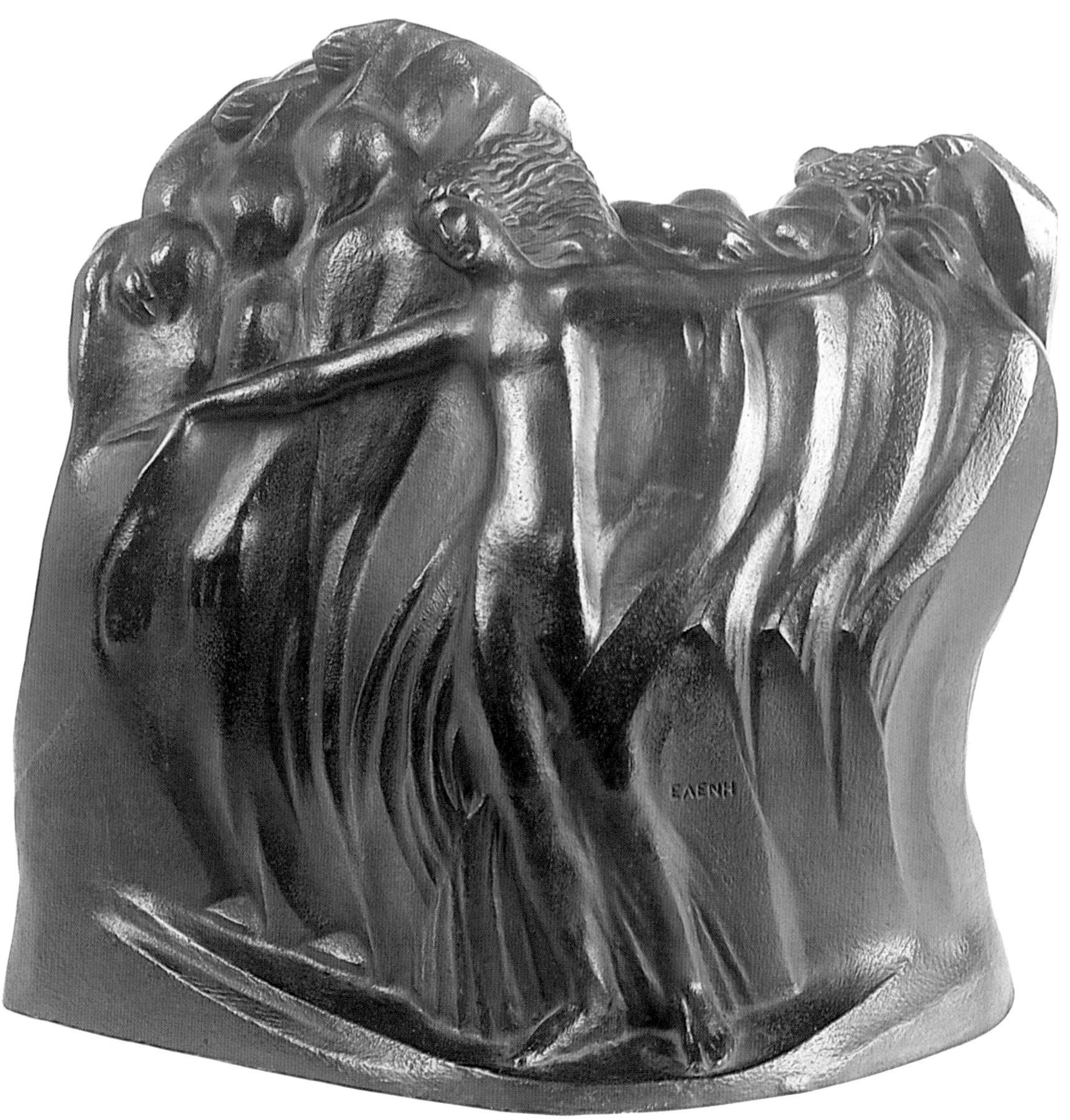

Decorative Arts

EVELYN RUMSEY CARY

(AMERICAN, 1855 – 1924)

**PAN-AMERICAN EXPOSITION POSTER,
1901**

color lithograph, 48 1/4 x 25 1/2" (122.6 x 64.8 cm.)
Collection Herbert F. Johnson Museum of Art
Cornell University, Ithaca, New York
Gift of Harry A. Starr, 78.057.021
CAT. NO. 60

Evelyn Rumsey Cary, at one time president of the Buffalo
Society of Artists and a prominent figure in Buffalo society
and culture around 1900, painted *The Spirit of Niagara*,
the original canvas from which this poster for the Pan-
American Exposition was made. Cary represented the
mighty Niagara Falls in the guise of the allegorical Maid
of the Mist, whose ethereal figure and flowing, watery
robes suggest both Symbolist and Art Nouveau influences.
The prominence of the beautiful Niagara – with the towers
of the city silhouetted behind her and a radiant rainbow
arching above all – aptly conveys the optimistic theme of
the Exposition's Rainbow City and the role of the great
Falls in providing power for the industrial progress and
plenty envisioned for the nation's future.

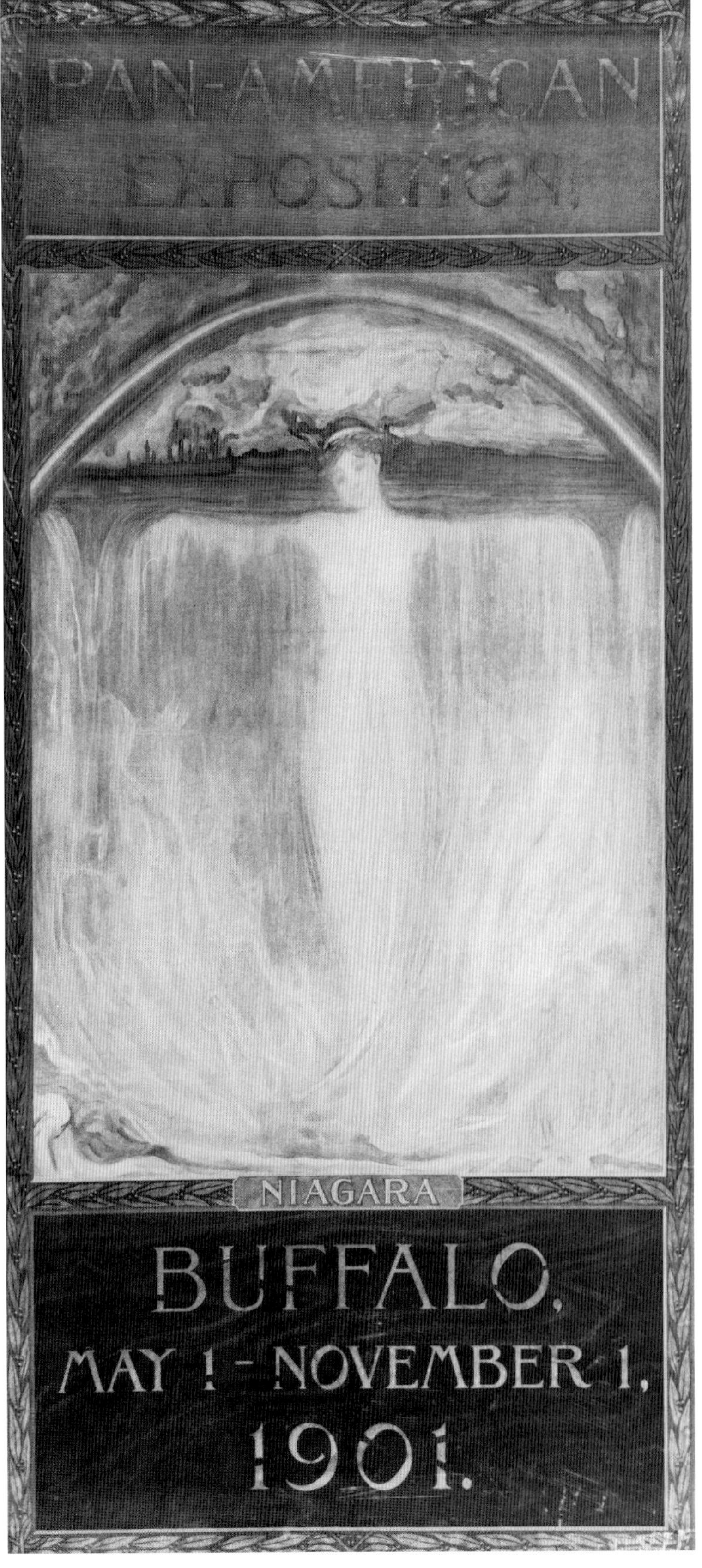

ROOKWOOD POTTERY (CINCINNATI, OHIO, 1880 — 1967)
KATARO SHIRAYAMADANI, DECORATOR

VASE WITH FERNS, 1890

earthenware, 10 1/2 high x 9 1/4" diam. (26.7 x 23.5 cm.)
Collection Everson Museum of Art, Syracuse, New York
Museum Purchase, 1977
CAT. NO. 46

In 1880, Maria Longworth Nichols founded Rookwood Pottery – destined to become one of the most important and productive of art potteries – in Cincinnati, Ohio, a city then already known for its artistic ceramics. From the outset, Japanese-inspired decoration emerged as the predominant aesthetic at Rookwood, and in 1887 Rookwood hired the Japanese artist Kataro Shirayamadani who (with the exception of an extended stay in Japan from 1911 to 1921) remained at the company until his death in 1948. The decoration on this classic, baluster-shaped vase, applied in the typical Rookwood manner of underglaze slip painting, epitomizes the naturalistic asymmetrical design, botanical motif, deep color, and lacquer-like surface of Rookwood's products of the period.

ROOKWOOD POTTERY (CINCINNATI, OHIO, 1880 — 1967)
SARA ELIZABETH (SALLIE) COYNE, DECORATOR

SCENIC VASE, 1916

earthenware, 10 3/4 high x 4" diam. (27.3 x 10.2 cm.)
Collection Everson Museum of Art, Syracuse, New York
Museum Purchase in Memory of Edward Beadle with Funds from Friends, 1984
CAT. NO. 45

During the first decade of the twentieth century, the most significant change occurring at Rookwood was the shift from high-gloss glazes to matte finishes, a shift intended to answer the cultural preference for honesty, harmony, and simplicity signified by the matte glaze. Sallie Coyne, like Shirayamadani a mainstay of the Rookwood firm (employed there from 1892 to 1931), decorated this vase with Vellum, the last and most select of the matte glazes developed in 1904, which combines the transparency of a high-gloss glaze with the soft, low-reflective surface of a matte glaze. Depicting an evergreen woodland bathed in winter twilight, the misty scene on this piece recalls the muted tones and soft focus of the Tonalist painting and Pictorial photography popular around 1900.

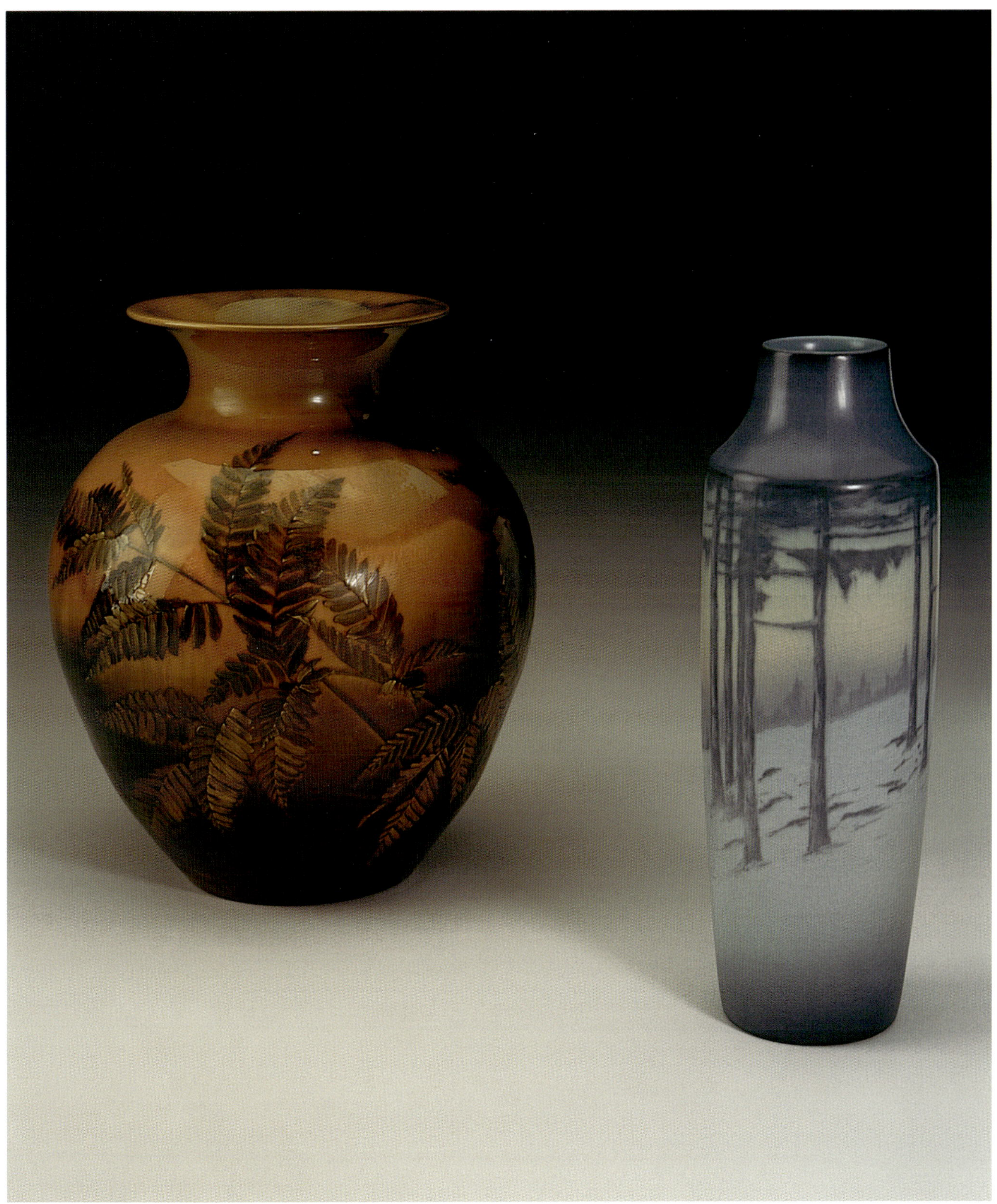

Zsolnay Pottery (Hungary)

Vase, 1890s

ceramic, 4 3/8 high x 5 1/8" diam. (11.1 x 13 cm.)
Collection Memorial Art Gallery of the University of Rochester, New York
Gift of the Estate of Eleanor Volpe Krass, 96.27
CAT. NO. 83

English artist and designer William Morris's belief in creating simple, beautiful, well-crafted, and useful objects lay at the heart of the Arts and Crafts movement that spread throughout Europe, as well as England and the United States, at the end of the nineteenth century. Crafted in Hungary, this curiously shaped, squat vase displays the Arts and Crafts aesthetic in general and its decoration, with its lively pattern of dots, flowers, and serpentine stems, the Art Nouveau style in particular.

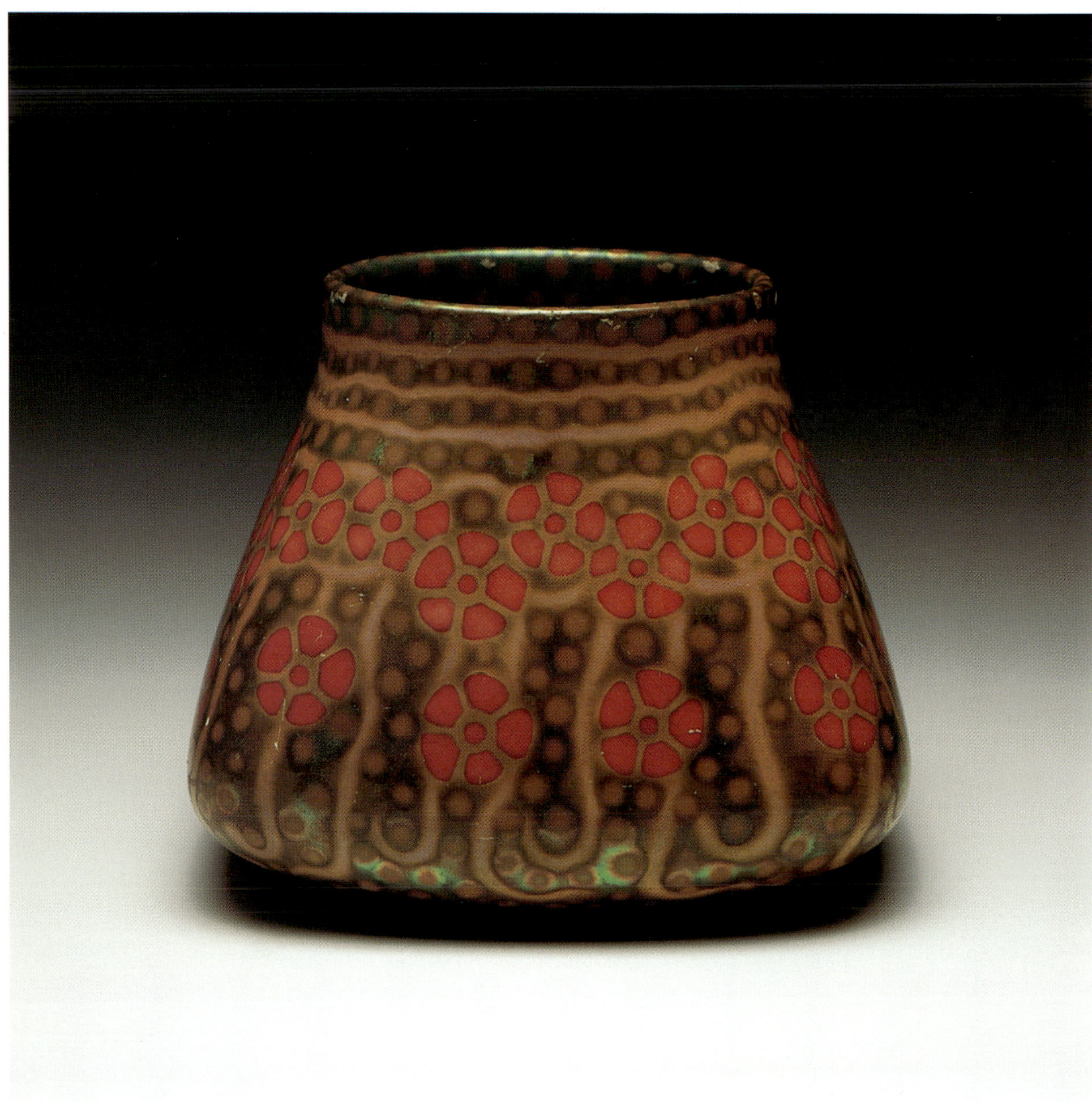

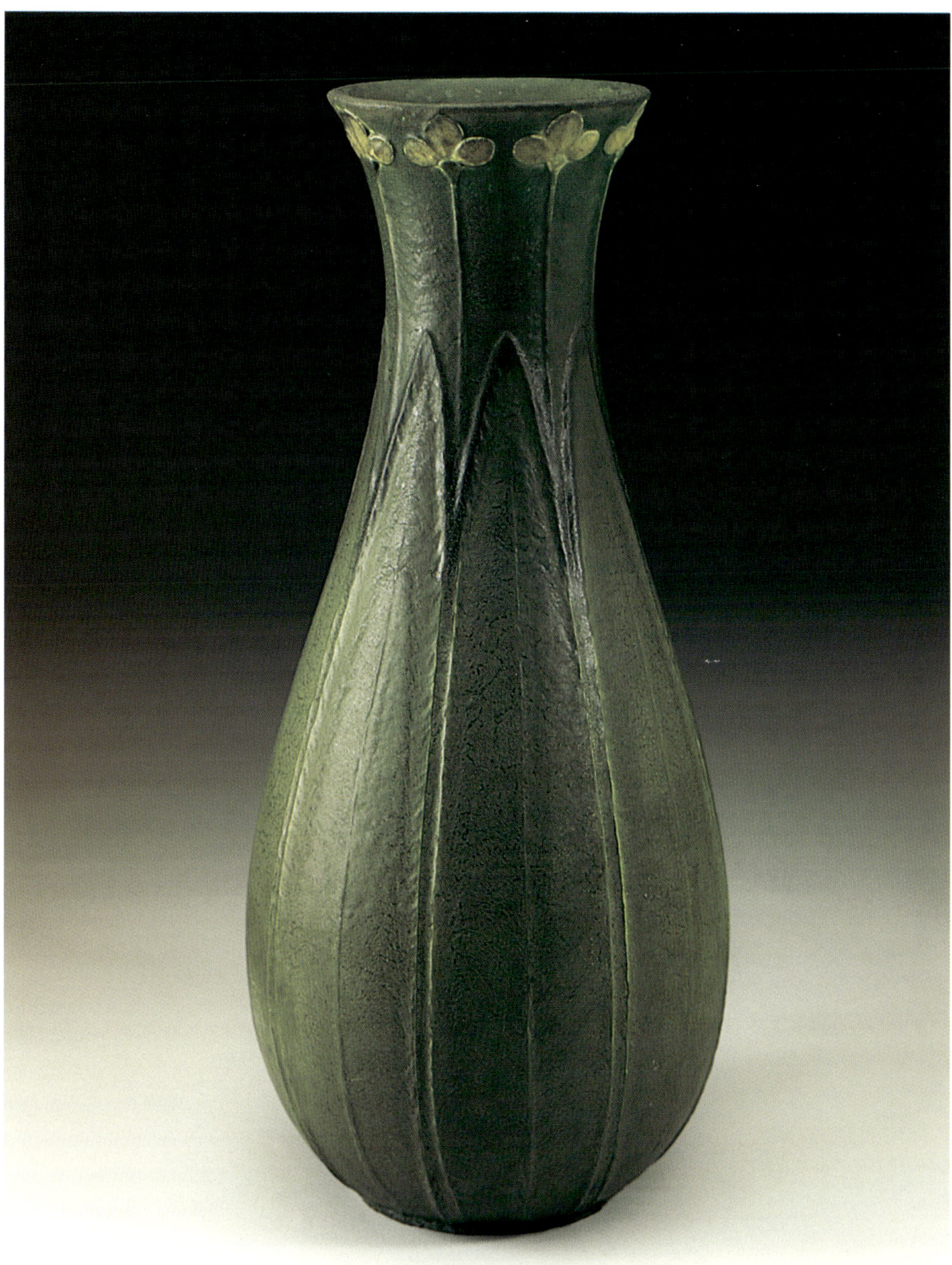

earthenware, 22 high x 9 1/2" diam. (55.8 x 24.1 cm.)
Collection Everson Museum of Art, Syracuse, New York
Museum Purchase, 1982
CAT. NO. 42

William Henry Grueby founded his first pottery company in Boston, Massachusetts, in 1894, initially concentrating on glazed bricks, tiles, and architectural terracotta, but by 1897 he had expanded his production to include art pottery. Grueby developed the matte glazes himself, like the popular green watermelon rind glaze used here. All Grueby Pottery pieces were handmade and decorated, featuring simple organic shapes and sculpted motifs like the broad leaves encompassing the pear-shaped body and the tri-petaled flowers circling the flared mouth of this vase. Gustav Stickley considered Grueby's wares ideal accessories to his furnishings and used Grubey tiles in some of his table tops. Both shared an exhibition space at the Pan-American Exposition, with Grueby winning gold medals there for his products.

WHITE'S POTTERY (UTICA, NEW YORK, 1838 – 1907)
MUG WITH PAN-AMERICAN EXPOSITION DECORATION, 1901

stoneware, 4 high x 3 1/4" diam. (10.2 x 8.3 cm.)
Collection Munson-Williams-Proctor Arts Institute, Museum of Art,
Utica, New York
Museum Purchase, 71.59
CAT. NO. 95

White's Pottery, established in Utica, New York, in the 1830s by Noah White and operated by White's heirs until 1910, became known early on for its superior salt-glazed stoneware fashioned from light fine clay and decorated with simple designs in bright cobalt blue. The company employed artist Hugo Billhardt from 1894 to 1901 to design jugs, jars, bowls, canteens, pitchers, crocks, and souvenirs for conventions and special events, like this mug bearing the ubiquitous logo – two allegorical maidens, representing North and South America, clasping hands in friendship – for the Pan-American Exposition. Although the bodies of these pieces were made from molds, the handles and decorations were applied by hand by female decorators.

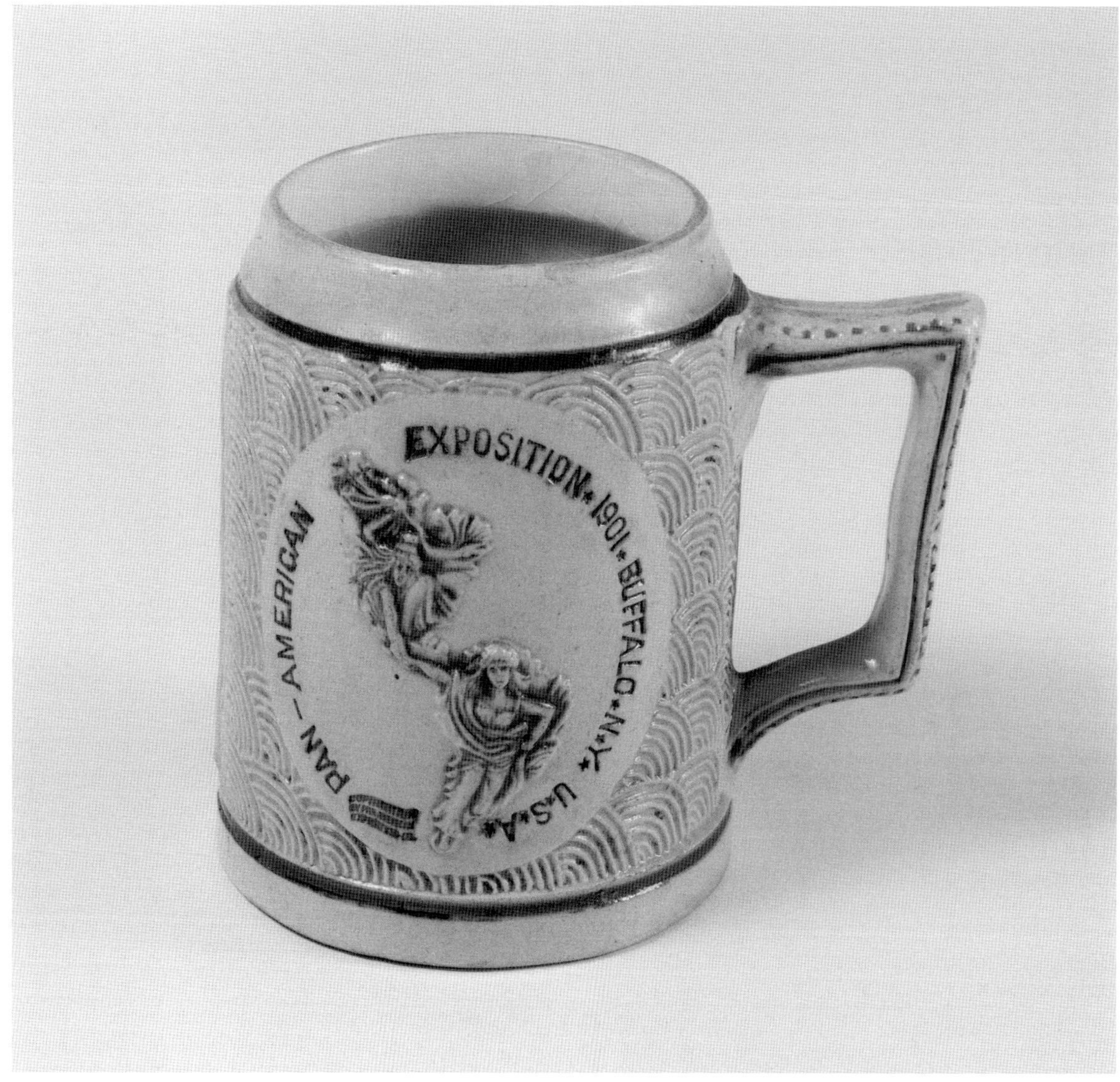

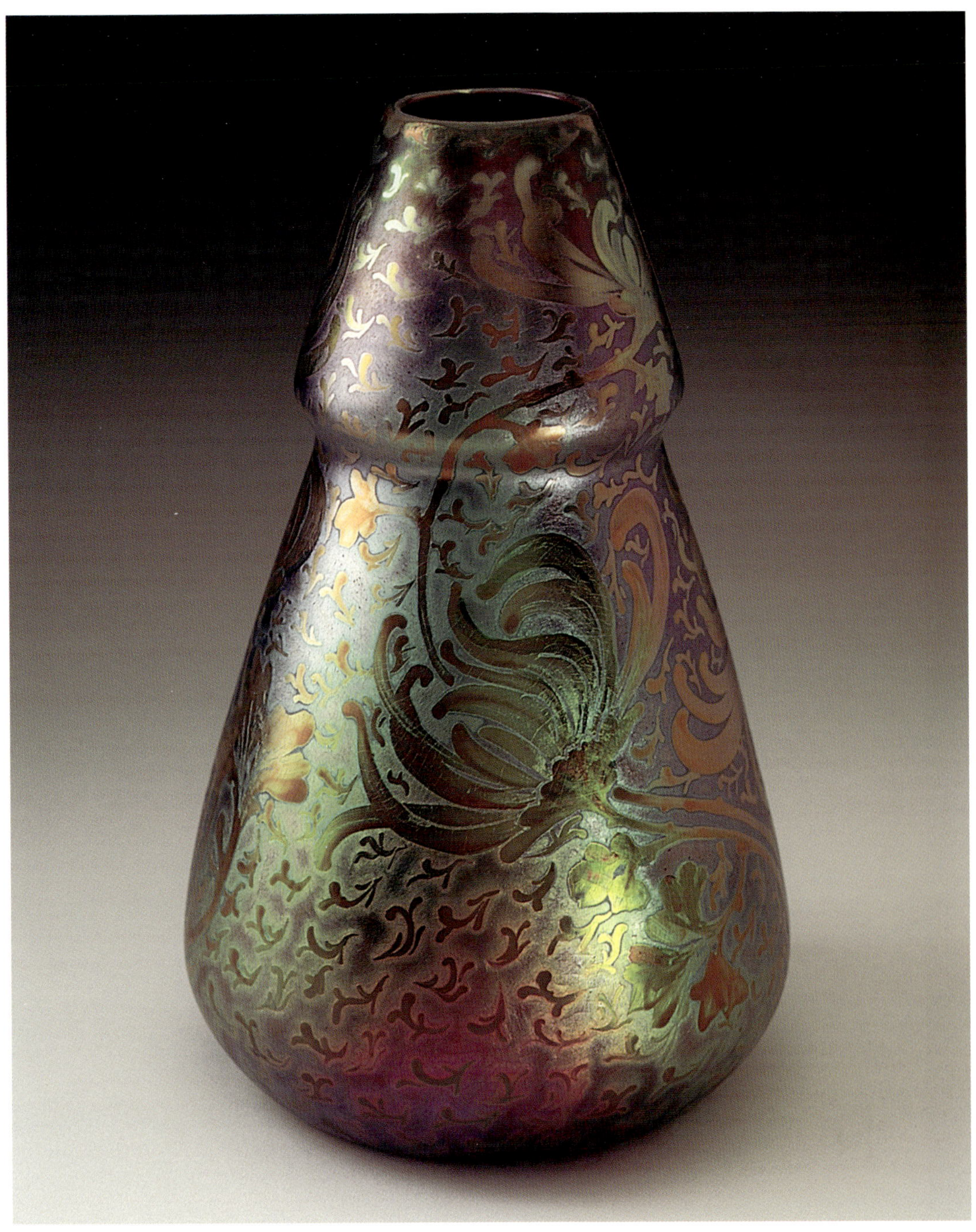

WELLER POTTERY (ZANESVILLE, OHIO, 1872 – 1949)
JACQUES SICARD, DECORATOR

VASE, 1901-10

earthenware, 22 high x 10" diam. (55.9 x 25.4 cm.)
Collection Everson Museum of Art, Syracuse, New York
Museum Purchase, the Dorothy and Robert Riester Ceramic Fund, 1988
CAT. NO. 48

Much of the art pottery produced by Samuel Weller's Zanesville, Ohio, business resembled Rookwood's in the use of the latter's Standard, a process employing underglaze slip painting and high-gloss glazes shading from ocher to brown (called Louwelsa by Weller). With the hiring in 1902 of Jacques Sicard, a French-trained artist, Weller introduced a new line of earthenware luxuriantly decorated with metallic lusters on an iridescent ground. Sicard worked in isolation to create exquisite pieces, such as this vase, until his return to France in 1907.

ADELAIDE ALSOP ROBINEAU (SYRACUSE, NEW YORK, 1901-1929)
AMERICAN, 1865 – 1929

JAR WITH COVER, 1919

porcelain, 7 1/2 high x 8" diam. (19.1 x 20.3 cm.)
Collection Everson Museum of Art, Syracuse, New York
Gift of Dr. Ethel T. Eltinge, 1982
CAT. NO. 44

CRAB VASE, 1908

porcelain, 7 3/8 high x 2 1/2" diam. (18.7 x 6.4 cm.)
Collection Everson Museum of Art, Syracuse, New York
Museum Purchase, 1916
CAT. NO. 43

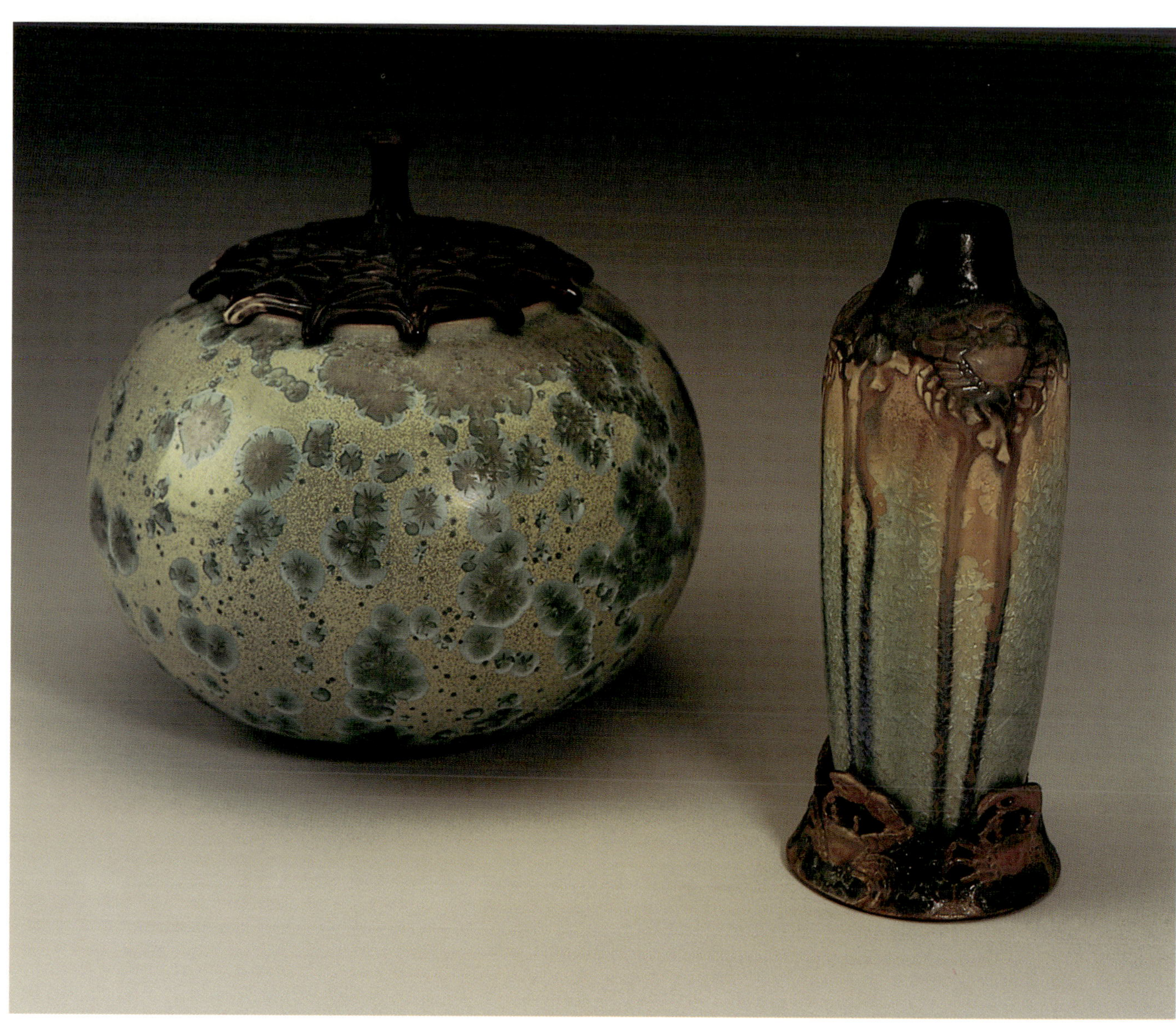

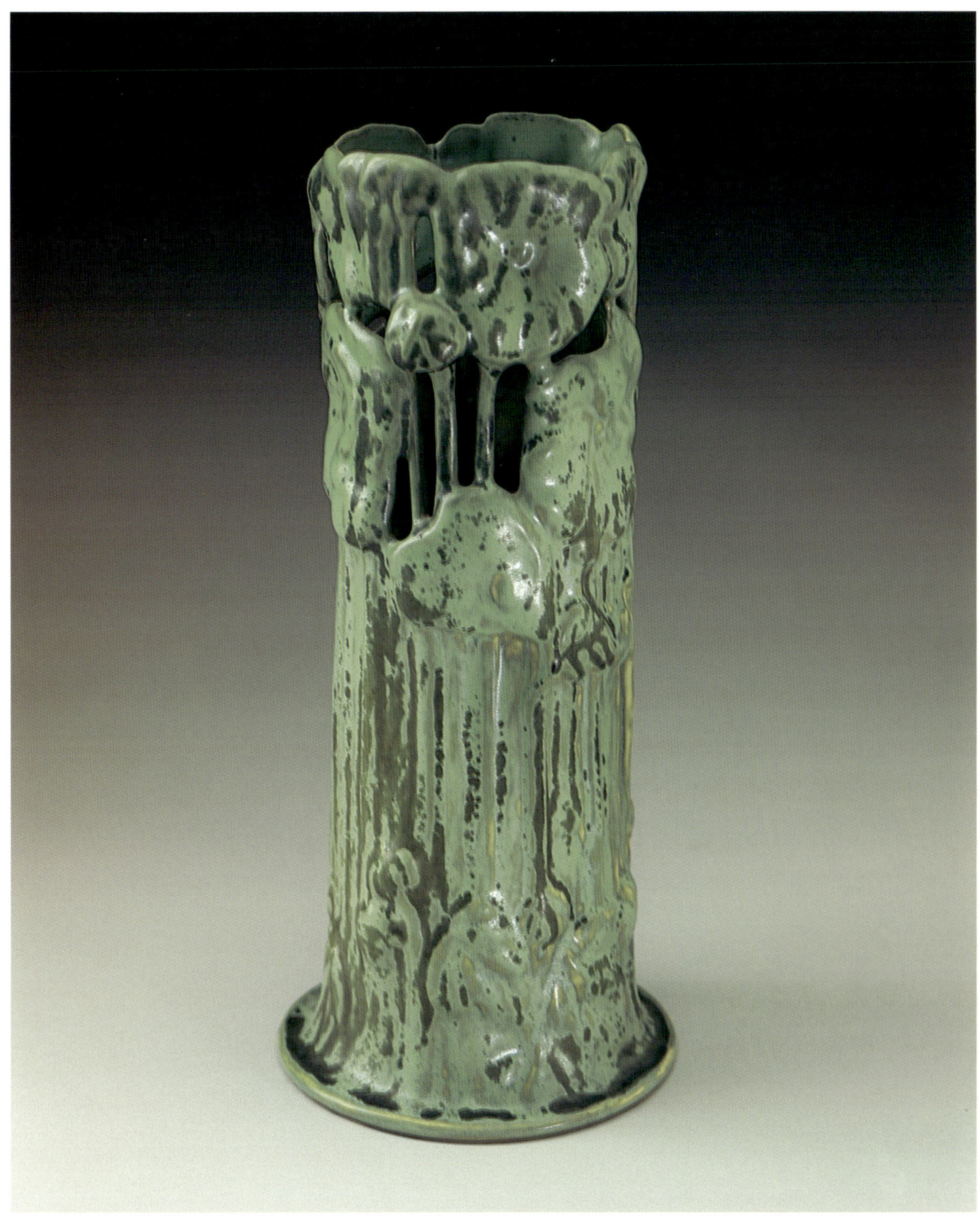

TIFFANY POTTERY (CORONA, NEW YORK, 1898 – 1920)

VASE WITH PANSIES, CA. 1910

stoneware, 10 3/8 high x 4 1/2" diam. (26.4 x 11.4 cm.)
Collection Everson Museum of Art, Syracuse, New York
Gift of Mr. and Mrs. Bronson A. Quackenbush, 1978
CAT. NO. 47

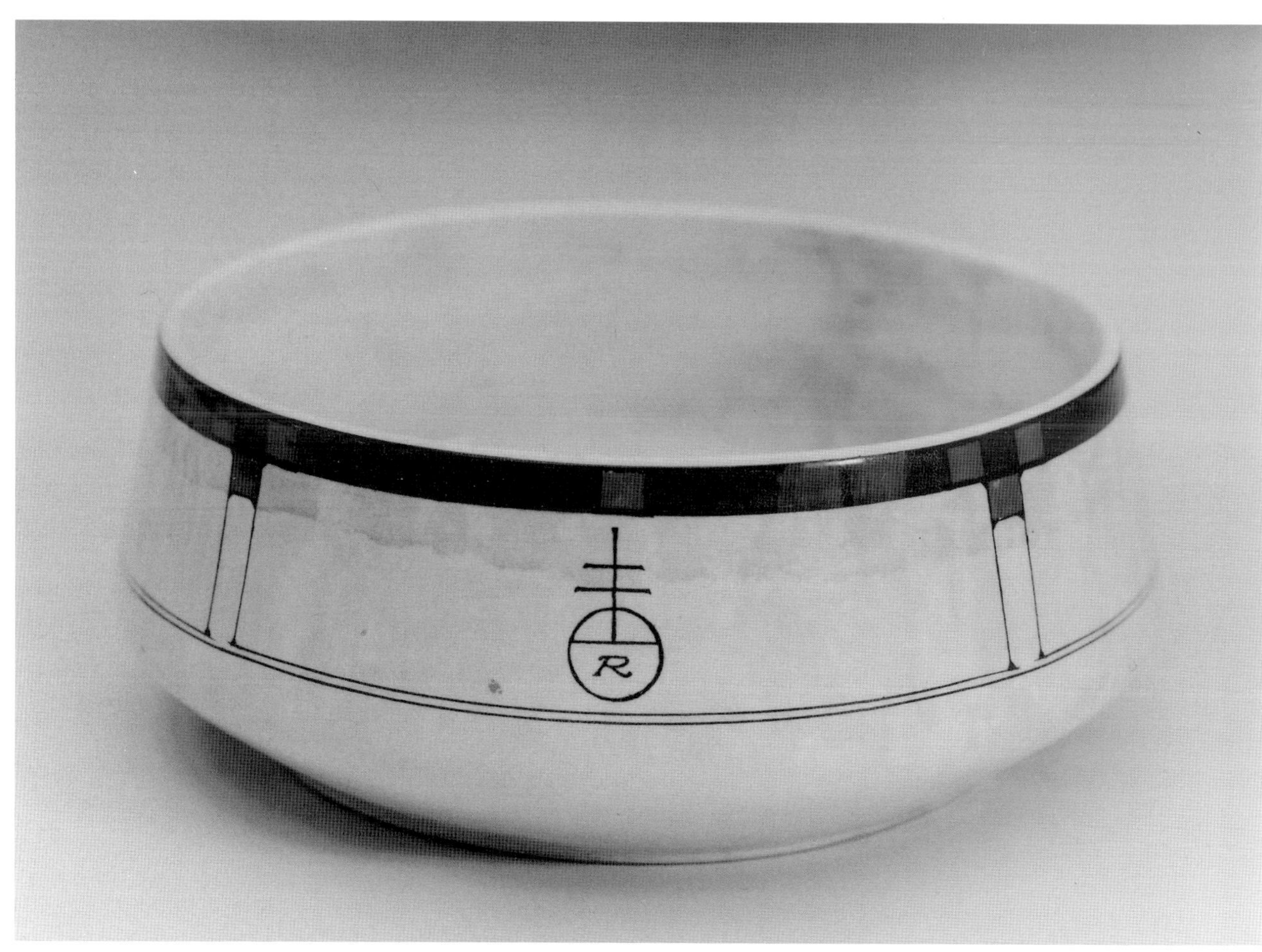

BUFFALO POTTERY (BUFFALO, NEW YORK, 1901– 1956)

BOWL, 1910-12

stoneware, 3 5/8 high x 9 1/8" diam. (9.2 x 23.2 cm.)
Collection Everson Museum of Art, Syracuse, New York
Museum Purchase, 1986
CAT. NO. 41

Chartered in 1901, Buffalo Pottery (later to become Buffalo China, Inc.) originated as an offshoot of the Larkin Soap Company, manufacturing pottery items to serve as promotional premiums for Larkin's soap products. Heir to the industrial promise of the Pan-American Exposition's electrical wonderland, Buffalo Pottery was the first in the world to run solely on electricity. Elegantly austere in form and decoration, this bowl bears the Roycroft symbol on its front, identifying it as part of a service made for the Roycroft Inn in East Aurora, New York.

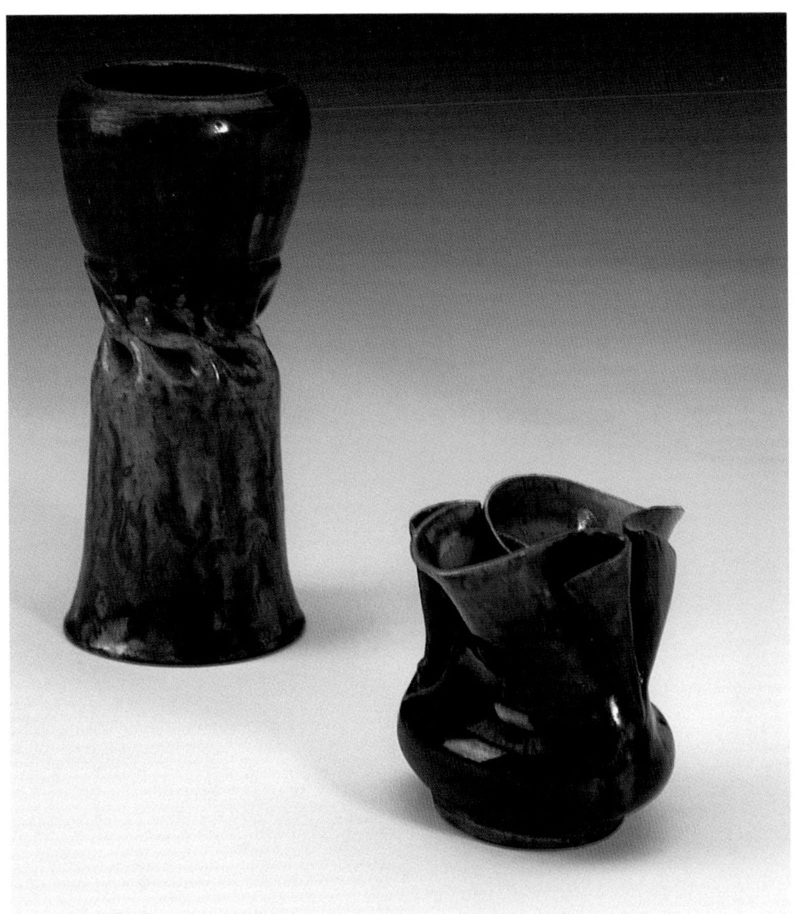

BILOXI ART POTTERY (MISSISSIPPI, CA. 1882 – 1910)
GEORGE E. OHR, AMERICAN, 1857 – 1919

UNTITLED (TWISTED VASE), N. D.

earthenware, 6 3/4 high x 3 1/4" diam. (17.1 x 8.3 cm.)
Collection Everson Museum of Art, Syracuse, New York
Museum Purchase, 1976
CAT. NO. 39

UNTITLED (FOLDED VASE), N. D.

earthenware, 3 1/2 high x 3 1/2" diam. (8.9 x 8.9 cm.)
Collection Everson Museum of Art, Syracuse, New York
The Paul and Mary Brandwein Collection, 1992
CAT. NO. 40

Known as "The Mad Potter of Biloxi," George E. Ohr engaged in eccentric behavior and promoted himself as a misunderstood genius. In the years just preceding and following 1900, the works he produced at his pottery in Biloxi, Mississippi, nonetheless gained international recognition. They were exhibited at major exhibitions, such as the World's Columbian Exposition in 1893 in Chicago and the Exposition Universelle in 1900 in Paris, and entered both private and public collections, such as those of Louis Comfort Tiffany and the Philadelphia Museum of Art. He was especially admired for his ability to create extraordinarily thin-walled vessels on the potter's wheel and for his unique tortoise-shell and metallic glazes. Perhaps the most exceptional quality of his work, however, was his dramatic alteration of the wheel-thrown earthenware pieces that he would gently crush, dent, or, as in the case of the untitled vases here, twist or fold. Although Ohr passionately embraced a purist belief in the importance of handcrafting, he eschewed the requirement of utility associated with the Arts and Crafts philosophy. For example, he often created nonfunctional items – teapots with two spouts or mugs with multiple handles – meant to be valued solely for their sculptural and expressive qualities. Nine years before his death in 1918, Ohr closed his pottery, packed away thousands of his best pieces, and faded from public memory. In 1972, an antique dealer came upon the cache and the Mad Potter's "mud babies" (as he called them) reentered the limelight.

LOUIS COMFORT TIFFANY (AMERICAN, 1848 – 1933)

GREEN MILLEFIORE VASE, N.D

glass, 6 1/2 high x 3" diam. (16.5 x 7.6 cm.)
Collection Herbert F. Johnson Museum of Art
Cornell University, Ithaca, New York
Gift of Louis Comfort Tiffany through the courtesy of A. Douglas Nash, 57.106
CAT. NO. 65

GOLD IRIDESCENT TULIP VASE, N.D.

glass, 15 1/4 high x 5 1/4" diam. (38.7 x 13.3 cm.)
Collection Herbert F. Johnson Museum of Art
Cornell University, Ithaca, New York
Edythe de Lorenzi Collection, Bequest of Otto de Lorenzi, 64.0887
CAT. NO. 64

BLUE BOWL WITH GREEN OVERTONES AND COARSE CRACKLE, N.D.

glass, 2 3/4 high x 7 1/2" diam. (7 x 19.1 cm.)
Collection Herbert F. Johnson Museum of Art
Cornell University, Ithaca, New York
Edythe de Lorenzi Collection, Bequest of Otto de Lorenzi, 64.0884
CAT. NO. 63

Tiffany premiered his Favrile glass before the public in 1895, winning an overwhelmingly positive response to the luminous, iridescent surfaces of his hand-blown glass (Favrile, derived from the Saxon word "febrile," meaning "handwrought"). To achieve the lustrous effect, an atomized mixture of metallic vapors was sprayed onto the surface of a finished piece placed within a heating chamber. Other techniques, such as the crackled texture that adds interest to the shallow bowl here, were also under constant development. Sometimes Tiffany combined traditional techniques with his newer discoveries; the tiny flowers gracing the green vase in this exhibition exemplify the use of a long-established Venetian practice. Cross-sections of millefiore rods (delicate rods composed of variously colored strands of glass) when encased in the glass body of the vase, create a design of small white petals surrounding a colored stamen, hence the name millefiore, or "thousand flowers."

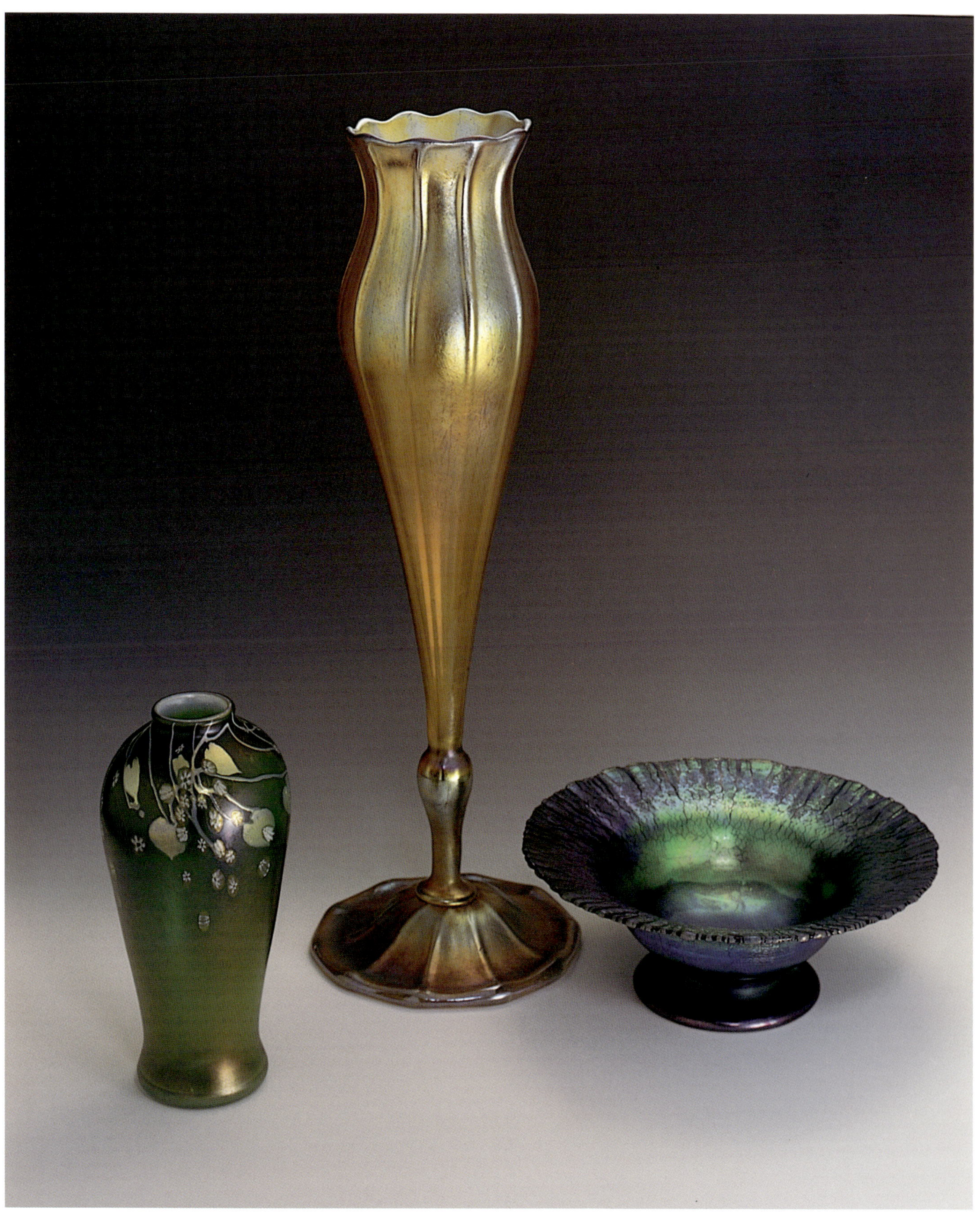

QUEZAL ART GLASS AND DECORATING COMPANY (BROOKLYN, NEW YORK)

COMPOTE, GOLD INTERIOR, WHITE AND GREEN LOTUS LEAVES, 20TH CENTURY

glass, 7 3/4 high x 8 1/4" diam. (19.7 x 21 cm.)
Collection Herbert F. Johnson Museum of Art
Cornell University, Ithaca, New York
Edythe de Lorenzi Collection, Bequest of Otto de Lorenzi, 64.0906
CAT. NO. 61

Named after the colorful Quetzal bird, the Quezal Art Glass and Decorating Company was founded in 1901 by Martin Bach, a disgruntled mixer at Louis Comfort Tiffany's firm. Bach's subsequent partner, Thomas Johnson, and many of their employees also abandoned Tiffany Glass for Quezal Art Glass. Apparently their dissatisfaction with Tiffany revolved around business rather than aesthetic issues, for their glassware, in both form and decoration, closely resembled that produced by their previous employer, as is evident in the shimmering colors and vibrant Art Nouveau design of the compote shown here.

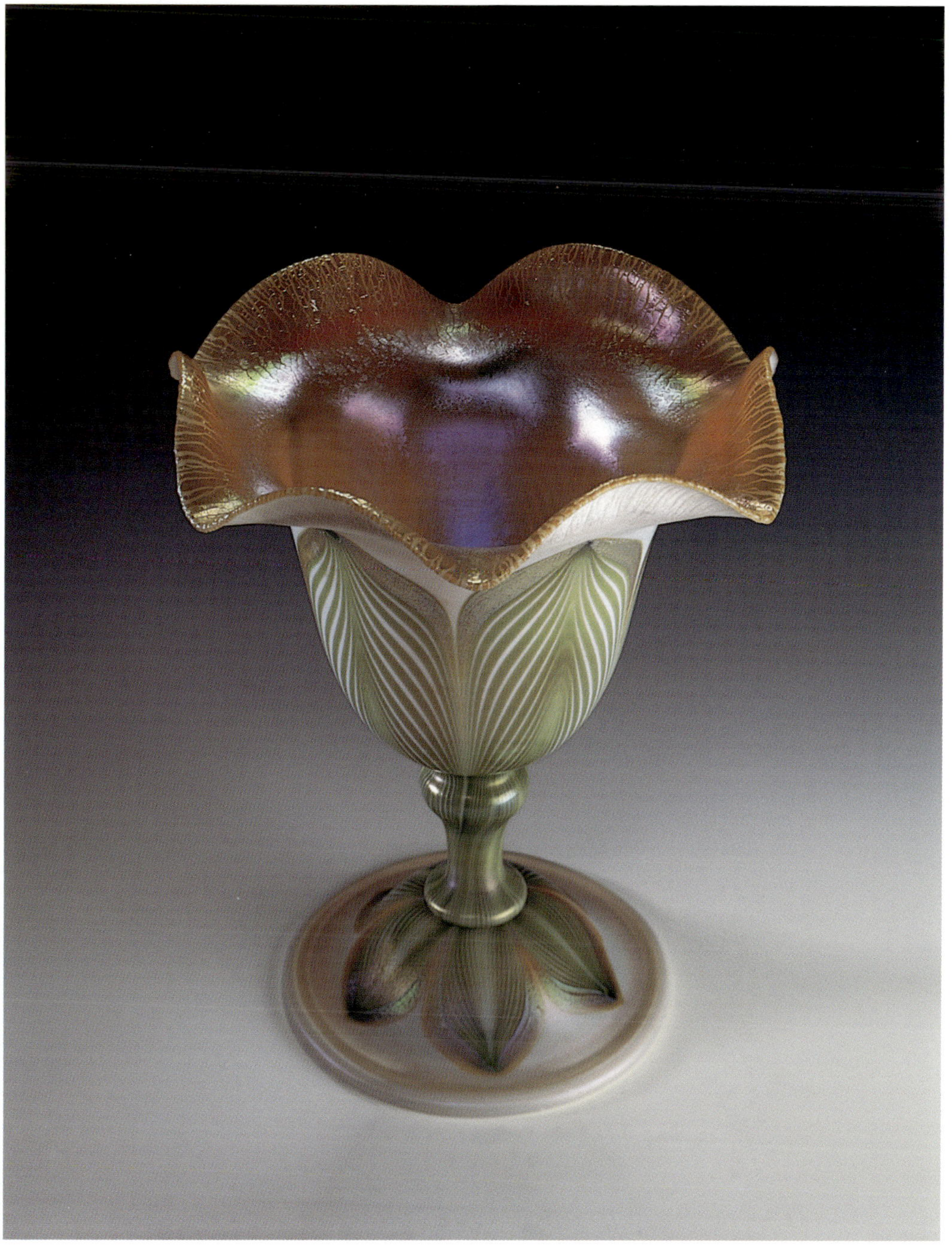

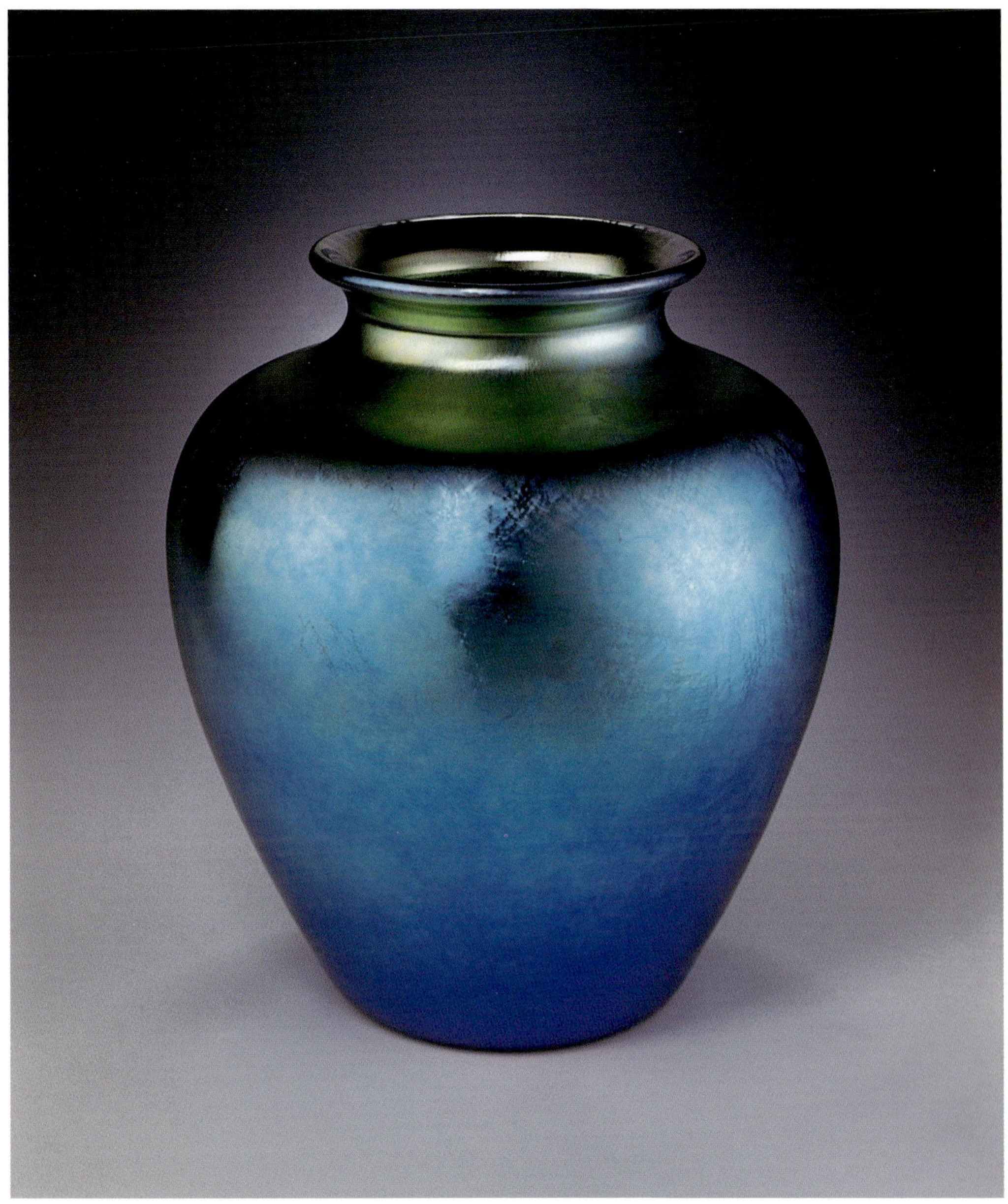

STEUBEN GLASS WORKS (CORNING, NEW YORK, 1903-PRESENT)

BLUE AURENE BULBOUS VASE, AFTER 1903

glass, 8 high x 7" diam. (20.3 x 17.8 cm.)
Collection Herbert F. Johnson Museum of Art
Cornell University, Ithaca, New York
Edythe de Lorenzi Collection, Bequest of Otto de Lorenzi, 64.0871
CAT. NO. 62

Another major competitor of Tiffany Glass was Steuben Glass Works in Corning, New York, founded in 1903 by Englishman Frederick Carder and Corning glass manufacturer T. G. Hawkes. Carder developed a beautiful blue-and-gold iridescent glass that he named Aurene, an appellation comprised of "aurum" (meaning "gold") and "schene"(meaning "sheen"). When the popularity of Steuben pieces, such as this voluptuous Aurene vase, began to rival that of Tiffany's Favrile glass, Tiffany filed a patent-infringement suit against Carder (although his effort ultimately proved fruitless).

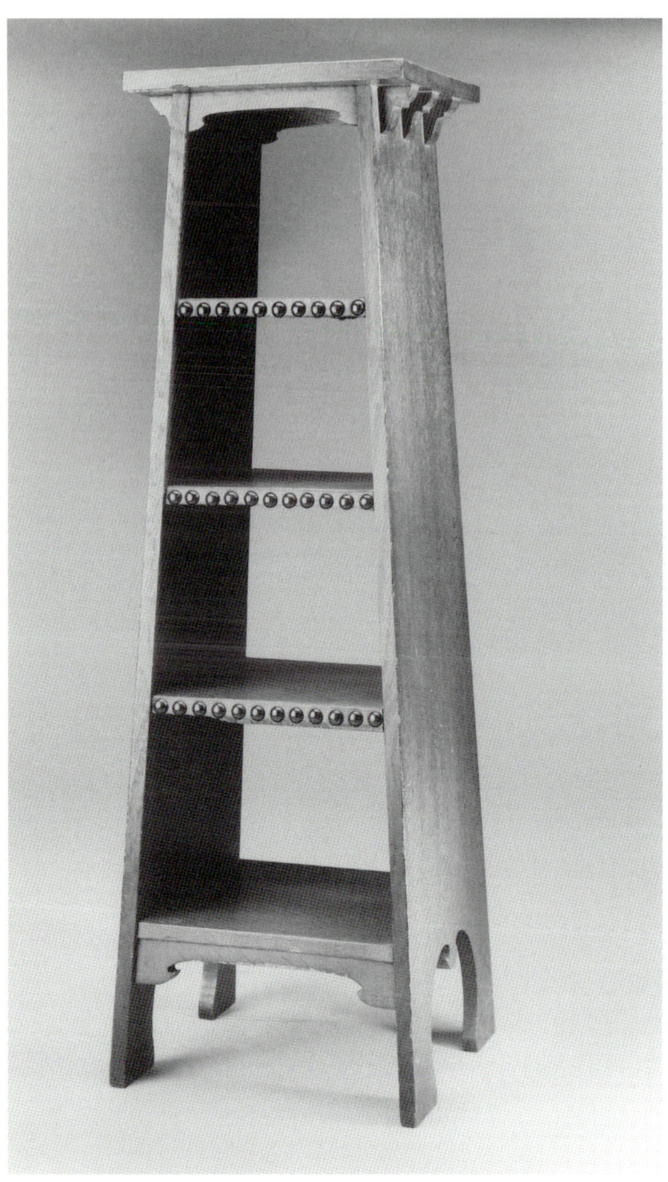

United Crafts (Eastwood, New York, 1899-1904)

Gustav Stickley, American, 1858-1942

Magazine Rack, ca. 1900

white oak, leather, and brass, 43 1/4 x 14 1/4 x 13 1/2"
(109.9 x 36.2 x 34.3 cm.)
Collection Everson Museum of Art, Syracuse, New York
Museum Purchase with Funds from Mr. and Mrs. Herbert Slotnick, 1983
CAT. NO. 50

Roycroft Shops (East Aurora, New York, 1895-1938)

Tall Back Chair, ca. 1900-1910

oak with leather seat and brass studs, 48 x 18 x 18"
(121.9 x 45.7 x 45.7 cm.)
Collection Everson Museum of Art, Syracuse, New York
Museum Purchase, 1982
CAT. NO. 49

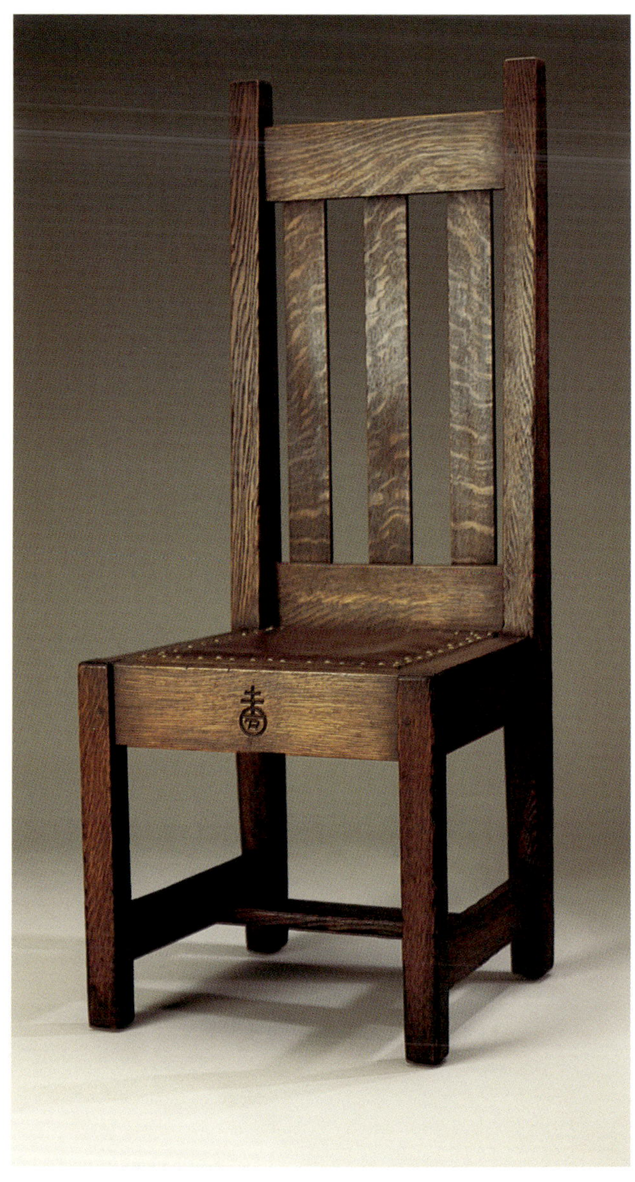

FRANK LLOYD WRIGHT (AMERICAN, 1867 – 1959)

ARMCHAIR, 1904

Wood with upholstered seat, 32 x 23 x 23" (81.3 x 58.4 x 58.4 cm.)
Collection Albright-Knox Art Gallery, Buffalo, New York
Gift of Mr. Darwin R. Martin, 1968
CAT. NO. 31

Although Frank Lloyd Wright was most closely associated with the Midwest at the beginning of the twentieth century when he was perfecting his Prairie Style, his connections with the Buffalo area at the time were significant. When Elbert Hubbard abdicated his position as vice-president of the Larkin Soap Company to eventually found the Roycroft Community, he was replaced by Darwin D. Martin, who knew Wright and engaged him to design the Martins' residence, the first of many commissions here for the architect. The barrel-shaped armchair he created for the Prairie–Style masterpiece is, indeed, a small masterpiece itself, unique in its simple lines yet complex in design, with the back curved in three directions and tapered in thickness from the center outward.

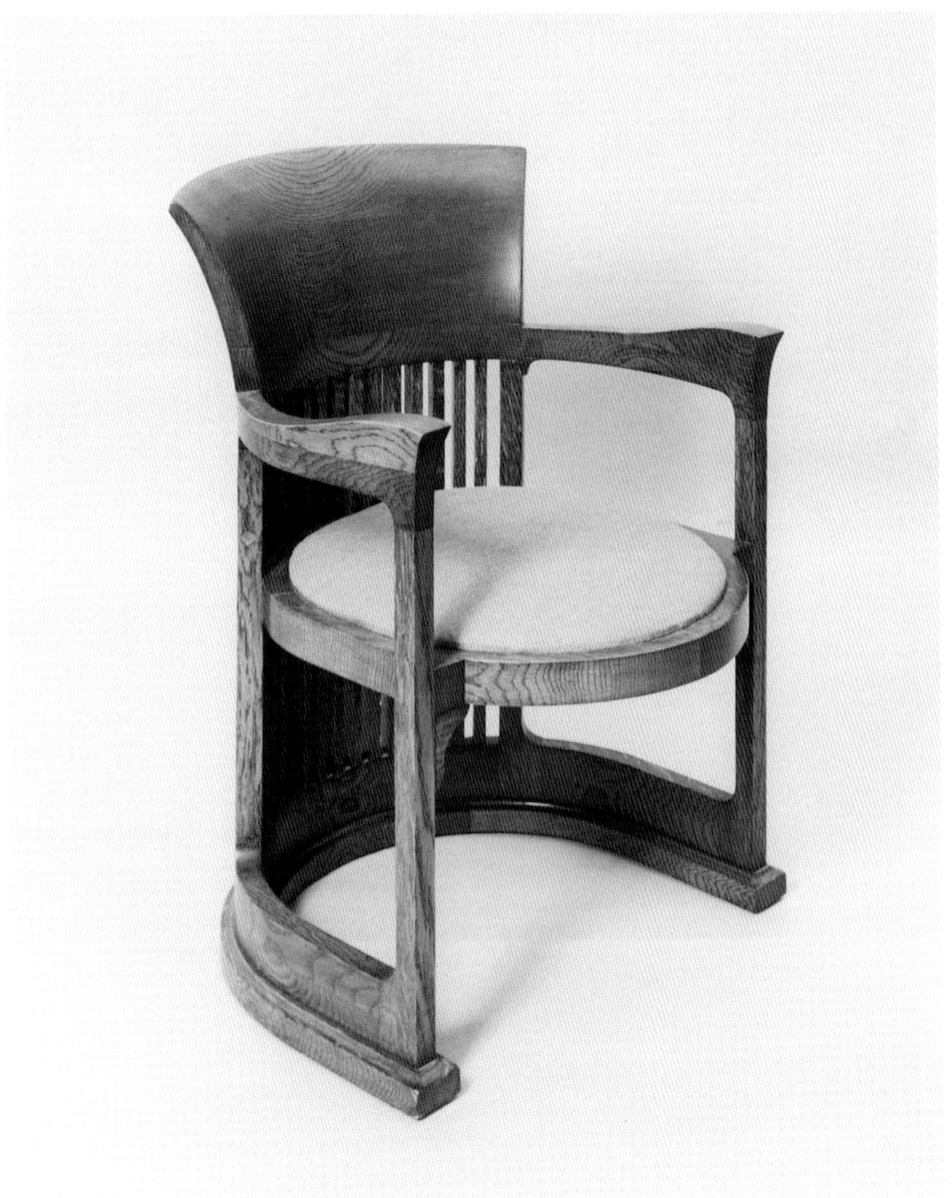

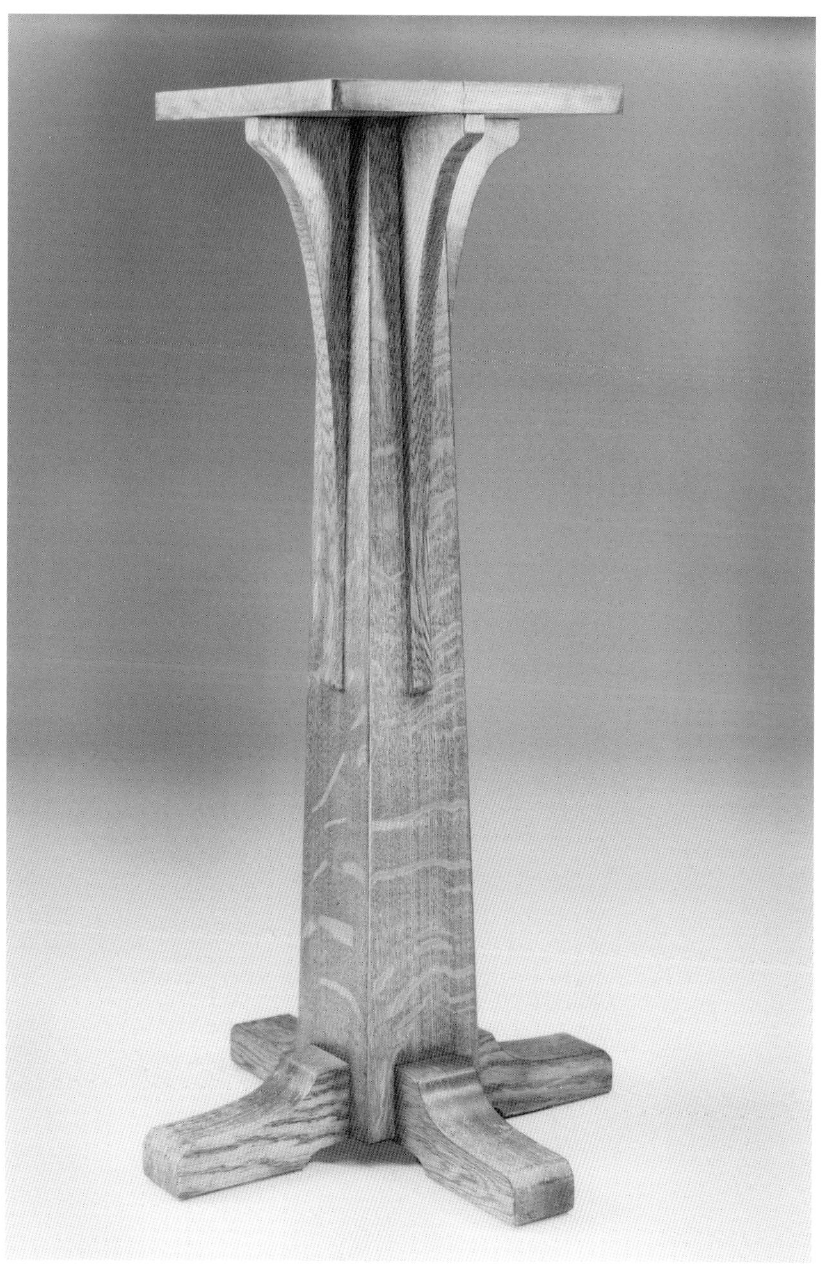

L. AND J.G. STICKLEY (FAYETTEVILLE, NEW YORK, FOUNDED 1902)

LEOPOLD STICKLEY, AMERICAN, 1869 – 1957

JOHN GEORGE STICKLEY, AMERICAN, 1871 – 1921

PEDESTAL, CA. 1910

white oak, 36 x 19 x 19" (91.4 x 48.3 x 48.3 cm.)
Collection Everson Museum of Art, Syracuse, New York
Gift of the Friends of Justin Beauchat in His Memory, 1982
CAT. NO. 51

Originally foreman at his brother Gustav's company, Leopold Stickley began his own furniture manufacturing business in Fayetteville, New York, in 1902 and took on his brother John George as a partner in 1904. More varied and adaptable to the demands of the market than Gustav, L. and J. G. Stickley incorporated the influences of Frank Lloyd Wright, Viennese architect-designers, and English Arts and Crafts proponents, as well as those of their brother, into their works. For example, the curves of the feet and the decorative supports at the top of the pedestal base, though understated, downplay the marked rectilinear character so central to Gustav's designs.

KARL KIPP, AMERICAN, 1882 – 1954

TRAPEZOIDAL VASE, CA. 1910

copper and German silver, 4 3/8 x 5 1/8 x 5 1/8" (11.1 x 13 x 13 cm.)
Collection Memorial Art Gallery of the University of Rochester, New York
Gift of Emily Sibley Watson, Walter Remington,
Arthur Stern II, and Bertha Buswell Bequest (by exchange), 93.1
CAT. NO. 82

Metalcrafting at Roycroft began with blacksmithing simple objects in iron, but by 1902, copper became the metal of choice. Copper was still an affordable commodity, easier to work with than iron, and reminiscent of colonial American crafts. In 1904, the arrival of the gifted designer Dard Hunter brought about a new sophistication in design that reflected his acquaintance with the geometric styles then flourishing in Austria and Scotland. Karl Kipp, who directed Roycroft's Copper Shop from 1908 until 1911, based the silver decoration on this vase on one of Hunter's geometric designs, thus further enhancing the object's unusual shape and setting off the hammered copper surface that signified its handcrafted origin.

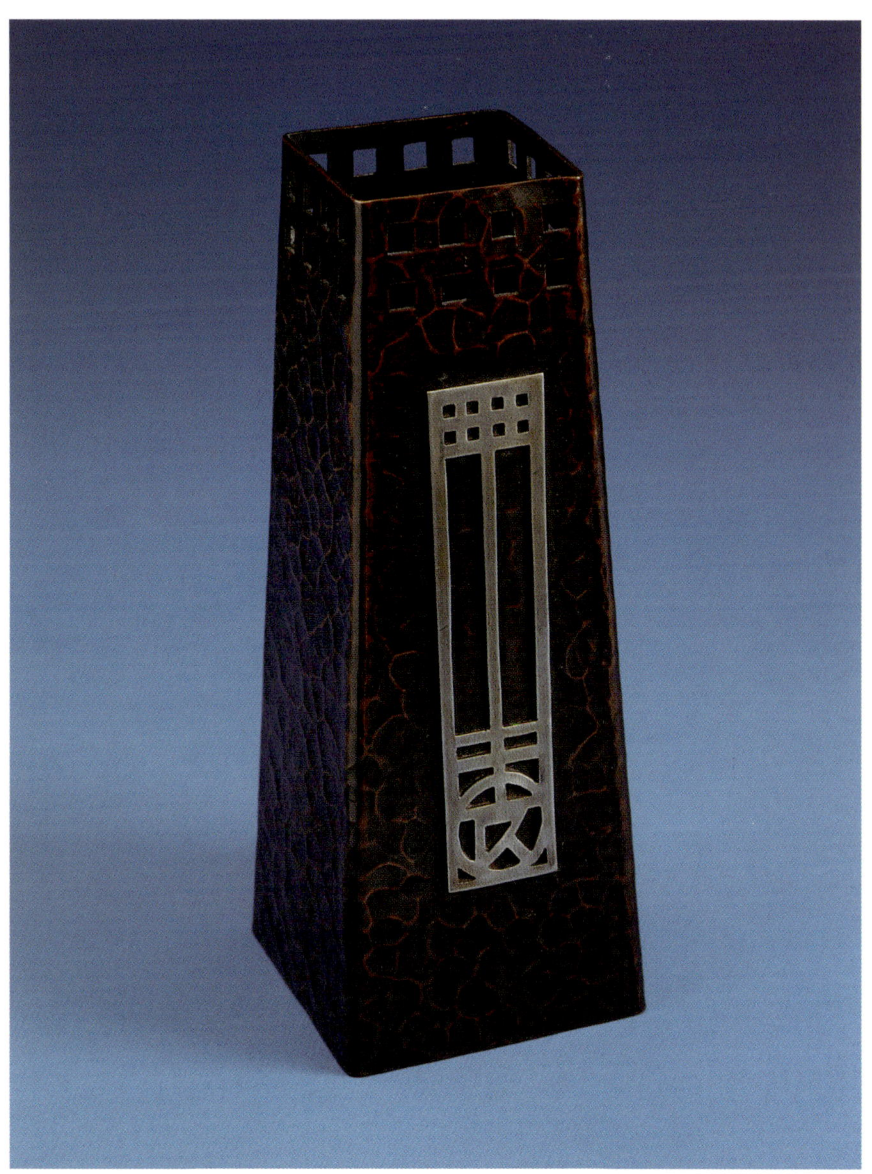

PHOTOGRAPHY

A Question of Intention: Photography Circa 1900

Claire Schneider

If the turn of a new century, and a new millennium, offers an interesting opportunity to reassess the state of the arts in the year 1900, now is a particularly fruitful time to reconsider photography. Many of the questions and internal wrangling that plagued photography when it first became available to a large spectrum of people, from serious artists to serious amateurs and scientific study, continue to surround this medium with a potential for both fantastic visual documentation and subjective expression. Questions about photography's role in the dissemination of knowledge, in the truth and fiction of its images, and in how photographs function in different spaces are as important today as they were a hundred years ago. In an attempt to validate itself as a fine art form, advocates of aesthetic photography at the turn of the last century answered these questions in specific ways. Photography should mirror art in content as well as style.

In reassessing photography with one hundred years of perspective, works have been included here that were not initially intended as fine-art photography. These images by amateurs, scientists, explorers, and commercial professionals have, with increasing frequency, entered museums' collections and been included in exhibitions because they offer not only perspective on the decisions made by fine-art photographers at the time, but also a rich and provocative array of new imagery to discover.

The group that fought to make photography a fine art circa 1900 was a wide-ranging and loose affiliation of serious amateurs known as the Pictorialists. Looking to other artistic movements of the day for models, they, like the Romantic writers, the Barbizon and Symbolist painters, and the Arts and Crafts movement, turned their renditions of people and places into grand metaphorical statements. These self-consciously artistic photographers, in addition, used a variety of techniques, including manipulating photographic images or muting their camera's focus, so that their photo-chemically created images resembled traditional forms of visual art such as prints and etchings.

By 1902, a small group known as the Photo-Secession had split off in pursuit of higher aesthetic standards, although their basic themes and pictorial values did not change significantly. Women continued to be idealized as symbols of motherhood and beauty in simplified compositions that recalled the Old Masters, Japanese prints, and such painters of the day as William Merritt Chase, John Singer Sargent, and James Abbott McNeill Whistler. See, for example, Gertrude Käsebier's *The Manger* (cat. no. 32) and Clarence Herbert White's *The Chiffonier* (cat. no. 36). Likewise, another traditional genre of painting, the still life with its emphasis on sensuous surfaces, elegance, and refinement was recreated by Baron Adolf de Meyer in *Still-Life (Lilies in a Glass Bowl)* (cat. no. 71) with a soft focus lens. And even when Photo-Secessionists took up a new subject – the city – their images continued to convey abstract themes. Edward Steichen's *Nocturne-Orangerie Staircase, Versailles* (cat. no. 33) retains the mystery and primacy he previously gave to the forest by using a limited tonal range and a delicacy of finish available from night photography and specialized photographic printing techniques. In *Tower Bridge, London* (cat. no. 67), Alvin Langdon Coburn makes his favorite architectural motif — the bridge — a symbol of the human conquest of nature. And even, the grand leader of this group, Alfred Stieglitz, juxtaposes the vitality of modern life between man and nature's struggle for existence. In *The Street, Fifth Avenue* (cat. no. 34), this artistic mood is however, recreated with the help of an overcast, snowy day, rather than technical wizardry.

After twenty years of advocating for photography, as an art on par with painting, sculpture, and printmaking, Stieglitz was finally able to show his and his followers' work in a fine arts setting — the Albright Art Gallery in Buffalo. The 1910 *International Exhibition of Pictorial Photography*, with more than 600 prints, was a validation of Stieglitz's extensive efforts. In fact, all but one of the works discussed above were collected directly from this exhibition. One contemporary work that was not shown is Augustus Thibaudeau's *Woman with Parasol* (cat. no. 35). Made by a member of the Photo-Pictorialists of Buffalo, a group that opposed Stieglitz's complete domination of the field, this idealization of a woman in a simple landscape, nevertheless, resembles in its elegance, nostalgic mood, and metaphorical aspirations the work of the Photo-Secessionists.

Ironically, while the Albright exhibition signified Stieglitz's domination of the field, it also signaled his turn away from photography to a broader interest in modern art and a more modernist aesthetic. And although the ideas of the Photo-Secessionists began to lose ground, they left an important legacy on the aesthetic that followed. The social activist Lewis Hine in *Doffer–Fall River, Massachusetts* (cat. no. 70) used grand compositional devices to compose powerful documents that not only recorded the horrible conditions of the working class but also gave these facts empathetic impact. Imogen Cunningham, influenced by Pictorialism when she was a student of Gertrude Käsebier, also used a documentary-like style to pursue the symbolist goal of imbuing concrete objects with higher meaning. Close-ups like *Stairway, Mills College* (cat. no. 68) retain a poetic sensibility despite her use of sharply focused, unmanipulated imagery.

While a more objective aesthetic began to dominate artistic photography by 1920, it had been the means of a whole new way to visually understand the world, since the beginning of this period. Eadweard Muybridge's sequential stop-action images not only established what a horse looks like when all its feet were off the ground, they also provided countless examples of how even ordinary activities can tell strange and whimsical tales. In *Animal Locomotion (woman at wash stand)* (cat. no. 72), the water frozen in time becomes a floating amoebae, a creature with its own independent fate. Conversely, the far-off and exotic become commonplace as a result of commercial studios like George Barker's. His *Falls of Niagara — General View, Niagara Falls, NY* (cat. no. 66) was seen in large numbers by people who might never have had the opportunity to personally view this natural phenomenon. Perhaps the most pervasive legacy of the visual revolution caused by photography was achieved by the amateur who produced works strictly for his own enjoyment. Like a page from a personal diary, Leslie Hamilton Wilson's *Changing a Tire* from "Scenes from Edwardian Life" (cat. no. 73) preserves this Edwardian gentleman's curiosity with a mundane aspect of life that seemed to be as exotic to him as his worldwide travels.

Technology, art, and intention are perhaps the most important words associated with photography. As one looks back at this photographic period, which is still often viewed with disdain for its likeness to second-rate painting, one must remember that it was also a time of drawing battle lines: between photography as a tool for knowing the world better and photography as an artistic medium for symbolic inquiry. Today, contemporary artists attempt to erase those lines by using and manipulating the vast array of images photography offers and by challenging the viewer's expectations of their intentions.

PETER HENRY EMERSON (BRITISH, 1856 – 1936)
TWIXT LAND AND WATER, 1886

platinum print, 7 x 11 1/4" (17.8 x 28.6 cm.)
Collection Herbert F. Johnson Museum of Art
Cornell University, Ithaca, New York
Class of 1962 Photography Fund, 80.031.007
CAT. NO. 69

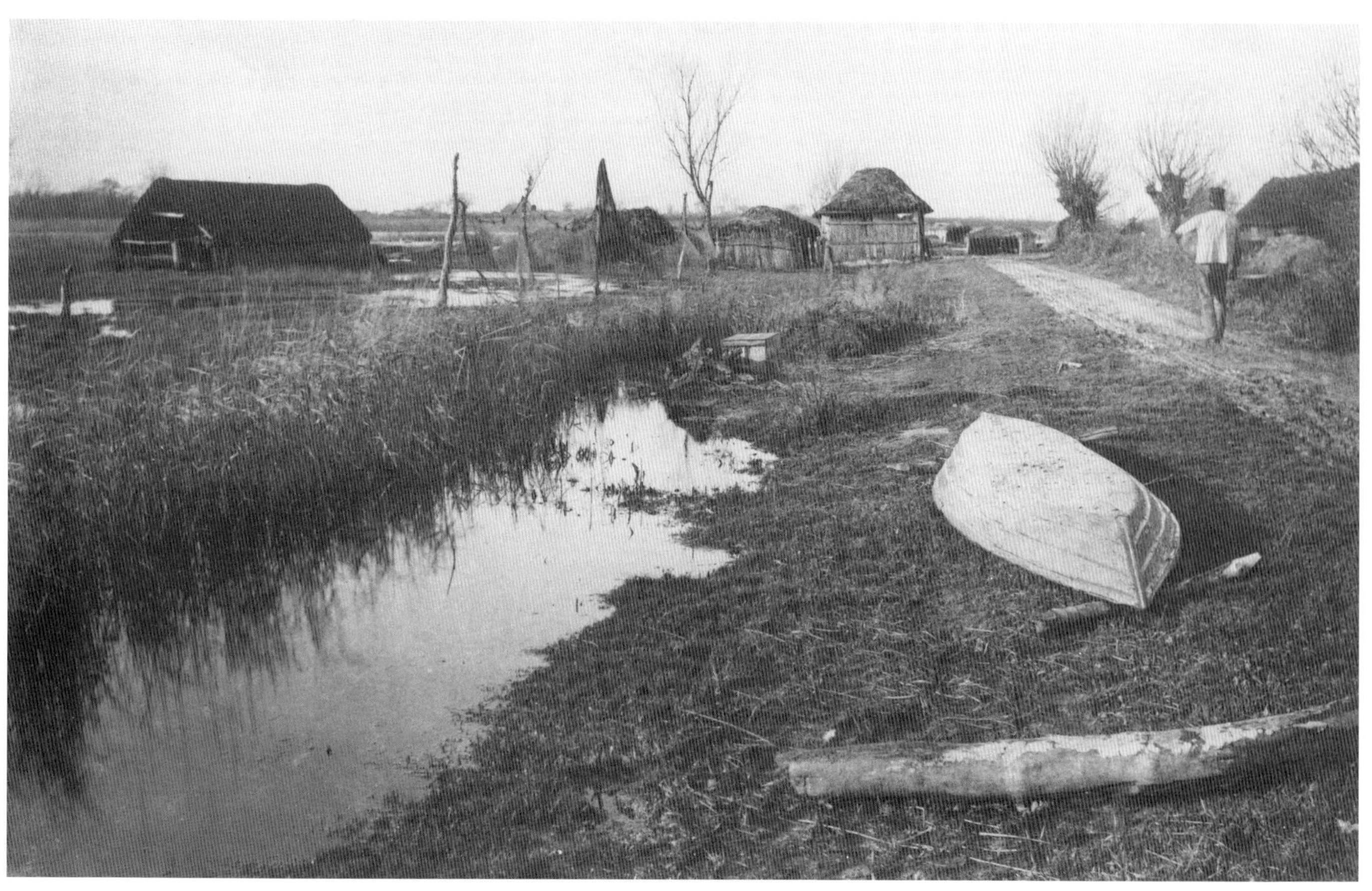

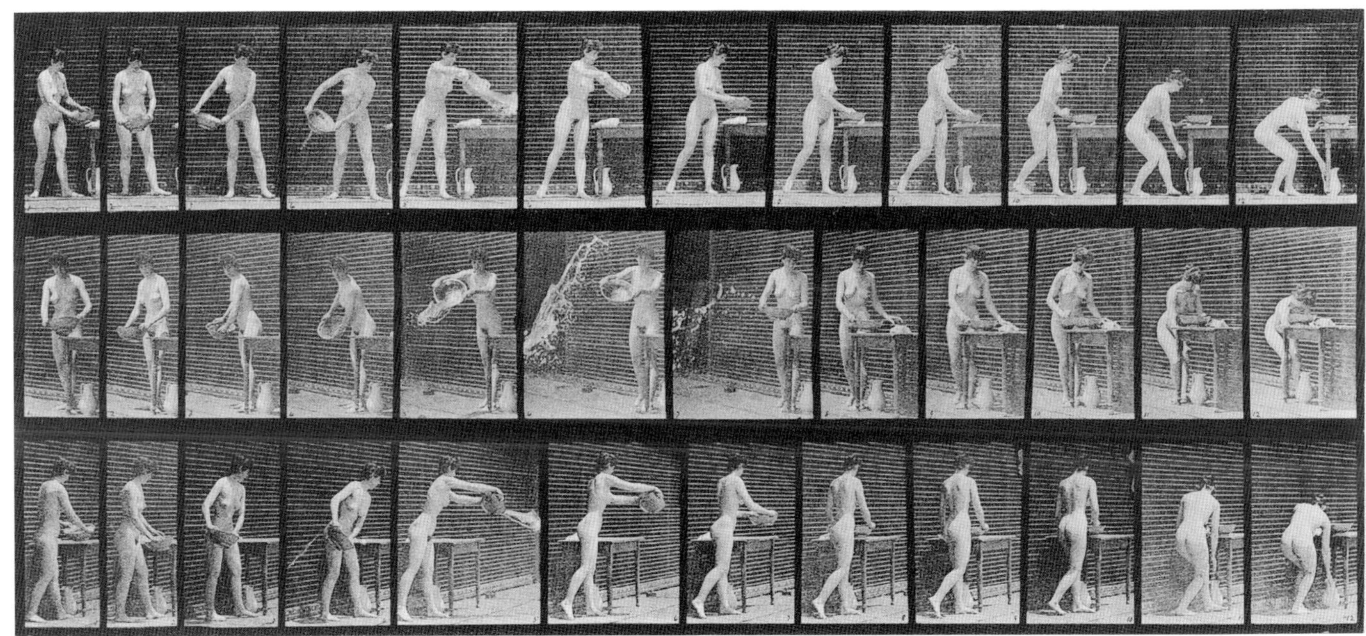

EADWEARD MUYBRIDGE (ENGLISH, 1830 – 1904)
ANIMAL LOCOMOTION (WOMAN AT WASH STAND), 1887

collotype, 18 3/4 x 23 1/2" (47.6 x 59.7 cm.)
Collection Herbert F. Johnson Museum of Art
Cornell University, Ithaca, New York
Gift of Diann and Thomas Mann, 96.038.003
CAT. NO. 72

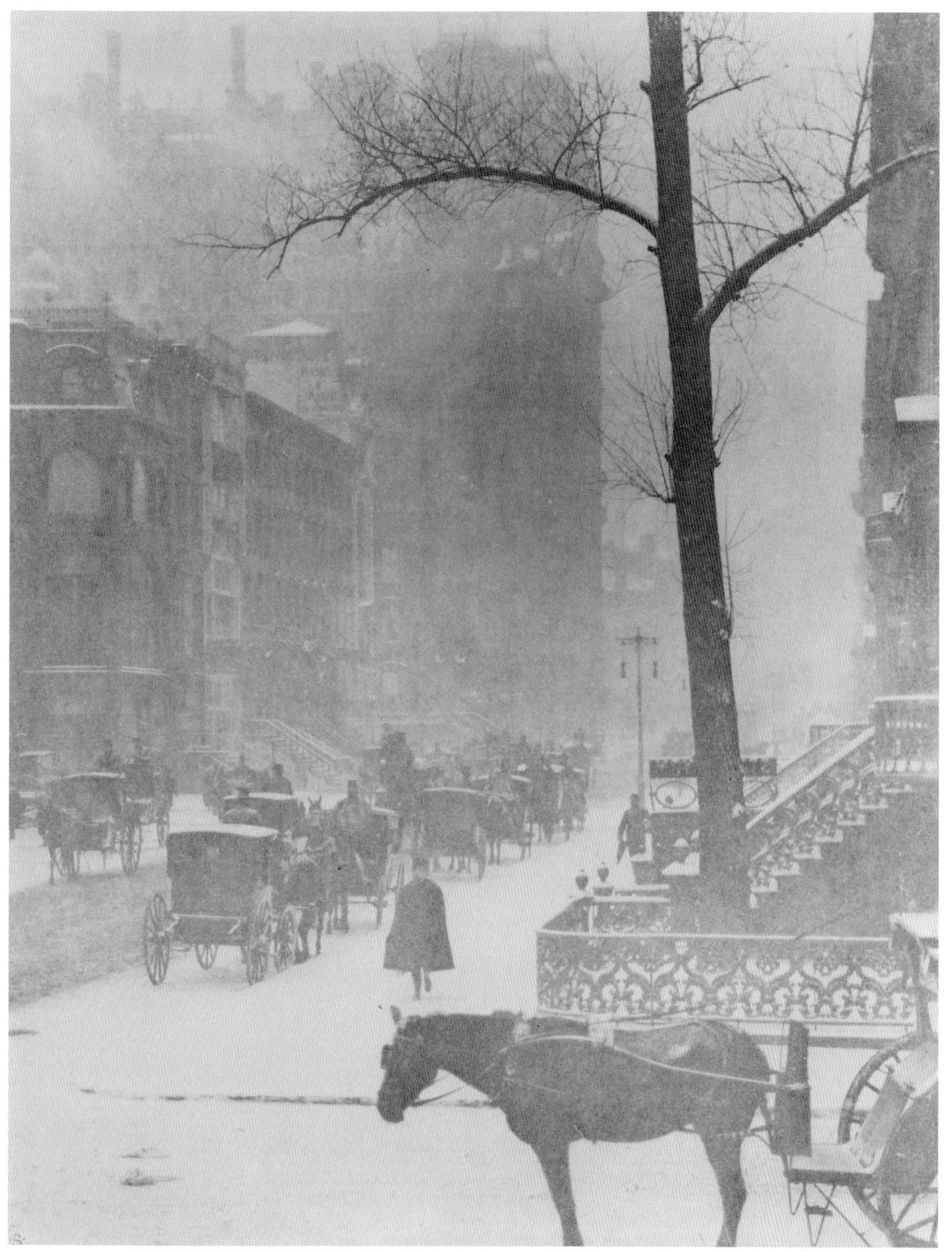

ALFRED STIEGLITZ (AMERICAN, 1864 – 1946)
THE STREET, FIFTH AVENUE, 1896

gravure, 12 x 9" (30.5 x 22.9 cm.)
Collection Albright-Knox Art Gallery, Buffalo, New York
General Purchase Fund, 1911
CAT. NO. 34

GERTRUDE KÄSEBIER (AMERICAN, 1852 – 1934)
THE MANGER, 1899 [PRINTED 1910]

platinum print on Japan tissue, 15 1/2 x 9 1/2" (39.4 x 24.2 cm.)
Collection Albright-Knox Art Gallery, Buffalo, New York
General Purchase Fund, 1911
CAT. NO. 32

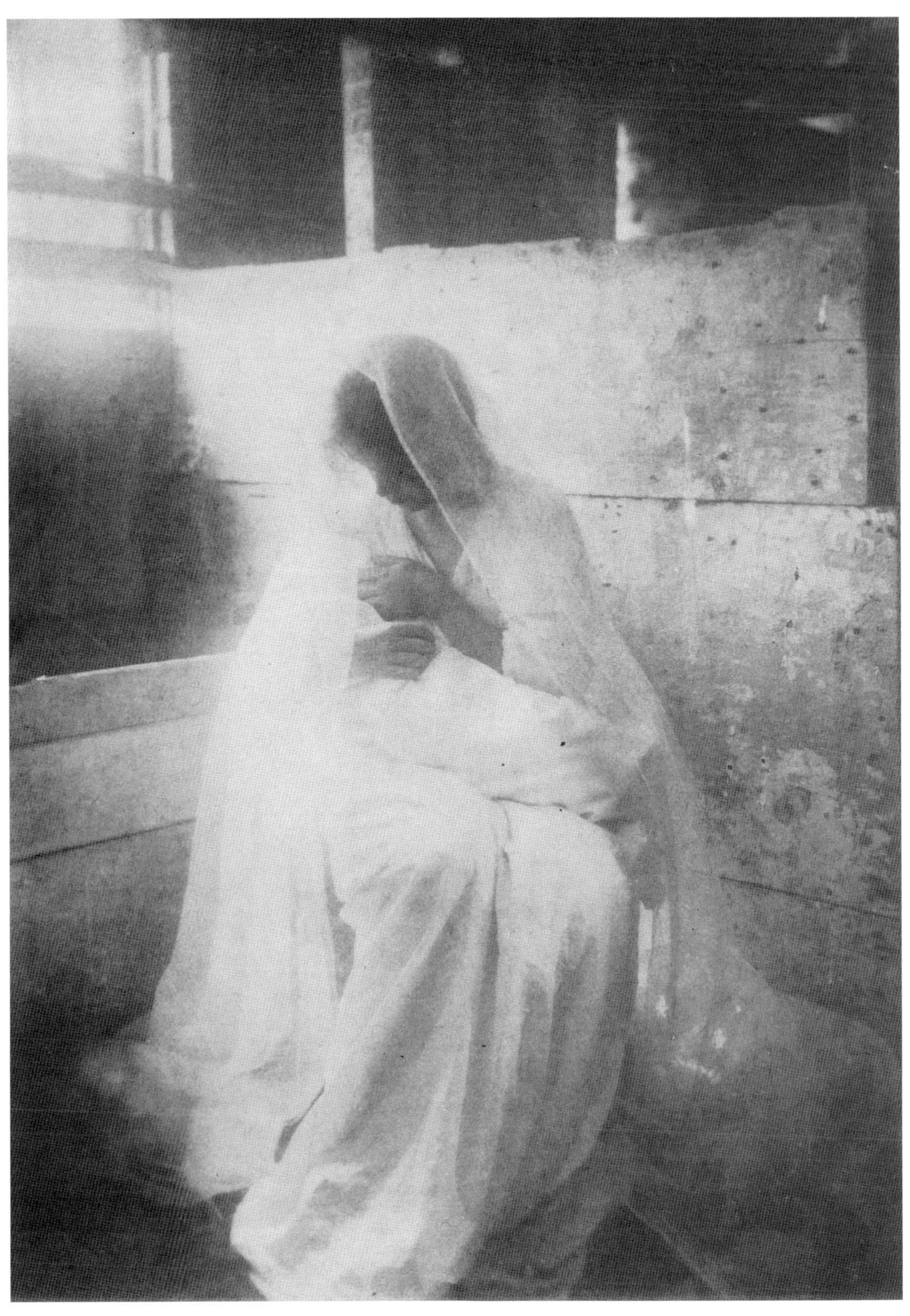

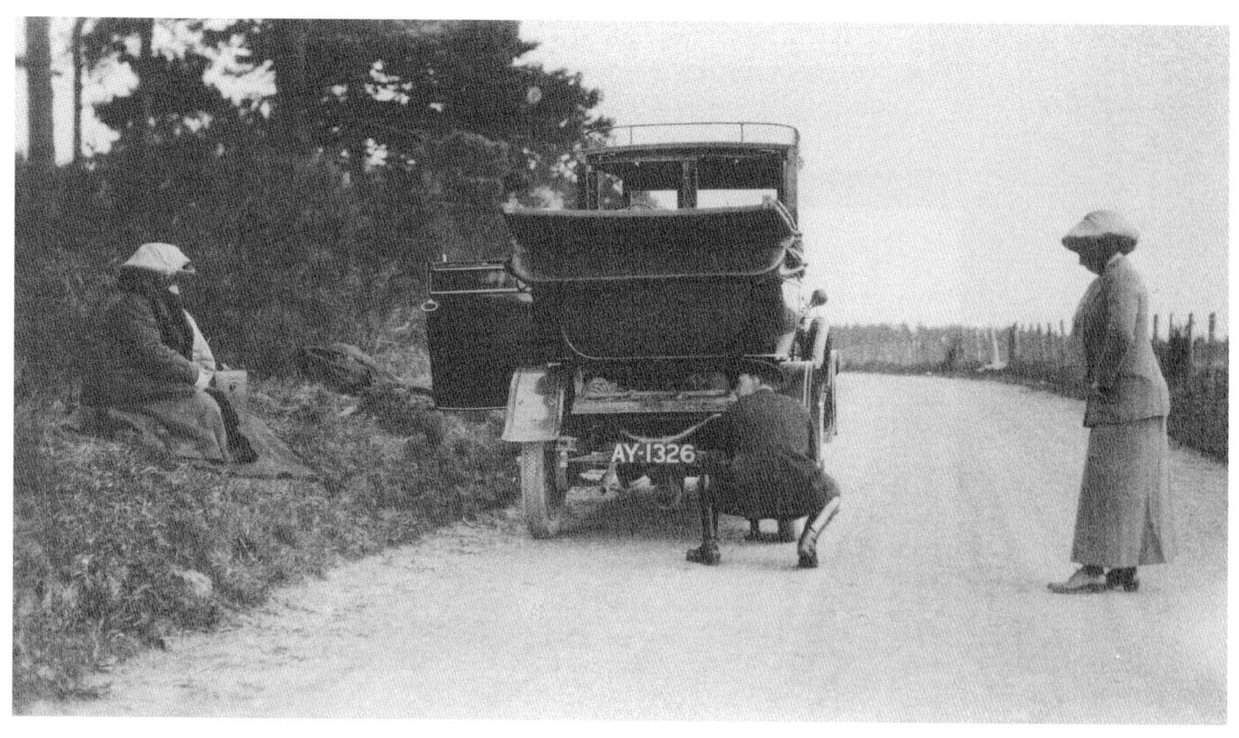

LESLIE HAMILTON WILSON (SCOTTISH, 1883 – 1968)
CHANGING A TIRE, FROM "SCENES FROM EDWARDIAN LIFE," 1899-1903

platinum print, 4 3/4 x 7 1/2" (12.1 x 19.1 cm.)
Collection Herbert F. Johnson Museum of Art
Cornell University, Ithaca, New York
Gift of Mr. and Mrs. Clark Worswick, 86.139.004.004
CAT. NO. 73

CLARENCE HERBERT WHITE (AMERICAN, 1871 – 1925)
THE CHIFFONIER, 1904

platinum print, 9 1/2 x 7 1/2" (24.1 x 19.1 cm.)
Collection Albright-Knox Art Gallery, Buffalo, New York
General Purchase Fund, 1911
CAT. NO. 36

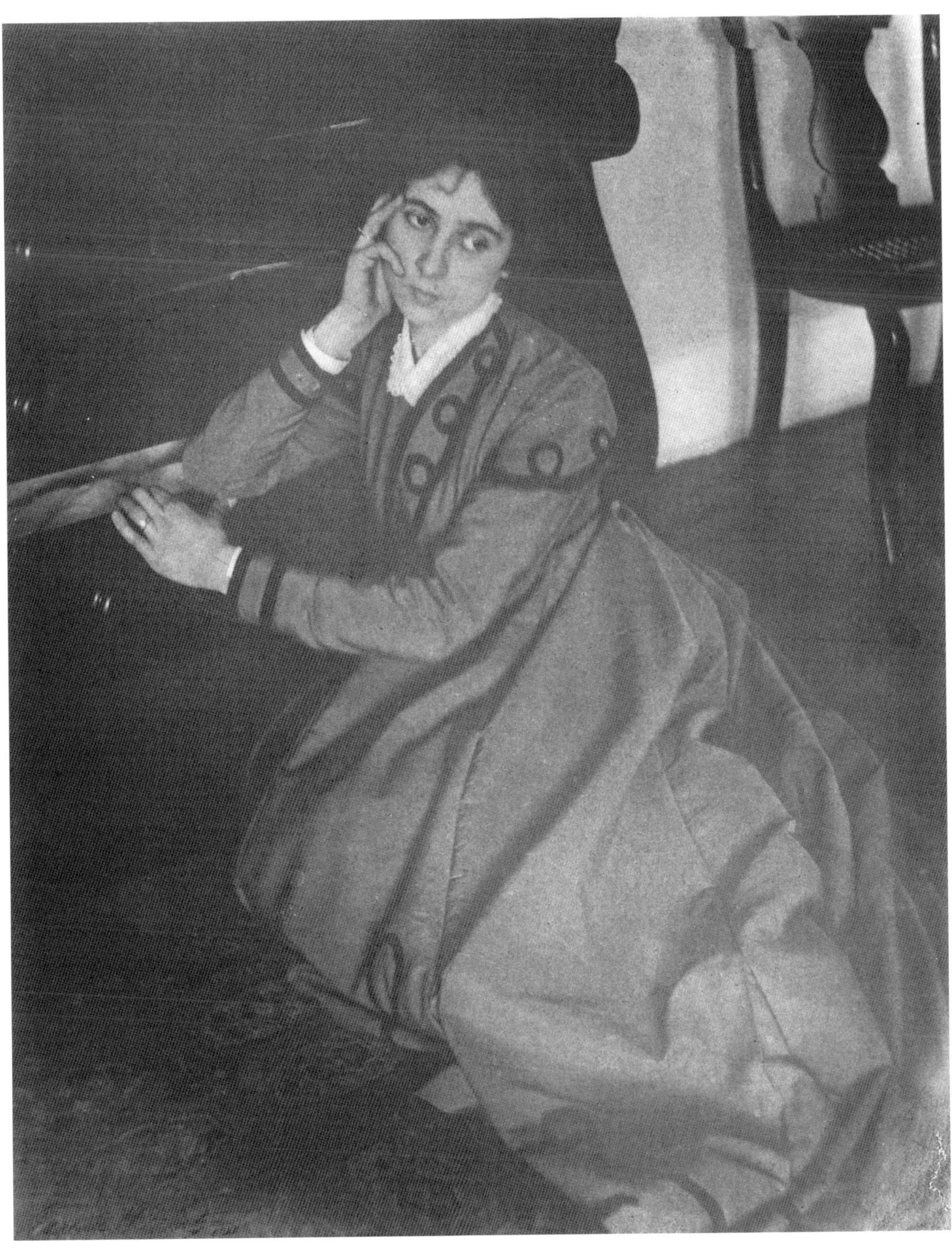

BARON ADOLF DE MEYER (GERMAN, 1868 – 1946)
STILL-LIFE (LILIES IN A GLASS BOWL), 1906

platinum print, 10 1/2 x 14" (26.7 x 35.6 cm.)
Collection Herbert F. Johnson Museum of Art
Cornell University, Ithaca, New York
Bequest of William P. Chapman, Jr., Class of 1895, 62.3315
CAT. NO. 71

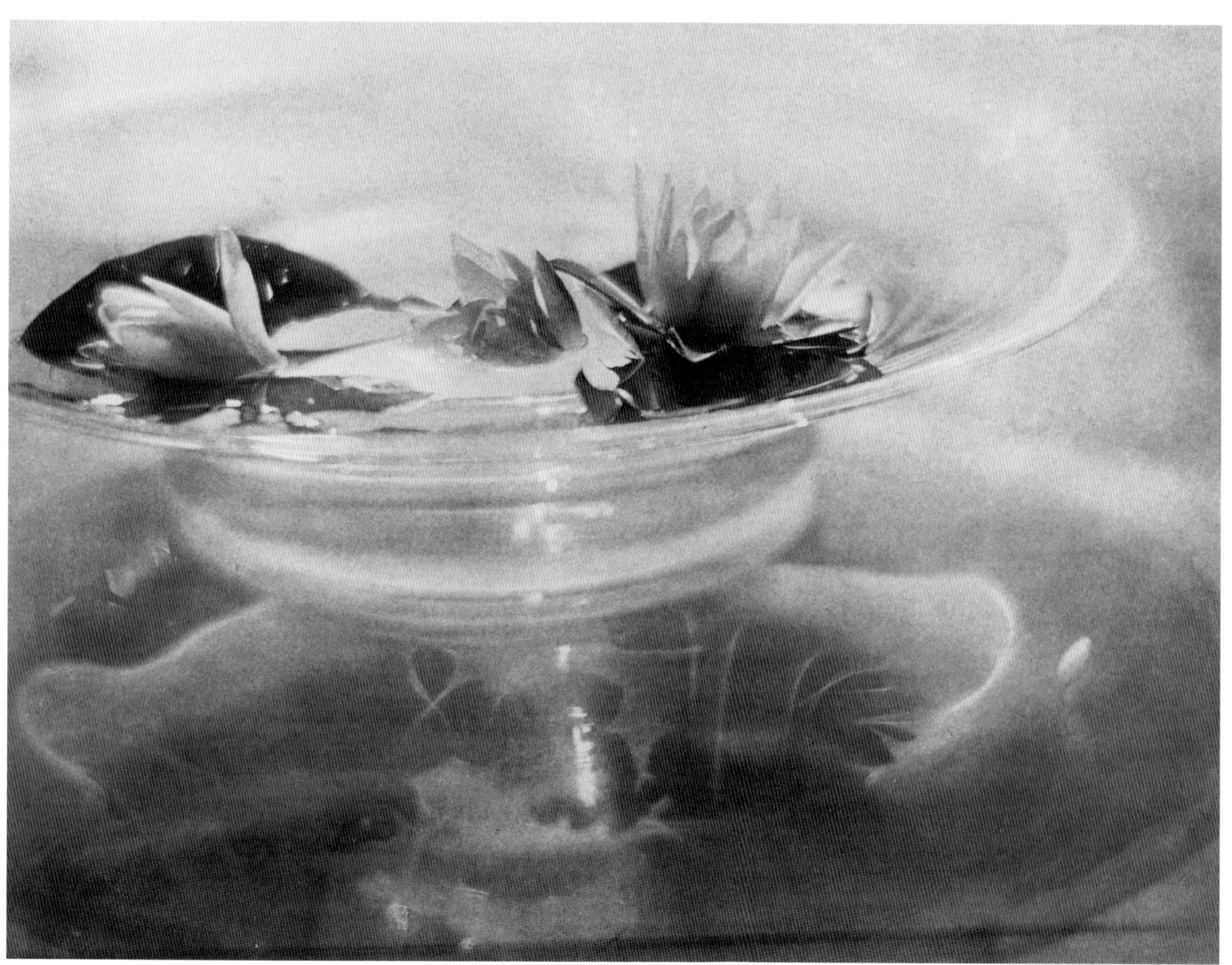

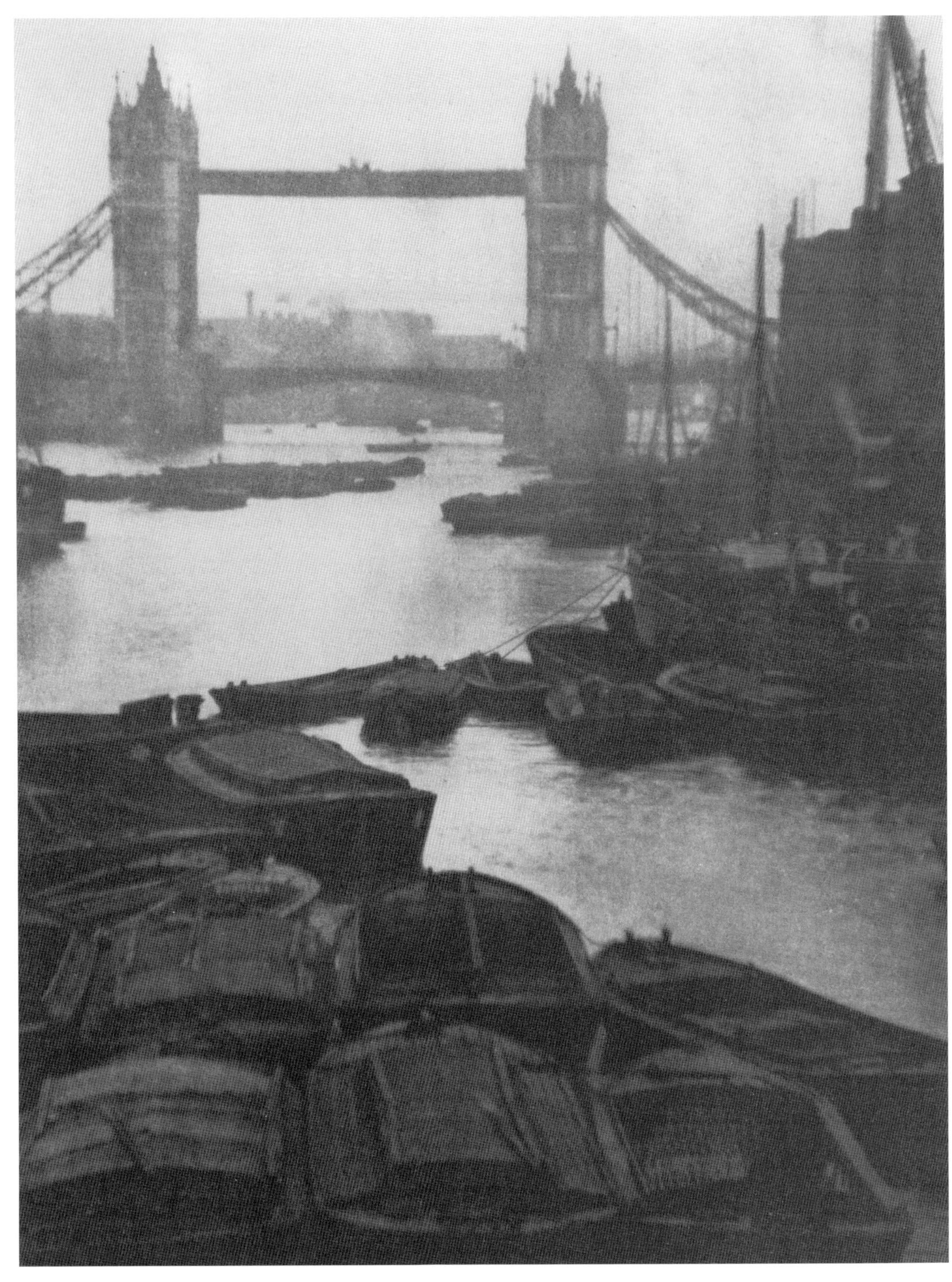

ALVIN LANGDON COBURN (AMERICAN, BORN ENGLAND, 1882 – 1966)
TOWER BRIDGE, LONDON, 1909

hand-pulled photogravure, 8 5/16 x 6 1/2 " (21.1 x 16.5 cm.)
Collection Herbert F. Johnson Museum of Art
Cornell University, Ithaca, New York
Gift of Jonathan Stein, Class of 1966, 82.098.011
CAT. NO. 67

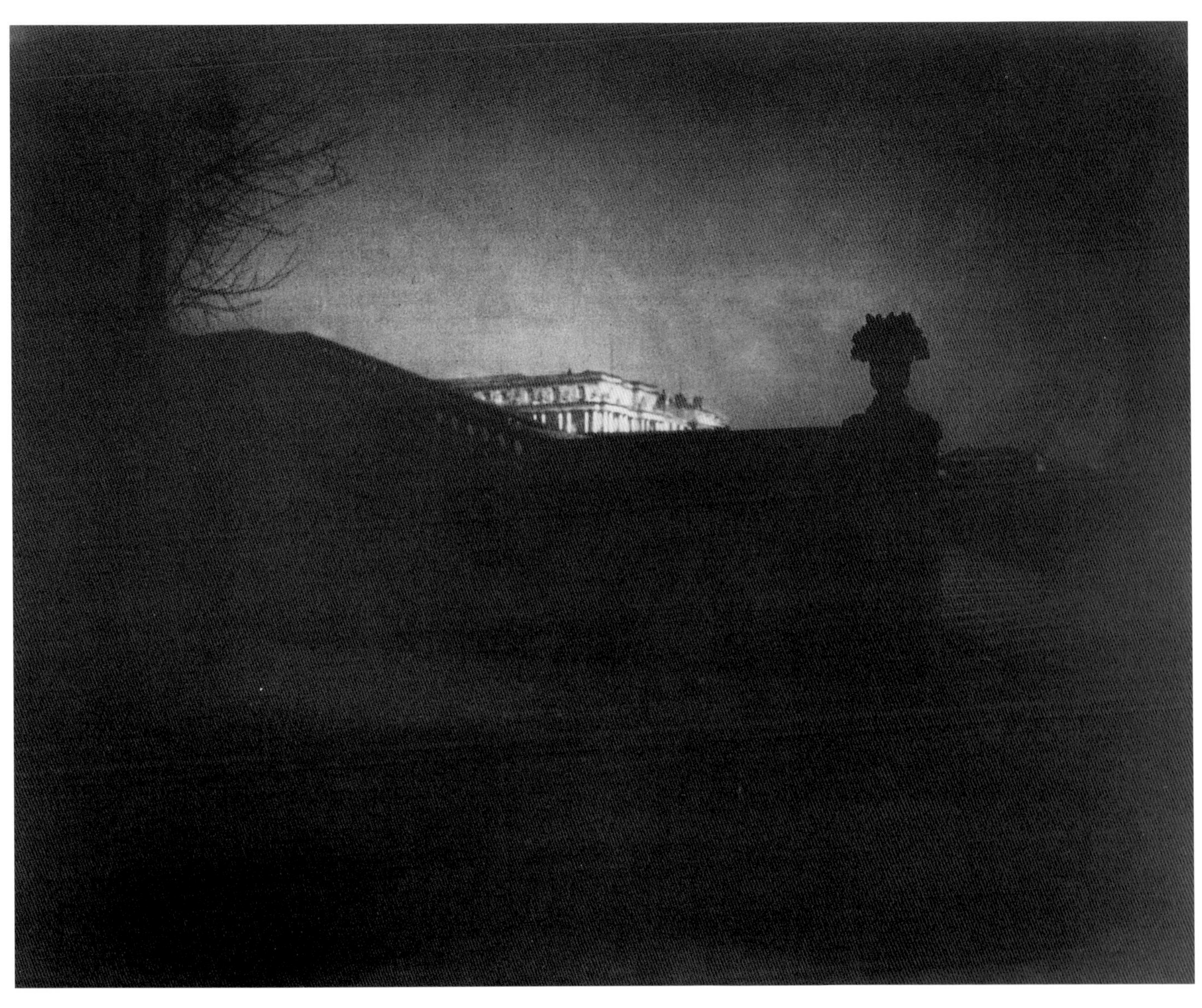

EDWARD J. STEICHEN (AMERICAN, 1879 – 1973)
NOCTURNE-ORANGERIE STAIRCASE, VERSAILLES, CA. 1910

pigment print, 12 1/2 x 15 3/4" (31.8 x 40 cm.)
Collection Albright-Knox Art Gallery, Buffalo, New York
General Purchase Fund, 1911
CAT. NO. 33

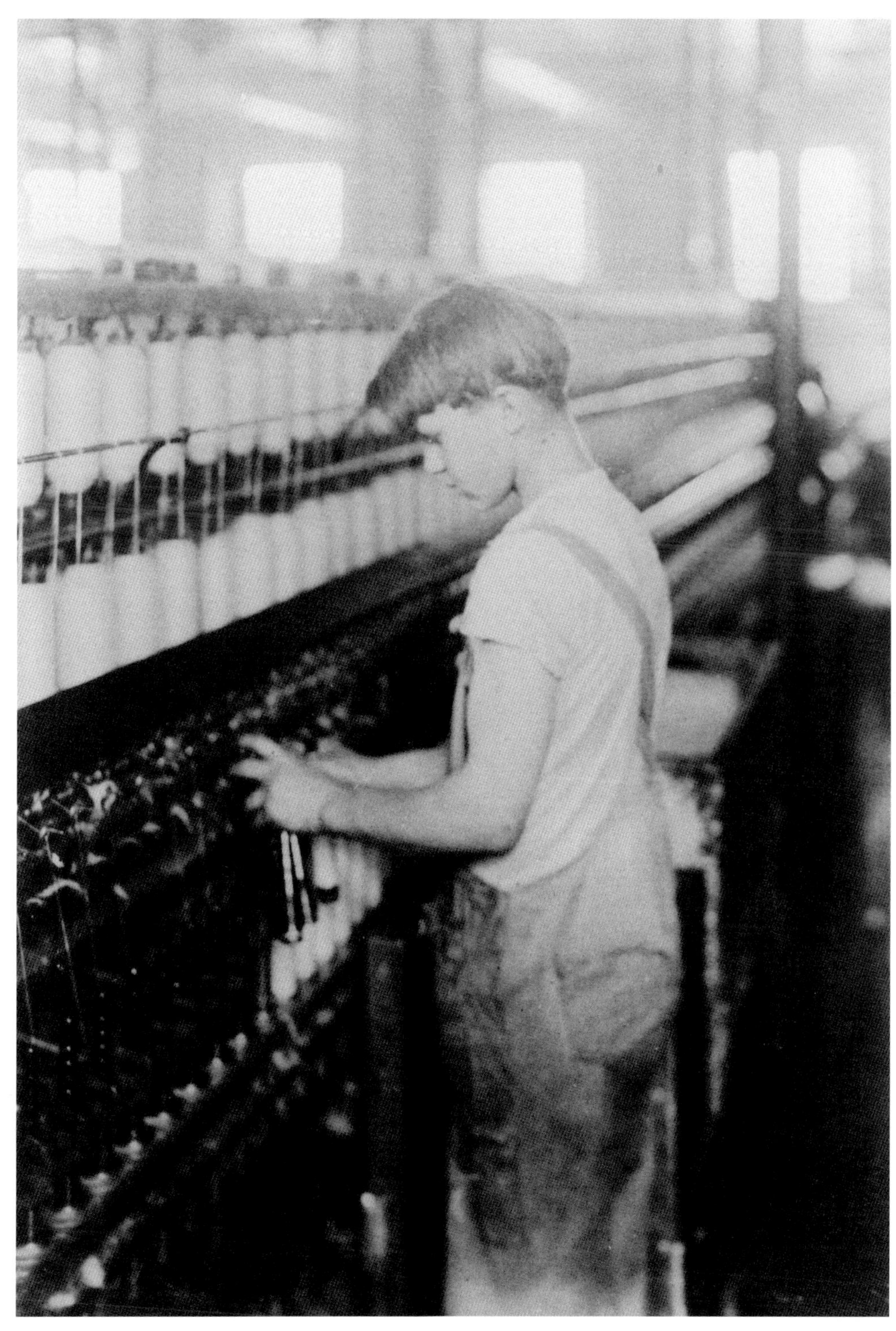

LEWIS W. HINE (AMERICAN, 1874 – 1940)
DOFFER—FALL RIVER, MASSACHUSETTS, 1916

gelatin silver print, 7 x 5" (17.8 x 12.7 cm.)
Collection Herbert F. Johnson Museum of Art
Cornell University, Ithaca, New York
Gift of Jonathan Stein, Class of 1966, 82.098.016
CAT. NO. 70

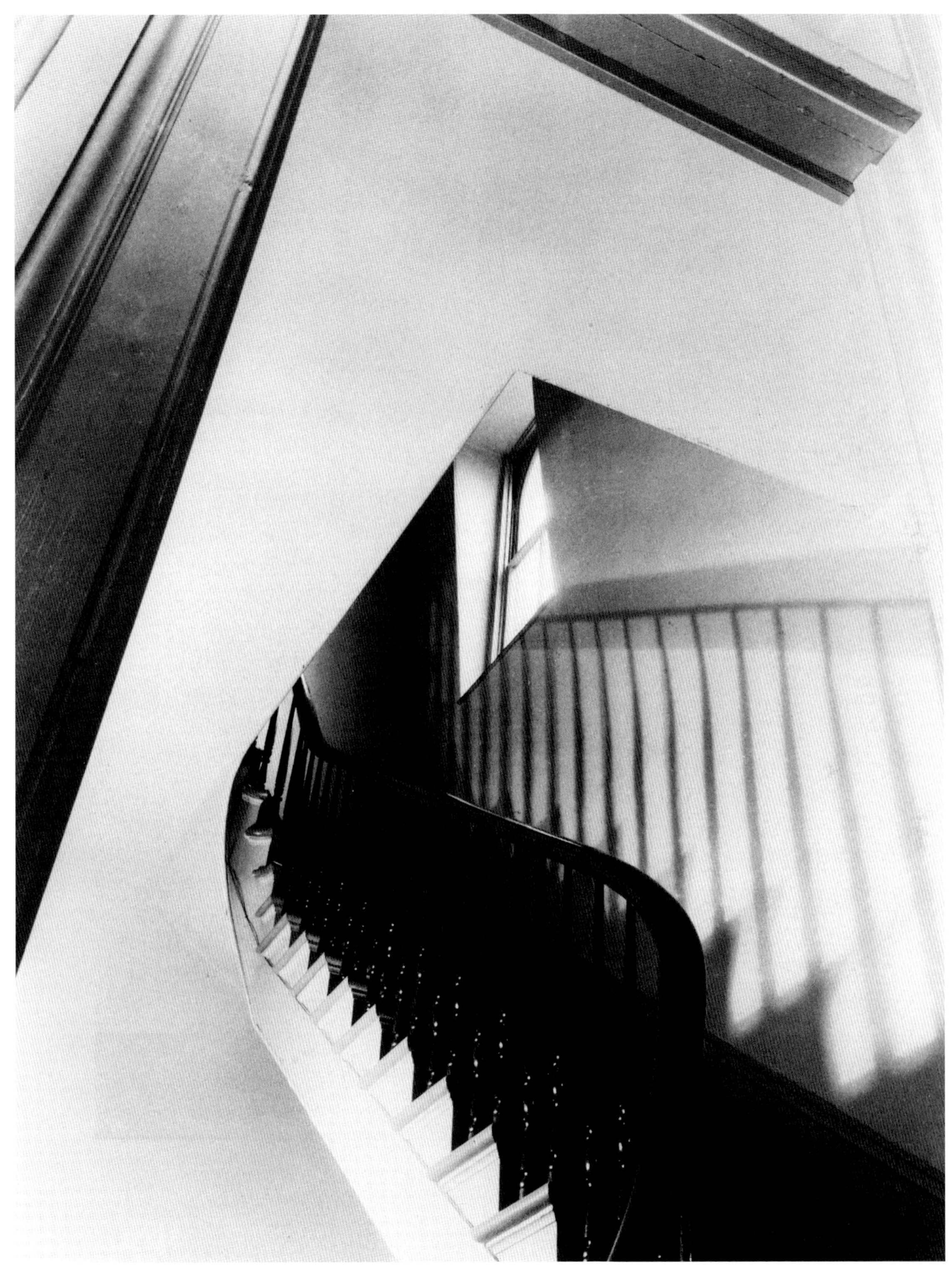

IMOGEN CUNNINGHAM (AMERICAN, 1883 – 1976)
STAIRWAY, MILLS COLLEGE, 1920

gelatin silver print, 11 x 8 3/4" (27.9 x 22.2 cm.)
Collection Herbert F. Johnson Museum of Art
Cornell University, Ithaca, New York
Friends of the Museum Purchase Fund, 75.015.003
CAT. NO. 68

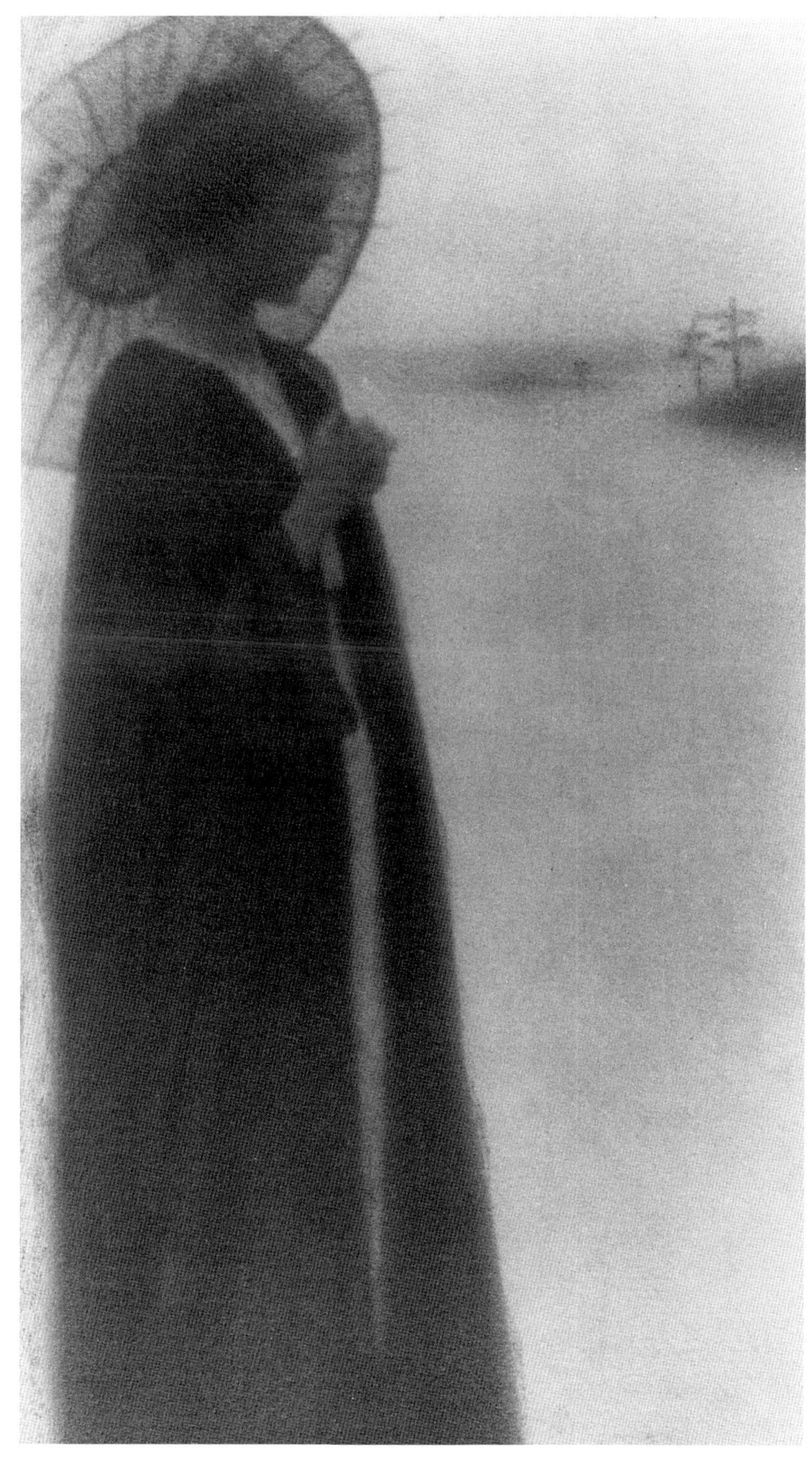

AUGUSTUS THIBAUDEAU (AMERICAN, 1866 – 1939)
WOMAN WITH PARASOL, N.D.

platinum print, 13 15/16 x 7 9/16" (35.4 x 19.2 cm.)
Collection Albright-Knox Art Gallery, Buffalo, New York
Gift of Marie Thibaudeau, 1979
CAT. NO. 35

140

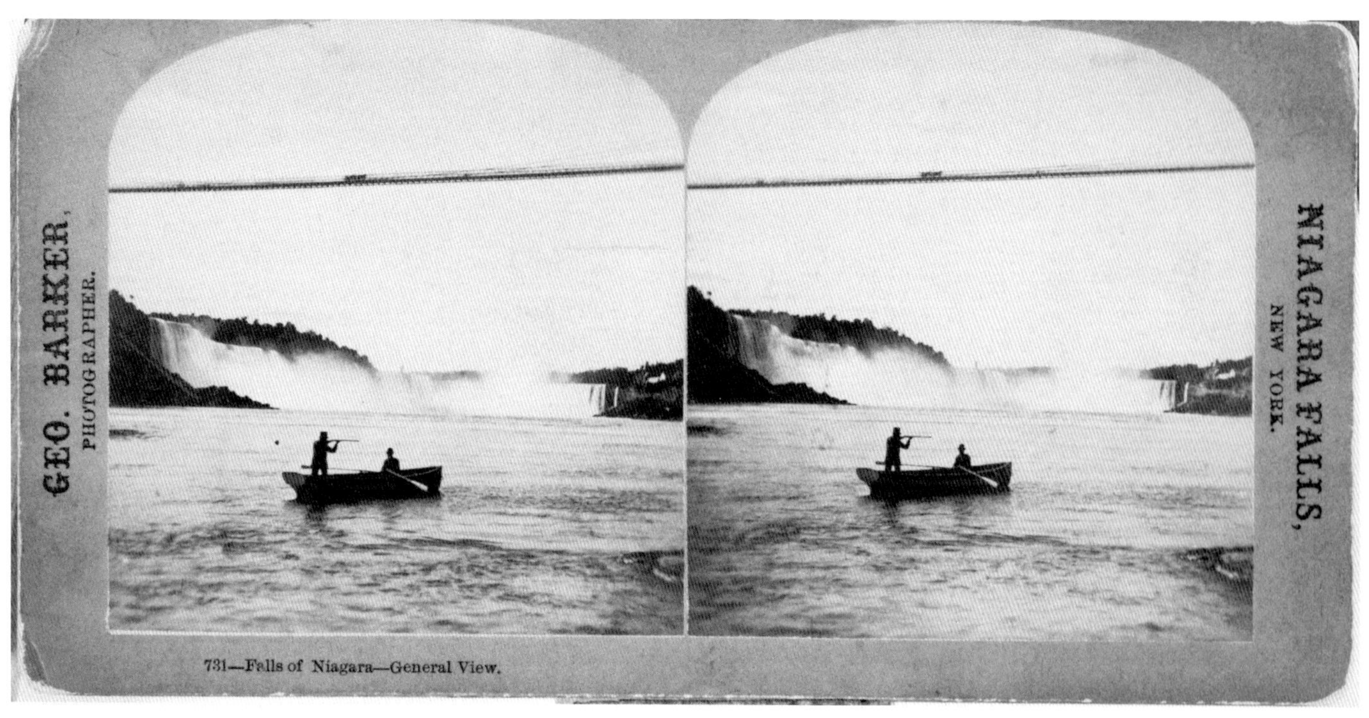

GEORGE BARKER (AMERICAN, 19TH CENTURY)
FALLS OF NIAGARA – GENERAL VIEW, NIAGARA FALLS, NY, N.D.

stereocard, 3 3/4 x 7" (9.5 x 17.8 cm.)
Collection Herbert F. Johnson Museum of Art
Cornell University, Ithaca, New York
Gift of Margaret and Frank Robinson, 96.045.011
CAT. NO. 66

WORKS IN THE EXHIBITION

Works are arranged by museum collection and then alphabetically by artist's last name within each medium. Dimensions are listed with height preceding width and depth.

ALBANY INSTITUTE OF HISTORY AND ART
Painting

1 **Will Hicok Low** (American, 1853 – 1932)
The Terrace Walls, 1901
oil on canvas, 19 1/2 x 25 7/8" (49.5 x 65.7 cm.)
Collection Albany Institute of History and Art, New York
Gift of John Townsend Lansing, 1908

2 **Walter Launt Palmer** (American, 1854 – 1932)
Autumn Morning, Mist Clearing Away, 1892
oil on canvas, 38 1/4 x 52 1/4" (97.2 x 132.7 cm.)
Collection Albany Institute of History and Art, New York
Gift of the Estate of Dr. Leonard G. Stanley, 1959

3 **Walter Launt Palmer** (American, 1854 – 1932)
Dwarf Sunflower, 1875-81
oil on wood panel, 9 x 9" (22.9 x 22.9 cm.)
painted border by Will H. Low, 1875, 13 1/8 x 13" (33.3 x 33 cm.)
Collection Albany Institute of History and Art, New York
Gift of Miss Louise A. Benson and William W. Benson, 1942

Sculpture

4 **Alice Morgan Wright** (American, 1881 – 1975)
Trojan Women, 1927
bronze, 23 x 12 x 22" (58.4 x 30.5 x 55.9 cm.)
Collection Albany Institute of History and Art, New York
Gift of Mrs. Clark Fleming, 1978

ALBRIGHT-KNOX ART GALLERY, BUFFALO
Painting

5 **Paul Cézanne** (French, 1839 – 1906)
Morning in Provence, ca. 1900-06
oil on canvas, 32 x 24 7/8" (81.3 x 63.2 cm.)
Collection Albright-Knox Art Gallery, Buffalo, New York
Gift of Mr. and Mrs. Charles A. Ribbel through the
Frank E. Ribbel Bequest, 1936
Traveling to Buffalo, Ithaca, Albany, Syracuse, and Rochester

6 **Thomas Couture** (French, 1815 – 1879)
Head of a Woman, 1876
oil on canvas, 18 x 15" (45.7 x 38.1 cm.)
Collection Albright-Knox Art Gallery, Buffalo, New York
Elisabeth H. Gates Fund, 1930

7 **Robert Delaunay** (French, 1885 – 1941)
Sun, Tower, Airplane, 1913
oil on canvas, 52 x 51 5/8" (132.1 x 131.1 cm.)
Collection Albright-Knox Art Gallery, Buffalo, New York
A. Conger Goodyear Fund, 1964

8 **André Derain** (French, 1880 – 1954)
The Trees, ca. 1906
oil on canvas, 23 3/8 x 28 1/2" (59.4 x 72.4 cm.)
Collection Albright-Knox Art Gallery, Buffalo, New York
Gift of Seymour H. Knox, Jr. in memory of Helen Northrup Knox, 1971

9 **Edward Dufner** (American, 1872 – 1957)
In the Studio, 1899
oil on canvas, 28 1/2 x 20" (72.4 x 50.8 cm.)
Collection Albright-Knox Art Gallery, Buffalo, New York
Sherman S. Jewett Fund, 1901

10 **Thomas Eakins** (American, 1844 – 1916)
Music, 1904
oil on canvas, 39 3/4 x 49 3/4" (101 x 126.4 cm.)
Collection Albright-Knox Art Gallery, Buffalo, New York
George Cary, Edmund Hayes, and James G. Forsyth Funds, 1955

11 **Roger de la Fresnaye** (French, 1885 – 1925)
Still Life with Three Handles, ca. 1912
oil on canvas, 18 x 24" (45.7 x 61 cm.)
Collection Albright-Knox Art Gallery, Buffalo, New York
Gift of A. Conger Goodyear, 1943

12 **Jean-Léon Gérôme** (French, 1824 – 1904)
Lion in the Desert, ca. 1885
oil on canvas, 27 x 36 3/8" (68.6 x 92.4 cm.)
Collection Albright-Knox Art Gallery, Buffalo, New York
Gift of Patricia Parkinson Neff and Grace de Cernea Reiniger
in memory of their mother, 1972

13 **Marsden Hartley** (American, 1877 – 1943)
Painting No. 46, 1914–15
oil on canvas, 39 1/4 x 32" (99.7 x 81.3 cm.)
Collection Albright-Knox Art Gallery, Buffalo, New York
Philip Kirwen Fund, 1956

14 **Daniel Ridgway Knight** (American, 1839 – 1924)
Springtime, ca. 1890
oil on canvas, 67 1/2 x 50" (171.5 x 127 cm.)
Collection Albright-Knox Art Gallery, Buffalo, New York
Gift of Mrs. Clara A. H. H. Smith in memory of her brother,
Frank Wayland Higgins, 1935

15 **Fernand Léger** (French, 1881 – 1955)
Smoke, 1912
oil on canvas, 36 1/4 x 28 3/4" (92.1 x 73 cm.)
Collection Albright-Knox Art Gallery, Buffalo, New York
Room of Contemporary Art Fund, 1940

16 **Gari Melchers** (American, 1860 – 1932)
The Wedding, ca. 1892
oil on canvas, 43 x 26" (109.2 x 66 cm.)
Collection Albright-Knox Art Gallery, Buffalo, New York
Charles W. Goodyear Fund, 1922

17 **Berthe Morisot** (French, 1841 – 1895)
Woman Sewing, ca. 1879
oil on canvas, 25 3/4 x 21 1/2" (65.4 x 54.6 cm.)
Collection Albright-Knox Art Gallery, Buffalo, New York
Fellows for Life Fund, 1926

18 **Georgia O'Keeffe** (American, 1887 – 1986)
Black Spot No. 3, 1919
oil on canvas, 24 x 16" (61 x 40.6 cm.)
Collection Albright-Knox Art Gallery, Buffalo, New York
George B. and Jenny R. Mathews and Charles Clifton Funds, 1973
Buffalo only

19 **Francis Picabia** (French, 1879 – 1953)
Figure Triste, 1912
oil on canvas, 46 1/2 x 47" (118.1 x 119.4 cm.)
Collection Albright-Knox Art Gallery, Buffalo, New York
Gift of The Seymour H. Knox Foundation, Inc., 1968

20 **Camille Pissarro** (French, born Virgin Islands, 1830 – 1903)
Peasants in the Fields, Eragny, 1890
oil on canvas, 25 3/8 x 31 5/8" (64.5 x 80.3 cm.)
Collection Albright-Knox Art Gallery, Buffalo, New York
Gift of A. Conger Goodyear, 1940

21 **Man Ray** (American, 1890 – 1976)
Symphony Orchestra, 1916
oil on canvas, 52 x 36" (132.1 x 91.4 cm.)
Collection Albright-Knox Art Gallery, Buffalo, New York
George B. and Jenny R. Mathews Fund, 1970

22 **Albert Pinkham Ryder** (American, 1847 – 1917)
The Temple of the Mind, ca. 1885
oil on wood, 17 3/4 x 16" (45.1 x 40.6 cm.)
Collection Albright-Knox Art Gallery, Buffalo, New York
Gift of R. B. Angus, 1918
Buffalo only

23 **John Singer Sargent** (American, 1856 – 1925)
Venetian Bead Stringers, 1880 or 1882
oil on canvas, 26 3/8 x 30 3/4" (67 x 78.1 cm.)
Collection Albright-Knox Art Gallery, Buffalo, New York
Friends of the Albright Art Gallery Fund, 1916

24 **Everett Shinn** (American, 1873 – 1953)
Theater Box, 1906
oil on canvas, 16 1/8 x 20 1/8" (41 x 51.1 cm.)
Collection Albright-Knox Art Gallery, Buffalo, New York
Gift of T. Edward Hanley, 1937

25 **Henri de Toulouse-Lautrec** (French, 1864 – 1901)
Woman Lifting Her Chemise, 1901
oil on wood panel, 22 x 16 5/8" (55.9 x 42.2 cm.)
Collection Albright-Knox Art Gallery, Buffalo, New York
Gift of A. Conger Goodyear, 1956

26 **Abraham Walkowitz** (American, born Russia, 1878 – 1965)
Improvisation of New York City, ca. 1916
oil on canvas, 44 x 33" (111.7 x 83.8 cm.)
Collection Albright-Knox Art Gallery, Buffalo, New York
George B. and Jenny R. Mathews,
Elisabeth H. Gates, and Edmund Hayes Funds, 1979

27 **Max Weber** (American, born Russia, 1881 – 1961)
Figure Study, 1911
oil on canvas, 24 x 40 1/2" (61 x 102.8 cm.)
Collection Albright-Knox Art Gallery, Buffalo, New York
Charles W. Goodyear Fund, 1959

Sculpture

28 **Henri Matisse** (French, 1869 – 1954)
Reclining Nude I, 1907
bronze, 13 11/16 x 19 3/4 x 11" (34.8 x 50.2 x 27.9 cm.)
Collection Albright-Knox Art Gallery, Buffalo, New York
Room of Contemporary Art Fund, 1945

29 **Constantin Meunier** (Belgian, 1831 – 1905)
The Hammerman, 1885
bronze, 46 1/2 x 21 1/2 x 13" (118.1 x 54.6 x 33 cm.) [including base]
Collection Albright-Knox Art Gallery, Buffalo, New York
Charles W. Goodyear Fund, 1913

30 **Pablo Picasso** (Spanish, 1881 – 1973)
Woman's Head, 1909
bronze, 16 1/4 x 10 3/8 x 10 3/4" (41.3 x 26.4 x 27.3 cm.)
Collection Albright-Knox Art Gallery, Buffalo, New York
Edmund Hayes Fund, 1948

Decorative Arts

31 **Frank Lloyd Wright** (American, 1867 – 1959)
Armchair, 1904
wood with upholstered seat, 32 x 23 x 23" (81.3 x 58.4 x 58.4 cm.)
Collection Albright-Knox Art Gallery, Buffalo, New York
Gift of Mr. Darwin R. Martin, 1968

Photography

32 **Gertrude Käsebier** (American, 1852 – 1934)
The Manger, 1899 [printed 1910]
platinum print on Japan tissue, 15 1/2 x 9 1/2" (39.4 x 24.2 cm.)
Collection Albright-Knox Art Gallery, Buffalo, New York
General Purchase Fund, 1911

33 **Edward J. Steichen** (American, 1879 – 1973)
Nocturne-Orangerie Staircase, Versailles, ca. 1910
pigment print, 12 1/2 x 15 3/4" (31.8 x 40 cm.)
Collection Albright-Knox Art Gallery, Buffalo, New York
General Purchase Fund, 1911

34 **Alfred Stieglitz** (American, 1864 – 1946)
The Street, Fifth Avenue, 1896
gravure, 12 x 9" (30.5 x 22.9 cm.)
Collection Albright-Knox Art Gallery, Buffalo, New York
General Purchase Fund, 1911

35 **Augustus Thibaudeau** (American, 1866 – 1939)
Woman with Parasol, n.d.
platinum print, 13 15/16 x 7 9/16" (35.4 x 19.2 cm.)
Collection Albright-Knox Art Gallery, Buffalo, New York
Gift of Marie Thibaudeau, 1979

36 **Clarence Herbert White** (American, 1871 – 1925)
The Chiffonier, 1904
platinum print, 9 1/2 x 7 1/2" (24.1 x 19.1 cm.)
Collection Albright-Knox Art Gallery, Buffalo, New York
General Purchase Fund, 1911

EVERSON MUSEUM OF ART, SYRACUSE
Painting

37 **Gifford Beal** (American, 1879 – 1956)
Freight Yards, 1915
oil on canvas, 35 1/4 x 47 1/2" (89.5 x 120.7 cm.)
Collection Everson Museum of Art, Syracuse, New York
Museum Purchase, Friends of American Art Fund, 1915

38 **Julian Alden Weir** (American, 1852 – 1919)
Portrait of a Woman, 1910
oil on canvas, 39 5/8 x 32 1/4" (100.6 x 81.9 cm.)
Collection Everson Museum of Art, Syracuse, New York
Museum Purchase, Friends of American Art Fund, 1913

Decorative Arts

39 **Biloxi Art Pottery,** Mississippi, ca. 1882 – 1910
George E. Ohr (American, 1857 – 1919)
Untitled (Twisted Vase), n. d.
earthenware, 6 3/4 high x 3 1/4" diam. (17.1 x 8.3 cm.)
Collection Everson Museum of Art, Syracuse, New York
Museum Purchase, 1976

40 **Biloxi Art Pottery,** Mississipi, ca. 1882 – 1910
George E. Ohr (American, 1857 – 1919)
Untitled (Folded Vase), n. d.
earthenware, 3 1/2 high x 3 1/2" diam. (8.9 x 8.9 cm.)
Collection Everson Museum of Art, Syracuse, New York
The Paul and Mary Brandwein Collection, 1992

41 **Buffalo Pottery,** Buffalo, New York, 1901– 1956
Bowl, 1910-12
stoneware, 3 5/8 high x 9 1/8" diam. (9.2 x 23.2 cm.)
Collection Everson Museum of Art, Syracuse, New York
Museum Purchase, 1986

42 **Grueby Pottery,** Boston, Massachusetts, 1897 – 1921
Monumental Vase, ca. 1900
earthenware, 22 high x 9 1/2" diam. (55.8 x 24.1 cm.)
Collection Everson Museum of Art, Syracuse, New York
Museum Purchase, 1982

43 **Adelaide Alsop Robineau,** Syracuse, New York, 1901-1929
(American, 1865 – 1929)
Crab Vase, 1908
porcelain, 7 3/8 high x 2 1/2" diam. (18.7 x 6.4 cm.)
Collection Everson Museum of Art, Syracuse, New York
Museum Purchase, 1916

44 **Adelaide Alsop Robineau,** Syracuse, New York, 1901-1929
(American, 1865 – 1929)
Jar With Cover, 1919
porcelain, 7 1/2 high x 8" diam. (19.1 x 20.3 cm.)
Collection Everson Museum of Art, Syracuse, New York
Gift of Dr. Ethel T. Eltinge, 1982

45 **Rookwood Pottery,** Cincinnati, Ohio, 1880 – 1967
Sara Elizabeth (Sallie) Coyne, decorator
Scenic Vase, 1916
earthenware, 10 3/4 high x 4" diam. (27.3 x 10.2 cm.)
Collection Everson Museum of Art, Syracuse, New York
Museum Purchase in Memory of Edward Beadle with Funds from
Friends, 1984

46 **Rookwood Pottery,** Cincinnati, Ohio, 1880 – 1967
Kataro Shirayamadani, decorator
Vase with Ferns, 1890
earthenware, 10 1/2 high x 9 1/4" diam. (26.7 x 23.5 cm.)
Collection Everson Museum of Art, Syracuse, New York
Museum Purchase, 1977

47 **Tiffany Pottery,** Corona, New York, 1898 – 1920
Vase with Pansies, ca. 1910
stoneware, 10 3/8 high x 4 1/2" diam. (26.4 x 11.4 cm.)
Collection Everson Museum of Art, Syracuse, New York
Gift of Mr. and Mrs. Bronson A. Quackenbush, 1978

48 **Weller Pottery,** Zanesville, Ohio, 1872 – 1949
Jacques Sicard, decorator
Vase, 1901-10
earthenware, 22 high x 10" diam. (55.9 x 25.4 cm.)
Collection Everson Museum of Art, Syracuse, New York
Museum Purchase, the Dorothy and Robert Riester Ceramic
Fund, 1988

49 **Roycroft Shops,** East Aurora, New York, 1895-1938
Tall Back Chair, ca. 1900-10
oak with leather seat and brass studs, 48 x 18 x 18"
(121.9 x 45.7 x 45.7 cm.)
Collection Everson Museum of Art, Syracuse, New York
Museum Purchase, 1982

50 **United Crafts,** Eastwood, New York, 1899-1904
Gustav Stickley (American, 1858 – 1942)
Magazine Rack, ca. 1900
white oak, leather, and brass, 43 1/4 x 14 1/4 x 13 1/2"
(109.9 x 36.2 x 34.3 cm.)
Collection Everson Museum of Art, Syracuse, New York
Museum Purchase with Funds from Mr. and Mrs. Herbert Slotnick, 1983

51 **L. and J.G. Stickley,** Fayetteville, New York, founded 1902
Leopold Stickley (American, 1869-1957)
John George Stickley (American, 1871-1921)
Pedestal, ca. 1910
white oak, 36 x 19 x 19" (91.4 x 48.3 x 48.3 cm.)
Collection Everson Museum of Art, Syracuse, New York
Gift of the Friends of Justin Beauchat in His Memory, 1982

HERBERT F. JOHNSON MUSEUM OF ART, CORNELL UNIVERSITY, ITHACA

Painting

52 **Adolphe William Bouguereau** (French, 1825 – 1905)
Madonna and Child with St. John, 1882
oil on canvas, 75 x 43 5/8" (190.5 x 110.8 cm.)
Collection Herbert F. Johnson Museum of Art
Cornell University, Ithaca, New York
Gift of Louis V. Keeler, Class of 1911, and Mrs. Keeler, 60.082

53 **Jean-Léon Gérôme** (French, 1824 – 1904)
Almeh Performing the Sword Dance, 1875
oil on canvas, 23 1/2 x 32 1/2" (59.7 x 82.6 cm.)
Collection Herbert F. Johnson Museum of Art
Cornell University, Ithaca, New York
Membership Purchase Fund, 73.009

54 **William Glackens** (American, 1870 – 1938)
The Water Slide, n.d.
oil on canvas, 29 1/2 x 24 1/2" (74.9 x 62.2 cm.)
Collection Herbert F. Johnson Museum of Art
Cornell University, Ithaca, New York
On loan from Willard Straight Hall, Cornell University, LOAN 56.071

55 **Frederick Childe Hassam** (American, 1859 – 1935)
Rocks and Sea, Isles of Shoals, 1912
oil on canvas, 23 1/4 x 25" (59.1 x 63.5 cm.)
Collection Herbert F. Johnson Museum of Art
Cornell University, Ithaca, New York
Gift of Lois Birrell Morrill, Hotel School Class of 1949, 84.074

56 **Theodore Robinson** (American, 1852 – 1896)
The Berme Road, 1893
oil on canvas, 18 x 22" (45.7 x 55.9 cm.)
Collection Herbert F. Johnson Museum of Art
Cornell University, Ithaca, New York
Purchased through the generosity of the H. A. Metzger, Class of 1921,
Bequest, 76.065

57 **Henry Ossawa Tanner** (American, 1859 – 1937)
Return of the Fisherman, ca. 1905
oil on canvas, 26 1/4 x 19 3/4" (66.7 x 50.2 cm.)
Collection Herbert F. Johnson Museum of Art
Cornell University, Ithaca, New York
Gift of Mrs. Stephen W. Jacobs, 79.029.001

Sculpture

58 **Auguste Rodin** (French, 1840 – 1917)
Head of Balzac "C", ca. 1897
bronze, 16 1/2 x 11 x 8" (41.9 x 27.9 x 20.3 cm.)
Collection Herbert F. Johnson Museum of Art
Cornell University, Ithaca, New York
Gift of the Cantor, Fitzgerald Art Foundation, 75.034

59 **Augustus Saint-Gaudens** (American, 1848 – 1907)
The Puritan, 1899
bronze, 30 3/4 x 20 x 11 1/2" (78.1 x 50.8 x 29.2 cm.)
Collection Herbert F. Johnson Museum of Art
Cornell University, Ithaca, New York
Museum Acquisition Purchase Fund, 72.083

Decorative Arts

60 **Evelyn Rumsey Cary** (American, 1855 – 1924)
Pan-American Exposition Poster, 1901
color lithograph, 48 1/4 x 25 1/2" (122.6 x 64.8 cm.)
Collection Herbert F. Johnson Museum of Art
Cornell University, Ithaca, New York
Gift of Harry A. Starr, 78.057.021

61 **Quezal Art Glass and Decorating Company,** Brooklyn, New York
Compote, gold interior, white and green lotus leaves, 20th century
glass, 7 3/4 high x 8 1/4" diam. (19.7 x 21 cm.)
Collection Herbert F. Johnson Museum of Art
Cornell University, Ithaca, New York
Edythe de Lorenzi Collection, Bequest of Otto de Lorenzi, 64.0906

62 **Steuben Glass Works,** Corning, New York, 1903-present
Blue Aurene Bulbous Vase, after 1903
glass, 8 high x 7" diam. (20.3 x 17.8 cm.)
Collection Herbert F. Johnson Museum of Art
Cornell University, Ithaca, New York
Edythe de Lorenzi Collection, Bequest of Otto de Lorenzi, 64.0871

63 **Louis Comfort Tiffany** (American, 1848 – 1933)
Blue Bowl with green overtones and coarse crackle, n.d.
glass, 2 3/4 high x 7 1/2" diam. (7 x 19.1 cm.)
Collection Herbert F. Johnson Museum of Art
Cornell University, Ithaca, New York
Edythe de Lorenzi Collection, Bequest of Otto de Lorenzi, 64.0884

64 **Louis Comfort Tiffany** (American, 1848 – 1933)
Gold Iridescent Tulip Vase, n.d.
glass, 15 1/4 high x 5 1/4" diam. (38.7 x 13.3 cm.)
Collection Herbert F. Johnson Museum of Art
Cornell University, Ithaca, New York
Edythe de Lorenzi Collection, Bequest of Otto de Lorenzi, 64.0887

65 **Louis Comfort Tiffany** (American, 1848 – 1933)
Green Millefiore Vase, n.d
glass, 6 1/2 high x 3" diam. (16.5 x 7.6 cm.)
Collection Herbert F. Johnson Museum of Art
Cornell University, Ithaca, New York
Gift of Louis Comfort Tiffany through the courtesy of A. Douglas
Nash, 57.106

Photography

66 **George Barker** (American, 19th century)
Falls of Niagara — General View, Niagara Falls, NY, n.d.
stereocard, 3 3/4 x 7" (9.5 x 17.8 cm.)
Collection Herbert F. Johnson Museum of Art
Cornell University, Ithaca, New York
Gift of Margaret and Frank Robinson, 96.045.011

67 **Alvin Langdon Coburn** (American, born England, 1882 – 1966)
Tower Bridge, London, 1909
hand-pulled photogravure, 8 5/16 x 6 1/2" (21.1 x 16.5 cm.)
Collection Herbert F. Johnson Museum of Art
Cornell University, Ithaca, New York
Gift of Jonathan Stein, Class of 1966, 82.098.011

68 **Imogen Cunningham** (American, 1883 – 1976)
Stairway, Mills College, 1920
gelatin silver print, 11 x 8 3/4" (27.9 x 22.2 cm.)
Collection Herbert F. Johnson Museum of Art
Cornell University, Ithaca, New York
Friends of the Museum Purchase Fund, 75.015.003

69 **Peter Henry Emerson** (British, 1856 – 1936)
Twixt Land and Water, 1886
platinum print, 7 x 11 1/4" (17.8 x 28.6 cm.)
Collection Herbert F. Johnson Museum of Art
Cornell University, Ithaca, New York
Class of 1962 Photography Fund, 80.031.007

70 **Lewis W. Hine** (American, 1874 – 1940)
Doffer–Fall River, Massachusetts, 1916
gelatin silver print, 7 x 5 " (17.8 x 12.7 cm.)
Collection Herbert F. Johnson Museum of Art
Cornell University, Ithaca, New York
Gift of Jonathan Stein, Class of 1966, 82.098.016

71 **Baron Adolf de Meyer** (German, 1868 – 1946)
Still-Life (Lilies in a Glass Bowl), 1906
platinum print, 10 1/2 x 14" (26.7 x 35.6 cm.)
Collection Herbert F. Johnson Museum of Art
Cornell University, Ithaca, New York
Bequest of William P. Chapman, Jr., Class of 1895, 62.3315

72 **Eadweard Muybridge** (English, 1830 – 1904)
Animal Locomotion (woman at wash stand), 1887
collotype, 18 3/4 x 23 1/2" (47.6 x 59.7 cm.)
Collection Herbert F. Johnson Museum of Art
Cornell University, Ithaca, New York
Gift of Diann and Thomas Mann, 96.038.003

73 **Leslie Hamilton Wilson** (Scottish, 1883 – 1968)
Changing a Tire, from "Scenes from Edwardian Life," 1899-1903
platinum print, 4 3/4 x 7 1/2" (12.1 x 19.1 cm.)
Collection Herbert F. Johnson Museum of Art
Cornell University, Ithaca, New York
Gift of Mr. and Mrs. Clark Worswick, 86.139.004.004

MEMORIAL ART GALLERY OF THE UNIVERSITY OF ROCHESTER

Painting

74 **Adolphe William Bouguereau** (French, 1825 – 1905)
Young Priestess, 1902
oil on canvas, 71 1/4 x 32" (181 x 81.3 cm.)
Collection Memorial Art Gallery of the University of Rochester, New York
Gift of Paul T. White in memory of Josephine Kryl White, 73.1

75 **Paul Cézanne** (French, 1839 – 1906)
The Sea at L'Éstaque, 1878-82
oil on canvas, 21 1/4 x 25 5/8" (54 x 65.1 cm.)
Collection Memorial Art Gallery of the University of Rochester, New York
Anonymous gift in tribute to Edward Harris and in memory of
H. R. Stirlin of Switzerland, 69.45
Traveling to Utica, Buffalo, and Rochester

76 **Thomas Wilmer Dewing** (American, 1851 – 1938)
Portrait in a Brown Dress, ca. 1908
oil on wood panel, 20 x 15 1/2" (50.8 x 39.4 cm.)
Collection Memorial Art Gallery of the University of Rochester, New York
Gift of Mr. and Mrs. Alexander Millar Lindsay, III, in memory of
Jesse Williams and Grace Curtice Lindsay and their daughter,
Carolyn Lindsay White, 57.79

77 **George Inness** (American, 1825 – 1894)
Early Moonrise in Florida, 1893
oil on canvas, 24 3/8 x 36 1/4" (61.9 x 92.1 cm.)
Collection Memorial Art Gallery of the University of Rochester, New York
George Eastman Collection of the University of Rochester, 36.61

78   **Ernest Lawson** (American, 1873 – 1939)
The Garden, 1914
oil on canvas, 20 x 24" (50.8 x 61 cm.)
Collection Memorial Art Gallery of the University of Rochester, New York
Gift of the Estate of Emily and James Sibley Watson, 51.36

79   **Willard Leroy Metcalf** (American, 1858 – 1925)
The Golden Carnival, 1910
oil on canvas, 36 x 39" (91.4 x 99.1 cm.)
Collection Memorial Art Gallery of the University of Rochester, New York
Gift of Emily Sibley Watson, 13.7

80   **Pierre-Auguste Renoir** (French, 1841 – 1919)
The Pond at Chaville (Étang de Chaville), 1911
oil on canvas, 18 3/16 x 22" (46.2 x 55.9 cm.)
Collection Memorial Art Gallery of the University of Rochester, New York
Gift of Dr. and Mrs. James H. Lockhart, Jr., 91.87

Sculpture

81   **Frederick William MacMonnies** (American, 1863 – 1937)
Bacchante with Infant Faun, 1894
bronze, 33 3/4 x 11" (85.7 x 27.9 cm.)
Collection Memorial Art Gallery of the University of Rochester, New York
Gift of Lawrence R. Klepper and Michelle P. Klepper;
and General Acquisition Funds, 86.17

Decorative Arts

82   **Roycroft Shops,** East Aurora, New York, 1895-1938
Karl Kipp (American, 1882 – 1954)
Trapezoidal Vase, ca. 1910
copper and German silver, 4 3/8 x 5 1/8 x 5 1/8" (11.1 x 13 x 13 cm.)
Collection Memorial Art Gallery of the University of Rochester, New York
Gift of Emily Sibley Watson, Walter Remington,
Arthur Stern II, and Bertha Buswell Bequest (by exchange), 93.1

83   **Zsolnay Pottery,** Hungary
Vase, 1890s
ceramic, 4 3/8 high x 5 1/8" diam. (11.1 x 13 cm.)
Collection Memorial Art Gallery of the University of Rochester, New York
Gift of the Estate of Eleanor Volpe Krass, 96.27

MUNSON-WILLIAMS-PROCTOR ARTS INSTITUTE, MUSEUM OF ART, UTICA
Painting

84   **William Merritt Chase** (American, 1849 – 1916)
Memories, 1885-86
oil on canvas, 50 1/2 x 37" (128.3 x 94 cm.)
Collection Munson-Williams-Proctor Arts Institute, Museum of Art,
Utica, New York
Museum Purchase, 57.305

85   **Arthur B. Davies** (American, 1862 – 1928)
Jewel-Bearing Tree of Amity, ca. 1912
oil on canvas, 18 1/4 x 40 3/8" (46.4 x 102.6 cm.)
Collection Munson-Williams-Proctor Arts Institute, Museum of Art,
Utica, New York
Museum Purchase, 56.5

86   **Charles Demuth** (American, 1883 – 1935)
Nospmas. M. Egiap Nospmas. M., 1921
oil on canvas, 24 x 20 1/4" (61 x 51.4 cm.)
Collection Munson-Williams-Proctor Arts Institute, Museum of Art,
Utica, New York
Museum Purchase, 68.29

87   **Preston Dickinson** (American, 1891 – 1930)
Fort George Hill, 1915
oil on canvas, 14 x 17" (35.6 x 43.2 cm.)
Collection Munson-Williams-Proctor Arts Institute, Museum of Art,
Utica, New York
Edward W. Root Bequest, 57.132

88   **Robert Henri** (American, 1865 – 1929)
Dutch Soldier, 1907
oil on canvas, 32 5/8 x 26 1/8" (82.9 x 66.4 cm.)
Collection Munson-Williams-Proctor Arts Institute, Museum of Art,
Utica, New York
Museum Purchase, 58.8

89   **George Luks** (American, 1867 – 1933)
Roundhouse at High Bridge, 1909-10
oil on canvas, 30 3/8 x 36 1/4" (77.2 x 92.1 cm.)
Collection Munson-Williams-Proctor Arts Institute, Museum of Art,
Utica, New York
Museum Purchase, 50.17

90   **Maurice B. Prendergast** (American, born Newfoundland, 1858 – 1924)
Landscape with Figures, ca. 1910-12
oil on canvas, 29 3/4 x 42 3/4" (75.6 x 108.6 cm.)
Collection Munson-Williams-Proctor Arts Institute, Museum of Art,
Utica, New York
Edward W. Root Bequest, 57.212

91   **Morgan Russell** (American, 1886 – 1953)
Cosmic Synchromy, 1913-14
oil on canvas, 16 1/4 x 13 1/8" (41.3 x 33.3 cm.)
Collection Munson-Williams-Proctor Arts Institute, Museum of Art,
Utica, New York
Museum Purchase, 57.26

92   **John Sloan** (American, 1871 – 1951)
Scrubwomen, Astor Library, ca. 1910-11
oil on canvas, 32 x 26" (81.3 x 66 cm.)
Collection Munson-Williams-Proctor Arts Institute, Museum of Art,
Utica, New York
Museum Purchase, 58.87

93   **John H. Twachtman** (American, 1853 – 1902)
Landscape, 1882
oil on canvas, 35 x 46" (88.9 x 116.8 cm.)
Collection Munson-Williams-Proctor Arts Institute, Museum of Art,
Utica, New York
Museum Purchase, 58.9

94   **James Abbott McNeill Whistler** (American, 1834 – 1903)
The Sea, Pourville, No. 2, ca. 1899
oil on wood, 5 3/8 x 9 3/16" (13.7 x 23.3 cm.)
Collection Munson-Williams-Proctor Arts Institute, Museum of Art,
Utica, New York
Museum Purchase with Funds from the Charles E. Merrill Trust,
73.114

Decorative Arts

95   **White's Pottery,** Utica, New York, 1838 – 1907
Mug with Pan-American Exposition decoration, 1901
stoneware, 4 high x 3 1/4" diam. (10.2 x 8.3 cm.)
Collection Munson-Williams-Proctor Arts Institute, Museum of Art,
Utica, New York
Museum Purchase, 71.59

Groft, Tammis K. and Mary Alice MacKay, eds. *Albany Institute of History & Art: 200 years of collecting.*
New York: Hudson Hills Press in association with Albany Institute of History & Art, 1998.

Herbert F. Johnson Museum of Art, Cornell University. *Handbook of the Collections.*
Ithaca, New York: Office of University Publications, 1981.

Herbert F. Johnson Museum of Art, Cornell University. *A Handbook of the Collection.*
Ithaca, New York: Herbert F. Johnson Museum of Art, 1998.

Krane, Susan, Robert Evren, and Helen Raye. *Albright-Knox Art Gallery: The Painting and Sculpture Collection: Acquisitions since 1972.* Edited by Karen Lee Spaulding.
New York: Hudson Hills Press in association with the Albright-Knox Art Gallery, 1987.

Marling, Karal Ann. *Looking Back: A Perspective on the 1913 Inaugural Exhibition.*
Rochester, New York: Memorial Art Gallery of the University of Rochester, 1988.

Nash, Steven A., Katy Kline, Charlotta Kotik, and Emese Wood. *Albright-Knox Art Gallery: Painting and Sculpture from Antiquity to 1942.*
New York: Rizzoli International Publications, Inc. in association with the Albright-Knox Art Gallery, 1979.

Perry, Barbara, ed. *American Ceramics: the Collection of Everson Museum of Art.*
New York: Rizzoli International Publications, Inc., 1989.

Peters, Susan Dodge, ed. *Memorial Art Gallery: An Introduction to the Collection.* Rochester,
New York: Memorial Art Gallery of the University of Rochester in association with Hudson Hills Press,
New York, 1988.

Schweizer, Paul D., ed. *Masterworks of American Art from the Munson-Williams-Proctor Institute.*
New York: Harry N. Abrams, Inc., 1989.

INDEX

PHOTOGRAPH CREDITS

Courtesy Albany Institute of History and Art: Page 59

Courtesy Albright-Knox Art Gallery, Buffalo: Pages 48, 54, 55, 57, 60, 65, 67, 69, 83, 84, 86, 93, 94, 95, 104, 123, 131, 134, 137, 141

Art Science Studio Lab: Page 70

Courtesy Buffalo and Erie County Historical Society: Pages 6, 10

Tony De Camillo: Pages 102, 119, 120, 121

Courtesy Everson Museum of Art, Syracuse: Pages 77, 91, 109, 111, 113, 114, 115, 117, 122 right

Gale Farley Photography: Page 112

G.R. Farley: Page 75

Greenberg-May Production, Inc., Courtesy Albright-Knox Art Gallery: Page 99

Biff Henrich/Keystone Productions: Pages 2, 50, 51, 58, 63, 71, 72, 81, 87, 103, 132

Courtesy Herbert F. Johnson Museum of Art, Cornell University, Ithaca: Pages 46, 52, 62, 82, 97, 101, 107, 129, 130, 133, 135, 136, 138, 139, 140

Joseph Levy: Pages 47, 66, 105

Courtesy Memorial Art Gallery of the University of Rochester: Page 61

Courtesy Munson-Williams-Proctor Arts Institute, Museum of Art, Utica: Pages 56, 64, 78, 85, 88, 96

David Revette Photography: Pages 53, 73, 79, 92

Runco Photo Studios, Inc.: Page 90

Hugh Tifft: Pages 116, 122 left, 124

James M. Via: Pages 49, 68, 74, 76, 80, 89, 100, 110, 125

Circa 1900

From the Genteel Tradition to the Jazz Age

Frank J. Mohring, Inc., Printing Production
Printer: Partners' Press, Kenmore, New York
Composed in Sabon and Engravers Roman fonts in Quark Xpress on Macintosh computers
Cover printed on 80 lb. Moistrite Matte Cover
Text printed on 100 lb. Moistrite Matte Text

1500 copies of this book were published by The Buffalo Fine Arts Academy,
Albright-Knox Art Gallery, Buffalo, New York, January 2001.